The definitive guide to the leading employers recruiting graduates during 2015-2016.

HIGH FLIERS PUBLICATIONS LTD
IN ASSOCIATION WITH THE TIMES

Published by High Fliers Publications Limited
King's Gate, 1 Bravingtons Walk, London N1 9AE
Telephone: 020 7428 9100   *Web:* www.Top100GraduateEmployers.com

Editor Martin Birchall
Publisher Gill Thomas
Production Director Robin Burrows
Production Manager Nathalie Abbott
Portrait Photography Sarah Merson

Printed and bound in Italy by L.E.G.O. S.p.A.

A CIP catalogue record for this book
is available from the British Library.
ISBN 978-0-9559257-6-4

Contents

Employer Entries

Foreword

By **Martin Birchall**
Editor, *The Times Top 100 Graduate Employers*

Welcome to the seventeenth edition of *The Times Top 100 Graduate Employers*, your guide to the most prestigious and sought-after employers that are recruiting graduates in 2015-2016.

The last five years have heralded a period of unprecedented change for the country's leading universities and students enrolling for degree courses, with the introduction of the new £9,000-a-year tuition fees and the associated sharp increase in the level of debt that undergraduates amass during their studies.

The first cohort of students to have paid the new tuition fees graduated in the summer of 2015 and, thankfully, during their time at university the graduate job market has improved dramatically.

Having begun their studies in the aftermath of the recession and the worst slump in graduate vacancies for fifteen years, the 'Class of 2015' emerged into something of a graduate recruitment boom. Over the past three recruiting seasons the number of entry-level jobs available at *The Times Top 100 Graduate Employers* has increased by a fifth, taking graduate employment to its highest level for over a decade.

Indeed in four key industries – consulting, IT & telecommunications, accounting & professional services and the public sector – there were at least 50 per cent more opportunities for graduates in 2015 than there were ten years previously.

This timely upturn in graduate employment mirrors Britain's wider economy which, according to the Office for National Statistics, has recorded growth of almost 6 per cent over the last two years – a faster growth rate than several other major economies, including Germany, France, the US and Canada.

News of this upbeat assessment of both the graduate job market and the broader economy beyond seems to have made a big impact on university campuses.

TOP 100
GRADUATE EMPLOYERS

&& This latest edition of the Top 100 includes the the one millionth copy printed since the book was launched in 1999. &&

The latest research with student job hunters for *The Times Top 100 Graduate Employers* shows that 26 per cent of final year students from the 'Class of 2015' expected to start a full-time graduate job straight after leaving university, the highest proportion for fourteen years. And there was a corresponding dramatic drop in the number of final year students who had 'no definite plans' for after university – just 9 per cent were undecided about their future, the lowest proportion since 1998.

If you're one of the 375,000 finalists due to graduate in 2016, then the outlook is even more optimistic. Employers featured within this edition of *The Times Top 100 Graduate Employers* expect to expand their graduate intake by a further 9.6 per cent during the 2015-2016 recruitment season, taking the number of graduate vacancies available in 2016 to an all-time high.

This year marks a major milestone for *The Times Top 100 Graduate Employers* – this latest edition includes the one millionth copy printed since the book was launched in 1999. Sixteen years on, the *Top 100* continues to provide an unrivalled, independent annual assessment of the graduate employers that university-leavers rate most highly.

This year's rankings have been compiled from face-to-face interviews with more than 18,000 final year students who graduated from universities across the UK in the summer of 2015. Students were asked to name the employer that they thought offered the best opportunities for new graduates.

Between them, the 'Class of 2015' named organisations in every key industry and business sector – consulting firms, City investment banks, IT & telecommunications companies, accounting & professional services firms, media groups, the country's leading charities, oil & energy groups, consulting firms, high street retailers and the top law firms. The one hundred employers that were mentioned most often during the research form *The Times Top 100 Graduate Employers* for 2015-2016.

This book is therefore a celebration of the employers who are judged to offer the brightest prospects for graduates. Whether through the perceived quality of their training programmes, the business success that they enjoy, the scale of their organisations, or by the impression that their recruitment promotions have made – these are the employers that were most attractive to graduate job hunters in 2015.

The Times Top 100 Graduate Employers won't necessarily identify which organisation you should join after graduation – only you can decide that. But it is an invaluable reference if you want to discover what Britain's leading employers have to offer.

Leaving university and finding your first graduate job can be quite a daunting process but it is one of the most important steps you'll ever take. Having a thorough understanding of the range of opportunities available must be a good way to start.

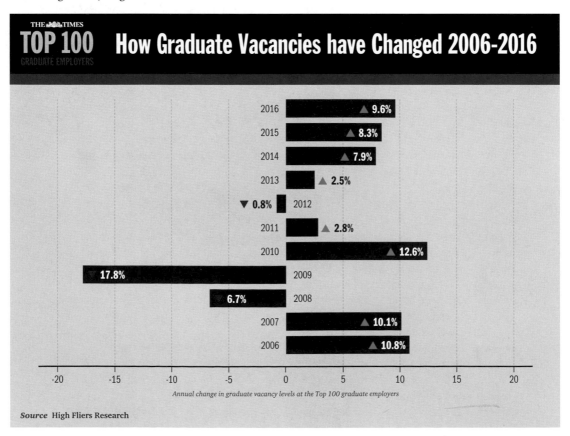

THE TIMES
TOP 100 **How Graduate Vacancies have Changed 2006-2016**
GRADUATE EMPLOYERS

2016	▲ 9.6%
2015	▲ 8.3%
2014	▲ 7.9%
2013	▲ 2.5%
2012	▼ 0.8%
2011	▲ 2.8%
2010	▲ 12.6%
2009	▼ 17.8%
2008	▼ 6.7%
2007	▲ 10.1%
2006	▲ 10.8%

-20   -15   -10   -5   0   5   10   15   20

Annual change in graduate vacancy levels at the Top 100 graduate employers

Source High Fliers Research

Toughest 12 months ever.

I only wish it was longer.

Industrial Placement Opportunities

- **£25,000 for a 12-month programme**
- **4 weeks' holiday allowance**
- **Chance to apply for the Graduate Area Manager Programme**

Crikey, Aldi's IP programme is *full on*. I knew it would be hard because they're the UK's fastest-growing supermarket. But it's only when you're here that you appreciate the pace and responsibility involved. There's a great mix of theory and hands-on experience, which is perfect for degree students who are fascinated by retail. You get loads of support but you've got to find your backbone, manage people who've been here for years and get everything working smoothly. You're even given the keys to a store and you think: "Hang on, I'm only 20!" But Aldi trust you and know what you're capable of. Sometimes before you do.

aldirecruitment.co.uk/industrial-placements

BECAUSE I'M ALDI. AND I'M LIKE NO OTHER.

SHOW YOUR

We're BDO.
Welcome to our world.

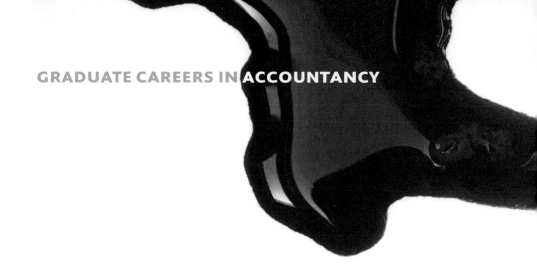

TRUE COLOURS

WHAT CAN YOU ADD TO OUR MIX? ▶

COLOURFUL CAREERS | COLOURFUL CHARACTERS

FIND OUT A SHADE MORE ABOUT BDO

f BDO-TraineesUK   t @BDO_TraineesUK
www: bdo.co.uk/careers | **e:** student.recruitment@bdo.co.uk

THE TIMES

TOP 100 GRADUATE EMPLOYERS 2008-2009
TOP 100 GRADUATE EMPLOYERS 2009-2010
TOP 100 GRADUATE EMPLOYERS 2010-2011
TOP 100 GRADUATE EMPLOYERS 2011-2012
TOP 100 GRADUATE EMPLOYERS 2012-2013
TOP 100 GRADUATE EMPLOYERS 2013-2014
TOP 100 GRADUATE EMPLOYERS 2014-2015
TOP 100 GRADUATE EMPLOYERS 2015-2016

Researching The Times Top 100 Graduate Employers

By **Gill Thomas**
Publisher, High Fliers Publications

Each year up to ten thousand employers, large and small, recruit graduates from the UK's leading universities. Some offer formal development programmes for new graduates, others are simply recruiting for vacancies which require a particular degree or qualification, but together they provide an estimated 200,000 entry-level jobs for university-leavers annually.

Such a wide range of potential opportunities can make finding the organisation that is 'right' for you quite a daunting challenge. What basis can you use to evaluate so many employers and their graduate roles? How can you assess all the different options and decide which offer the best career paths?

There are few simple answers to these questions and no single employer can ever hope to be right for every graduate – everyone makes their own judgement about the organisations they want to work for and the type of job they find the most attractive.

So how then can anyone produce a meaningful league table of Britain's leading graduate employers? What criteria can define whether one individual organisation is 'better' than another? To compile the new edition of *The Times Top 100 Graduate Employers*, the independent market research company, High Fliers Research,

interviewed 18,412 final year students who left UK universities in the summer of 2015.

Students from the 'Class of 2015' who took part in the study were selected at random to represent the full cross-section of finalists at their universities, not just those who had already secured graduate employment. The research examined students' experiences during their search for a graduate job and asked them about their attitudes to employers.

> **"** *In an outstanding achievement, PwC has been voted the UK's leading graduate employer for the twelfth year running.* **"**

The key question used to produce the *Top 100* was "Which employer do you think offers the best opportunities for graduates?". The question was deliberately open-ended and students were not shown a list of employers to choose from or prompted in any way.

Across the full survey sample, finalists named more than 1,500 different organisations – from the smallest local or regional employers, to some of the world's best-known companies. The responses were analysed and the one hundred organisations that were mentioned most often make up the *The Times Top 100 Graduate Employers* for 2015.

It is clear from the variety of answers given by finalists from the 'Class of 2015' that students used several criteria to determine which employer they considered offered the best opportunities for

THE TIMES TOP 100 GRADUATE EMPLOYERS
The Times Top 100 Graduate Employers 2015

	2014			2014	
1.	1	PWC	51.	36	ROYAL BANK OF SCOTLAND GROUP
2.	4	ALDI	52.	45	BRITISH AIRWAYS
3.	9	GOOGLE	53.	44	BOSTON CONSULTING GROUP
4.	2	TEACH FIRST	54.	97	DIAGEO
5.	6	CIVIL SERVICE	55.	98	NEWTON EUROPE
6.	3	DELOITTE	56.	50	BAIN & COMPANY
7.	5	NHS	57.	39	SAINSBURY'S
8.	11	EY	58.	73	POLICE
9.	7	KPMG	59.	69	DEUTSCHE BANK
10.	8	BBC	60.	90	DLA PIPER
11.	10	JOHN LEWIS PARTNERSHIP	61.	83	HOGAN LOVELLS
12.	15	GLAXOSMITHKLINE	62.	55	AIRBUS
13.	12	UNILEVER	63.	67	BAKER & MCKENZIE
14.	18	J.P. MORGAN	64.	72	EXXONMOBIL
15.	17	GOLDMAN SACHS	65.	86	BLOOMBERG
16.	13	BARCLAYS	66.	NEW	DANONE
17.	20	ACCENTURE	67.	53	LOCAL GOVERNMENT
18.	21	HSBC	68.	59	MCDONALD'S
19.	16	JAGUAR LAND ROVER	69.	63	TRANSPORT FOR LONDON
20.	14	BP	70.	88	BOOTS
21.	22	IBM	71.	NEW	MOTT MACDONALD
22.	29	MCKINSEY & COMPANY	72.	38	WPP
23.	19	ROLLS-ROYCE	73.	66	SIEMENS
24.	23	TESCO	74.	94	DYSON
25.	31	LIDL	75.	NEW	ASTRAZENECA
26.	25	SHELL	76.	NEW	NETWORK RAIL
27.	26	PROCTER & GAMBLE	77.	60	ASDA
28.	41	L'ORÉAL	78.	64	NESTLÉ
29.	24	MICROSOFT	79.	61	BLACKROCK
30.	30	LLOYDS BANKING GROUP	80.	91	MONDELĒZ INTERNATIONAL
31.	27	ARUP	81.	NEW	AMAZON
32.	40	FRESHFIELDS BRUCKHAUS DERINGER	82.	NEW	FIRST DERIVATIVES
33.	32	CLIFFORD CHANCE	83.	52	MI5 – THE SECURITY SERVICE
34.	33	MARKS & SPENCER	84.	65	BANK OF AMERICA MERRILL LYNCH
35.	28	ARMY	85.	82	PENGUIN RANDOM HOUSE
36.	37	MORGAN STANLEY	86.	78	OXFAM
37.	42	APPLE	87.	87	NORTON ROSE FULBRIGHT
38.	48	MARS	88.	99	GE
39.	35	ALLEN & OVERY	89.	NEW	FACEBOOK
40.	76	FRONTLINE	90.	62	GRANT THORNTON
41.	34	LINKLATERS	91.	75	CENTRICA
42.	49	ATKINS	92.	81	UBS
43.	54	SKY	93.	85	LLOYD'S
44.	43	BT	94.	NEW	BDO
45.	70	EUROPEAN COMMISSION (EU CAREERS)	95.	NEW	WELLCOME TRUST
46.	56	CANCER RESEARCH UK	96.	84	HERBERT SMITH FREEHILLS
47.	68	ROYAL NAVY	97.	NEW	AECOM
48.	47	CITI	98.	NEW	NATIONAL GRID
49.	46	BAE SYSTEMS	99.	57	CREDIT SUISSE
50.	58	SLAUGHTER AND MAY	100.	NEW	BANK OF ENGLAND

Source **High Fliers Research** 18,412 final year students leaving UK universities in the summer of 2015 were asked the open-ended question 'Which employer do you think offers the best opportunities for graduates?' during interviews for *The UK Graduate Careers Survey 2015*

graduates. Some evaluated employers based on the information they had seen during their job search – the quality of recruitment promotions, the impression formed from meeting employers' representatives, or their experiences during the application and selection process.

Others focused on employers' general reputations – their public image, their business profile or their commercial success. Finalists also considered the level of vacancies that organisations were recruiting for as an indicator of possible employment prospects, or were influenced by employers' profiles at their university.

Many final year students, however, used the 'employment proposition' as their main guide – the quality of graduate training and development an employer offers, the starting salary and remuneration package available, and the practical aspects of a first graduate job, such as location or working hours.

Regardless of the criteria that students used to arrive at their answer, the hardest part for many was just selecting a single organisation. To some extent, choosing two or three, or even half a dozen employers, would have been much easier. But the whole purpose of the exercise was to replicate the reality that everyone faces – you can only work for one organisation. And at each stage of the graduate job search there are choices to be made as to which direction to take and which employers to pursue.

The resulting *Top 100* is a dynamic league table of the UK's most exciting and well-respected graduate recruiters in 2015. In an outstanding achievement, the accounting and professional services firm, PwC, has been voted the UK's leading graduate employer for the twelfth year running. The firm polled 8.2 per cent of finalists' votes this year, more than double the number of any other employer in this year's league table.

There are a number of significant changes within the new top ten rankings. Aldi's popular trainee area manager programme has moved up to second place, its highest-ever position in the *Top 100*. And internet giant, Google, has jumped six places to reach the top three for the first time, having moved up the rankings in nine of the last ten years since first appearing as a new entry in 85th place in 2005. The widely acclaimed Teach First scheme that recruited more than 1,800 graduates for its 2015 graduate intake – the highest number

ever recruited in a single year by an individual UK employer – has slipped back to fourth place. The Civil Service, best known for its prestigious Fast Stream programme, has returned to fifth place but Deloitte, the accounting and professional services firm that spent eight consecutive years in second place until 2013, has moved out of the top five to sixth place.

The NHS is ranked lower too this year, but EY, the accountancy firm which rebranded from Ernst & Young in 2013, has reappeared in the top ten and is now in eighth place, overtaking rivals KPMG for the first time in seventeen years. The BBC remains in the top ten but the John Lewis Partnership slips to 11th place. Healthcare company GSK has moved up to 12th position, its best ranking for fifteen years. J.P. Morgan has climbed another four places to its highest rating in the *Top 100* since 2001, overtaking rival investment bank Goldman Sachs.

Having dropped down the rankings for six years running, Accenture has moved back up two places this year and HSBC has returned to the top twenty, in 18th place. It has been another good year for strategic consultants McKinsey & Company – the firm has climbed up the table for the third consecutive year, taking it to just outside the top twenty employers, its best-ever *Top 100* position.

There have been mixed fortunes though for the leading City banking and financial institutions – just six of the fifteen employers featured within the new *Top 100* have improved their ratings and Credit Suisse, Bank of America Merrill Lynch, BlackRock and UBS are among those that are ranked lower in the new list.

The highest climbers in this year's *Top 100* are led by the international drinks company, Diageo, and consulting firm Newton Europe, which have both jumped forty-three places, to 54th and 55th places respectively. Frontline, the new children's social work programme that launched in autumn 2013 and was a new entry in last year's *Top 100*, has climbed an impressive thirty-six places to 40th position. But WPP, Grant Thornton and MI5 – The Security Service have each dropped at least thirty places in the new rankings.

There are a total of twelve new entries or re-entries in this year's *Top 100*, the highest being for consumer goods company Danone, which has had a convincing return to the rankings in 66th place. Engineering firm Mott Macdonald, pharmaceutical

Think you know us?

Asparagus Applauders

Graduate Opportunities
Leaders for Business Programme

From deciding on new menus for our in-flight meals, to being duty manager at JFK New York or developing sales in new markets, the graduates on our programme are rising to all kinds of fascinating challenges. And in a business as large and complex as ours, the possibilities are many and varied. So if you thought it was all about pilots and cabin crew, maybe you'd like to get to know us a little better?

group AstraZeneca and Network Rail are back in the league table in 71st, 75th and 76th places.

Online retailer Amazon, Facebook, engineering consultancy AECOM and the Wellcome Trust are each ranked in the *Top 100* for the first time, as is the Northern Ireland-based technology and consulting company, First Derivatives. Professional services firm BDO, National Grid and the Bank of England have each reappeared in 94th, 98th and 100th places respectively, after dropping out of the list in previous years.

Organisations leaving the *Top 100* in 2015 include Morrisons, Channel Four, EDF Energy, Red Bull, Santander, Arcadia Group, the RAF, the Department for International Development and three graduate employers that were new or re-entries in last year's rankings – E.ON, Savills and British Sugar.

It's now sixteen years since the original edition of *The Times Top 100 Graduate Employers* was produced in 1999 and in that time there have been just three organisations at number one. Andersen Consulting (now Accenture) held onto the top spot for the first four years and its success heralded a huge surge in popularity for careers in consulting – at its peak in 2001, almost one in six graduates applied for jobs in the sector.

In the year before the firm changed its name from Andersen Consulting to Accenture, it astutely introduced a new graduate package that included a £28,500 starting salary (a sky-high figure for graduates in 2000) and a much talked-about £10,000 bonus, helping to assure the firm's popularity, irrespective of its corporate branding.

In 2003, after two dismal years in graduate recruitment when vacancies for university-leavers dropped by more than a fifth following the terrorist attacks of 11th September 2001, the Civil Service was named Britain's leading graduate employer. Just a year later it was displaced by PricewaterhouseCoopers, the accounting and professional services firm formed from the merger of Price Waterhouse and Coopers & Lybrand in 1998. At the time, the firm was the largest private-sector recruiter of graduates, with an intake in 2004 of more than a thousand trainees.

Now known simply as PwC, the firm has remained at number one ever since, increasing its share of the student vote from five per cent in 2004 to more than 10 per cent in 2007 and fighting off the stiffest of competition from rivals Deloitte in 2008, when just seven votes separated the two employers.

PwC's reign as the leading employer represents a real renaissance for the entire accounting & professional services sector. Whereas fifteen years ago, a career in accountancy was regarded as a safe, traditional employment choice, today's profession is viewed in a very different light. The training required to become a chartered accountant is now

THE TIMES TOP 100 GRADUATE EMPLOYERS — Number Ones, Movers & Shakers in the Top 100

NUMBER ONES		HIGHEST CLIMBING EMPLOYERS		HIGHEST NEW ENTRIES	
1999	ANDERSEN CONSULTING	1999	SCHLUMBERGER (UP 13 PLACES)	1999	PFIZER (31st)
2000	ANDERSEN CONSULTING	2000	CAPITAL ONE (UP 32 PLACES)	2000	MORGAN STANLEY (34th)
2001	ACCENTURE	2001	EUROPEAN COMMISSION (UP 36 PLACES)	2001	MARCONI (36th)
2002	ACCENTURE	2002	WPP (UP 36 PLACES)	2002	GUINNESS UDV (44th)
2003	CIVIL SERVICE	2003	ROLLS-ROYCE (UP 37 PLACES)	2003	ASDA (40th)
2004	PRICEWATERHOUSECOOPERS	2004	J.P. MORGAN (UP 29 PLACES)	2004	BAKER & MCKENZIE (61st)
2005	PRICEWATERHOUSECOOPERS	2005	TEACH FIRST (UP 22 PLACES)	2005	PENGUIN (70th)
2006	PRICEWATERHOUSECOOPERS	2006	GOOGLE (UP 32 PLACES)	2006	FUJITSU (81st)
2007	PRICEWATERHOUSECOOPERS	2007	PFIZER (UP 30 PLACES)	2007	BDO STOY HAYWARD (74th)
2008	PRICEWATERHOUSECOOPERS	2008	CO-OPERATIVE GROUP (UP 39 PLACES)	2008	SKY (76th)
2009	PRICEWATERHOUSECOOPERS	2009	CADBURY (UP 48 PLACES)	2009	BDO STOY HAYWARD (68th)
2010	PRICEWATERHOUSECOOPERS	2010	ASDA (UP 41 PLACES)	2010	SAATCHI & SAATCHI (49th)
2011	PWC	2011	CENTRICA (UP 41 PLACES)	2011	APPLE (53rd)
2012	PWC	2012	NESTLÉ (UP 44 PLACES)	2012	EUROPEAN COMMISSION (56th)
2013	PWC	2013	DFID (UP 40 PLACES)	2013	SIEMENS (70th)
2014	PWC	2014	TRANSPORT FOR LONDON (UP 36 PLACES)	2014	FRONTLINE (76th)
2015	PWC	2015	DIAGEO, NEWTON EUROPE (UP 43 PLACES)	2015	DANONE (66th)

Source High Fliers Research

CAN WE INSPIRE THE

leader

IN YOU?

No. 1
worldwide
in Fresh **DAIRY**
PRODUCTS

No. 1
in Western Europe
in **MEDICAL**
NUTRITION

No. 2
worldwide in
WATERS (packaged
& by volume)

No. 2
worldwide
in **EARLY LIFE**
NUTRITION

SALES & MARKETING /// BUSINESS PARTNERING /// NUTRITION

FIND OUT MORE ONLINE
DANONE.CO.UK/GRADUATES

DANONE

seen as a prized business qualification and the sector's leading firms are regularly described as 'dynamic' and 'international' by undergraduates looking for their first job after university.

A total of 208 different organisations have now appeared within *The Times Top 100 Graduate Employers* since its inception and over forty of these have made it into the rankings every year since 1999. The most consistent performers have been PwC, KPMG and the Civil Service, each of which have never been lower than 9th place in the league table. The NHS has also had a formidable record, appearing in every top ten since 2003, and the BBC, Goldman Sachs and EY (formerly Ernst & Young) have all remained within the top twenty throughout the last decade.

Google is the highest-climbing employer within the *Top 100*, having risen over eighty places during the last decade, to reach the top three for the first time this year. But car manufacturer Jaguar Land Rover holds the record for the fastest-moving employer, after jumping more than seventy places in just five years, between 2009 and 2014.

Other employers haven't been so successful, though. British Airways, ranked in sixth place in 1999, dropped out of the *Top 100* altogether a decade later and Ford, which was once rated as high as 14th, disappeared out of the list in 2006 after cancelling its graduate recruitment programme two years previously.

Thirty-four graduate employers – including Nokia, Maersk, the Home Office, Cable & Wireless, United Biscuits, Nationwide, Capgemini and the Met Office – have the dubious record of having only been ranked in the *Top 100* once during the last fifteen years. And Marconi had the unusual

THE TIMES TOP 100 GRADUATE EMPLOYERS — Winners & Losers in the Top 100

MOST CONSISTENT EMPLOYERS	HIGHEST RANKING	LOWEST RANKING
ANDERSEN (FORMERLY ARTHUR ANDERSEN)	2nd (1999-2001)	3rd (2002)
PWC	1st (FROM 2004)	3rd (1999-2001, 2003)
KPMG	3rd (2006-2008, 2011-2012)	9th (2015)
CIVIL SERVICE	1st (2003)	8th (2011)
BBC	5th (2005-2007)	14th (1999)
GLAXOSMITHKLINE	11th (2000)	22nd (2002-2003)
IBM	13th (2000)	24th (2012)
EY (FORMERLY ERNST & YOUNG)	7th (2013)	20th (2001)
BP	14th (2013-2014)	32nd (2004)
ACCENTURE (FORMERLY ANDERSEN CONSULTING)	1st (1999-2002)	20th (2014)

EMPLOYERS CLIMBING HIGHEST	NEW ENTRY RANKING	HIGHEST RANKING
GOOGLE	85th (2005)	3rd (2015)
JAGUAR LAND ROVER	87th (2009)	16th (2014)
LIDL	89th (2009)	25th (2015)
ALDI	65th (2002)	2nd (2015)
MI5 – THE SECURITY SERVICE	96th (2007)	33rd (2010)
TEACH FIRST	63rd (2004)	2nd (2014)
APPLE	87th (2009)	27th (2012)
ATKINS	94th (2004)	37th (2009)
ARCADIA GROUP	99th (2001)	47th (2007)
SLAUGHTER AND MAY	90th (2001)	39th (2010)

EMPLOYERS FALLING FURTHEST	HIGHEST RANKING	LOWEST RANKING
BRITISH AIRWAYS	6th (1999)	Not ranked (2010, 2011)
FORD	11th (1999)	Not ranked (FROM 2006)
THOMPSON REUTERS	22nd (2001)	Not ranked (2009-2012)
ASTRAZENECA	24th (2003)	Not ranked (2012-2014)
RAF	32nd (2005)	Not ranked (2015)
MINISTRY OF DEFENCE	35th (2003)	Not ranked (2007, FROM 2012)
MARCONI	36th (2001)	Not ranked (FROM 2002)
DIAGEO	37th (2004)	Not ranked (2008-2009)
ICI	39th (2000)	Not ranked (2001, 2004, FROM 2006)
LOGICA	39th (1999)	Not ranked (FROM 2003)

Source High Fliers Research

distinction of being one of the highest-ever new entries in 36th place in 2001, only to vanish from the list entirely the following year.

One of the most spectacular ascendancies within the *Top 100* has been the rise of Aldi, which joined the list in 65th place in 2002, rose to third place in 2009 – helped in part by its memorable remuneration package for new recruits (currently £41,000 plus an Audi A4 car) – and is now in second place in 2015. And Teach First, which appeared as a new entry in 63rd place in 2003, climbed the rankings in each of the years following and achieved second place in the *Top 100* in 2014.

This year's edition of *The Times Top 100 Graduate Employers* has produced a number of significant changes within the rankings and the results provide a unique insight into how graduates from the 'Class of 2015' rated the UK's leading employers. Almost all of these organisations are featured in the 'Employer Entry' section of this book – from page 53 onwards, you can see a two-page profile for each employer, listed alphabetically for easy reference.

The editorial part of the entry includes a short description of what the organisation does, its opportunities for graduates and its recruitment programme for 2015-2016. A fact file for each employer gives details of the business functions that graduates are recruited for, the number of graduate vacancies on offer, likely starting salaries for 2016, their minimum academic requirements, application deadlines, the universities that the employer is intending to visit during the year, plus details of their graduate recruitment website and how to follow the employer on Facebook, Twitter and LinkedIn. The right-hand page of each employer entry contains a display advert promoting the organisation.

If you would like to find out more about any of the employers featured in *The Times Top 100 Graduate Employers*, then simply register with **www.Top100GraduateEmployers.com** – the official website showcasing the latest news and information about *Top 100* organisations.

Registration is entirely free and as well as being able to access the website, you'll receive regular email updates about the employers you are most interested in – this includes details of the careers events they're holding at your university during the year, upcoming job application deadlines, and the very latest business news about each of the organisations.

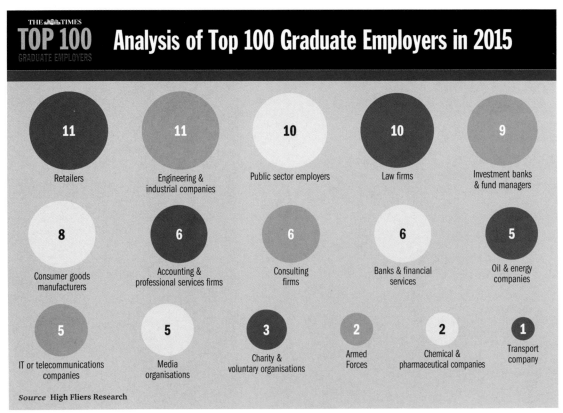

THE TIMES

TOP 100
GRADUATE EMPLOYERS

Analysis of Top 100 Graduate Employers in 2015

11	**11**	**10**	**10**	**9**
Retailers	Engineering & industrial companies	Public sector employers	Law firms	Investment banks & fund managers
8	**6**	**6**	**6**	**5**
Consumer goods manufacturers	Accounting & professional services firms	Consulting firms	Banks & financial services	Oil & energy companies
5	**5**	**3**	**2**	**2**	**1**
IT or telecommunications companies	Media organisations	Charity & voluntary organisations	Armed Forces	Chemical & pharmaceutical companies	Transport company

Source **High Fliers Research**

THE TIMES
TOP 100 The Top 10 Graduate Employers 2000-2014
GRADUATE EMPLOYERS

2000
1. ANDERSEN CONSULTING
2. ARTHUR ANDERSEN
3. PRICEWATERHOUSECOOPERS
4. PROCTER & GAMBLE
5. KPMG
6. CIVIL SERVICE
7. ARMY
8. UNILEVER
9. MARS
10. BBC

2001
1. ACCENTURE (FORMERLY ANDERSEN CONSULTING)
2. ANDERSEN (FORMERLY ARTHUR ANDERSEN)
3. PRICEWATERHOUSECOOPERS
4. PROCTER & GAMBLE
5. GOLDMAN SACHS
6. CIVIL SERVICE
7. KPMG
8. UNILEVER
9. ARMY
10. MARS

2002
1. ACCENTURE
2. PRICEWATERHOUSECOOPERS
3. ANDERSEN
4. CIVIL SERVICE
5. ARMY
6. KPMG
7. UNILEVER
8. PROCTER & GAMBLE
9. GOLDMAN SACHS
10. MARS

2003
1. CIVIL SERVICE
2. ACCENTURE
3. PRICEWATERHOUSECOOPERS
4. ARMY
5. KPMG
6. HSBC
7. BBC
8. PROCTER & GAMBLE
9. NHS
10. DELOITTE & TOUCHE

2004
1. PRICEWATERHOUSECOOPERS
2. CIVIL SERVICE
3. ACCENTURE
4. KPMG
5. NHS
6. BBC
7. ARMY
8. PROCTER & GAMBLE
9. HSBC
10. DELOITTE (FORMERLY DELOITTE & TOUCHE)

2005
1. PRICEWATERHOUSECOOPERS
2. CIVIL SERVICE
3. ACCENTURE
4. KPMG
5. BBC
6. DELOITTE
7. NHS
8. HSBC
9. GOLDMAN SACHS
10. PROCTER & GAMBLE

2006
1. PRICEWATERHOUSECOOPERS
2. DELOITTE
3. KPMG
4. CIVIL SERVICE
5. BBC
6. NHS
7. HSBC
8. ACCENTURE
9. PROCTER & GAMBLE
10. GOLDMAN SACHS

2007
1. PRICEWATERHOUSECOOPERS
2. DELOITTE
3. KPMG
4. CIVIL SERVICE
5. BBC
6. NHS
7. ACCENTURE
8. HSBC
9. ALDI
10. GOLDMAN SACHS

2008
1. PRICEWATERHOUSECOOPERS
2. DELOITTE
3. KPMG
4. ACCENTURE
5. NHS
6. CIVIL SERVICE
7. BBC
8. ALDI
9. TEACH FIRST
10. GOLDMAN SACHS

2009
1. PRICEWATERHOUSECOOPERS
2. DELOITTE
3. ALDI
4. CIVIL SERVICE
5. KPMG
6. NHS
7. ACCENTURE
8. TEACH FIRST
9. BBC
10. ERNST & YOUNG

2010
1. PRICEWATERHOUSECOOPERS
2. DELOITTE
3. CIVIL SERVICE
4. KPMG
5. ALDI
6. NHS
7. TEACH FIRST
8. ACCENTURE
9. BBC
10. ERNST & YOUNG

2011
1. PWC (FORMERLY PRICEWATERHOUSECOOPERS)
2. DELOITTE
3. KPMG
4. ALDI
5. NHS
6. BBC
7. TEACH FIRST
8. CIVIL SERVICE
9. ACCENTURE
10. ERNST & YOUNG

2012
1. PWC
2. DELOITTE
3. KPMG
4. TEACH FIRST
5. ALDI
6. NHS
7. CIVIL SERVICE
8. ERNST & YOUNG
9. BBC
10. JOHN LEWIS PARTNERSHIP

2013
1. PWC
2. DELOITTE
3. TEACH FIRST
4. KPMG
5. CIVIL SERVICE
6. ALDI
7. EY (FORMERLY ERNST & YOUNG)
8. NHS
9. JOHN LEWIS PARTNERSHIP
10. GOOGLE

2014
1. PWC
2. TEACH FIRST
3. DELOITTE
4. ALDI
5. NHS
6. CIVIL SERVICE
7. KPMG
8. BBC
9. GOOGLE
10. JOHN LEWIS PARTNERSHIP

Source High Fliers Research

Your ambition...

Taking a career journey with limitless possibilities.

Thousands of employers around the world train graduates to become ICAEW Chartered Accountants. In fact, 97% of the best global brands employ our members.

Discover how you can achieve more as a chartered accountant.

icaew.com/careers

ICAEW

Insight day
1 day

Students of all years

Talent academies
2-5 days

First to final year students

Boost your employability

We've got lots of different work experience programmes for every year of study, so you can learn more about us and boost your employability. They'll help you make an informed decision about which of our career opportunities is best for you. To find out more visit our website.

Take the opportunity of a lifetime
pwc.com/uk/work-experience

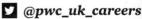

Graduate job with PwC

Diversity in business
1-2 weeks • Paid

Students of all years

Summer internships
6-8 weeks • Paid

Penultimate year students

Work placement
11 months • Paid

Sandwich or placement students

Create value through diversity. Be yourself, be different.

Careers Servic
where opportunities be

Welc

Caree

What next?
Looking to life after university

www.

Successful Job Hunting

By **Marc Lintern**
Director of Employability and Student Success, Newcastle University

An important part of going to university is the opportunity to start to shape your future and explore what you want to do as a graduate. Your degree subject and academic studies are, of course, a big part of this but universities offer so much more and your careers service can help you to get the most from your university experience.

Many students start their degree with the intention that it will be the first step of their chosen career and will lead to a good graduate job at the end of their studies. However, the competition for places at the most popular organisations is fierce and it's all too easy to put career preparations and planning on the back burner.

Employers are looking for graduates who really stand out – those with plenty of experience on their CV, whether it's part-time jobs, relevant work experience, taking part in employer competitions, participation in extra-curricular activities at university or commitments outside of university life.

This means that the earlier you can begin thinking about your career plans – preferably during your first year – the more chance you'll have to explore your ideas and options, and to start gaining experience that will help you achieve the job you desire.

" If you've applied to a job that you really believe you'll be suited to, then everything's going to go well. "

A great place to start is your university careers service. Every university in the UK has one, providing careers guidance and support for its students, from freshers' week until after graduation so try and visit as soon as you can to find out about the resources and advice that they offer.

Staff at the careers service can guide you to a wealth of information about different job types, business sectors and industries, part-time vacancies, voluntary work, paid summer internships, overseas schemes, business start-up support, and the latest graduate vacancies, as well as helping you with your immediate questions and queries.

Professional careers advisers are usually available for one-to-one discussions on the potential career paths or employment options that might interest you, or to check through your CV and help you prepare application forms. If you're not sure what you want to do or need help to practice for interviews, longer appointments will be available with a careers adviser, either booked on a same-day basis or at some universities in advance, particularly at the busiest times of the year.

Much of the information that careers services provide is available on their website and it is well worth spending time exploring what is available. Services work hard to curate huge amounts of

MY WORK IS
HELPING PREVENT
FEMALE GENITAL MUTILATION.
HOW MANY GRADUATE MANAGEMENT SCHEMES OFFER THAT?

The NHS Graduate Management Training Scheme is nothing less than a life defining experience. Whether you join our HR, Finance, Health Informatics or General Management streams, you'll receive everything you need to make a positive impact on the lives of 53 million people across England.

These aren't clinical opportunities, but this is about developing exceptional healthcare leaders. High-calibre management professionals who will lead the NHS through a profound transformation and shape our services around ever-evolving patient needs. Inspirational people who will push up standards, deliver deeper value for money and continue the drive towards a healthier nation.

nhsgraduates.co.uk

Life Defining

NHS
Leadership Academy

**Graduate Management
Training Scheme**

information and make it as accessible as possible, so don't be afraid to ask if there's something you're looking for that you can't find. And it's worth checking whether you can register to receive email updates from your careers service. At some universities these are sent out automatically while others enable you to opt in to receive details of upcoming careers events, application deadlines and vacancy information that is specific to your interests.

Getting the most out of your careers service is a bit like taking out a gym membership – if you want a six-pack, it's not enough to just join the gym, you need to take advantage of your membership and go along regularly. The same is true for developing your career options. For most students a job offer or career step doesn't just 'happen' to them, it comes from making the effort to take advantage of opportunities on offer, including from the careers service. Remember, there is no question too small and no question that careers staff haven't been asked before.

Once you've begun to get a sense of the type of job you're interested in, the next step is to look into individual employers and, where relevant, their graduate programmes. Careers fairs, skills workshops and employer presentations on campus can be a great way to meet employers from different organisations. Look out too for job opportunities and placement schemes that your careers service offers with small and medium-sized businesses, often in your local region.

Careers fairs typically feature 30-80 employers at a single event while the busiest universities will offer more than 150 employer presentations during the year. Careers services will advertise in advance the types of employers who will be attending the fairs and it can make a big difference if you take the time to do some research beforehand, so you know which employers to try and speak to on the day. Graduate employers hope to see a level of preparedness and many careers services have useful information on their websites and run training sessions providing strategies on how to approach recruiters at these events.

Many of the careers fair stands will be staffed by new graduates who were in the same position as you a couple of years ago and are back at their old university to help you understand what it's really like to work there. So, fairs are a great way to find out which employers are recruiting, what

opportunities are available and what recruiters are looking for in the graduates they hire.

Try and keep an open mind about potential future employers. Go along to employer presentations or speak to recruiters at careers fairs to see if you *might* be interested in their organisations, rather than simply attending those where you know you definitely *are* interested in the company. It's a more time-consuming approach but attending lots of presentations will give you a much better idea of what type of employment opportunities are likely to suit your interests.

When you're at a careers fair or looking at the list of employers holding events at your university, it's easy to think 'there aren't any employers who are interested in me', especially if you're studying a degree that doesn't seem relevant to the graduate jobs on offer. But don't be put off – many employers hire graduates from 'any discipline' and are just as interested in arts & humanities students as those who are studying business or management. It's what you have to offer in addition to your degree which will make you stand out.

If you're in your first or second year and there are already specific employers that you know you'd like to work for, it's a good idea to find out how you can gain early experience with the company, such as through paid internships or work placements, either in your holidays or as part of your degree course.

More importantly, you should check whether there are particular routes that they use for their graduate recruitment. For example, some employers recruit summer interns and/or placement students and then offer the best of these candidates a graduate job for after university – if you're not in at the start and don't get on these work experience programmes, your likelihood of getting recruited can be significantly reduced.

You don't necessarily need to do a full internship or placement to get a sense of what it'd be like to work for an organisation as work shadowing, doing a 'taster' week, mentoring and open days can all be helpful. Look out for opportunities to gain experience with a local business or a voluntary organisation, and bear in mind that as well as the large national and international employers, many graduates often prefer to work for small or medium-sized businesses after university, as well as for charities and other 'third sector' non-profit organisations.

Increasing numbers of students and graduates are also exploring whether to start their own businesses and your university careers service will be able to help you explore all of these options, as well as provide practical support and advice if you are interested in the idea of working for yourself. Many careers services offer competitions for students interested in the idea of starting their own business and these can be a great way for any student to develop their business awareness while demonstrating the enterprising attitude that all employers desire.

Writing your CV is an important first step before you begin applying to employers, whether for a paid internship or a graduate position. Even though many of the bigger employers will have their own online application forms and don't accept CVs directly, the process of compiling information for a CV will help you record all your achievements, experiences, skills and knowledge in one place, giving you a repository that you can draw on when you're preparing individual job applications. With employers increasingly using LinkedIn to source potential candidates and advertise their vacancies, having a well prepared CV will also make it easy to set up your profile.

If you are applying direct to employers with a CV, don't forget that you will need to tailor this to every position you apply for, highlighting your suitability for that particular role. Your careers service can guide you as to what to include and if you do need a CV to submit to employers, they will help you prepare a polished, carefully formatted document that highlights your strengths and qualities. They can also assist you when you're preparing what to write for online applications and adding a summary to your LinkedIn profile.

If your initial application is successful, then the next selection stage for many larger employers could be to complete one or more psychometric tests. Common test topics include verbal reasoning, numeracy and situational judgement and these are usually done online. It's essential that before you attempt to complete them, you find out exactly what the rules of the test are and any preparation you can do in advance.

Although psychometric tests are measuring your innate aptitude or ability, if you've never taken tests before doing some practice tests can make a difference to how well you do by helping you get over the uncertainty and unfamiliarity of tests and the test situation. If you're an arts student who doesn't usually do much maths and you're due to do a numeracy test, working through practice tests can help you get up to speed and re-acquainted with your calculator. Many employers provide sample

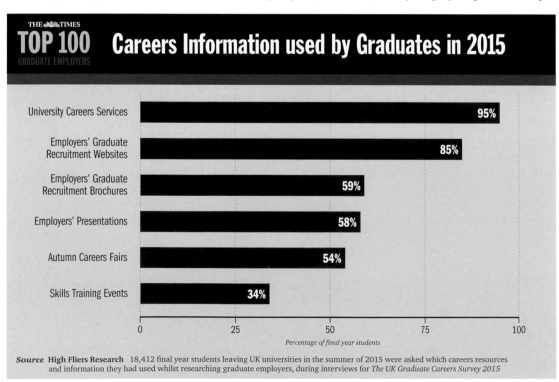

THE TIMES TOP 100 GRADUATE EMPLOYERS

Careers Information used by Graduates in 2015

Resource	Percentage
University Careers Services	95%
Employers' Graduate Recruitment Websites	85%
Employers' Graduate Recruitment Brochures	59%
Employers' Presentations	58%
Autumn Careers Fairs	54%
Skills Training Events	34%

Percentage of final year students

Source **High Fliers Research** 18,412 final year students leaving UK universities in the summer of 2015 were asked which careers resources and information they had used whilst researching graduate employers, during interviews for *The UK Graduate Careers Survey 2015*

Institute
and Faculty
of Actuaries

Why a career as an actuary adds up for me

"My job is to work out the risk of an event taking place and then to calculate what the impact of that would be for the business I'm working for.

I could be analysing weather patterns, the housing market in Brazil, London traffic trends or attendances at music festivals.

It's challenging, offers lots of opportunities for progression and it's well paid right from the start."

What you'll need to become an actuary

Actuaries love numbers. A degree in maths, statistics, actuarial science, economics or a related discipline such as physics is required alongside a maths A level.

You can rely on the support of the Institute and Faculty of Actuaries. We have over 25,000 members worldwide who call on our support, information resources and networking opportunities throughout their careers.

What can I earn?

Graduate Actuarial Trainees earn £35,219.

Where can I find out more?

e: careers@actuaries.org.uk
w: www.actuaries.org.uk/becoming-actuary/ pages/becoming-actuary

tests and past examples of the most widely used tests should be available from your careers service.

Regardless of whether you've applied to large or small employers, if your initial application and test results impress you'll be invited for a first interview. This could be face-to-face, by phone, over Skype or even an automated online recorded interview. Again, it's really useful to practice beforehand and your careers service website will provide guidance on what to expect for different types of interview and the sort of questions to expect.

Many careers services offer practice interviews with advisers or visiting graduate employers, either on a one-to-one basis or as a group session, and will give you feedback about how you've performed. And you may even be able to do a videoed practice interview so you can see yourself in action.

The final selection round at many organisations is an assessment day, often held at the employers' head office or a regional centre. The format varies considerably from employer to employer but most include group exercises, further interviews, more testing and sometimes preparing and delivering a presentation. It's essential you know what to expect

from the day so that you can prepare yourself. Most careers services offer practice group exercises to give you tips and feedback on your performance.

The other thing to remember is that you're being assessed the whole time, from the moment you arrive to the moment you leave, even during informal parts of the day like lunchtime or breaks. Be yourself – if you've applied to a job that you really believe you'll be suited to, then everything is going to go well. And however nervous you feel, remember to smile! As well as assessing your skills and experience, recruiters are trying to find out whether you'll fit into their organisation and somebody who seems positive is going to make a much better first impression.

Employers generally make job offers quite quickly after assessment centres, so you shouldn't have to wait long to hear if you've been successful. And, if you're in the fortunate position of having more than one job offer to consider, don't feel pressurised to make a decision too quickly. Talking through your options with a careers adviser can help you decide which offer to accept, ready to begin your new life as a graduate.

THE TIMES TOP 100 GRADUATE EMPLOYERS — Job Applications made by Graduates in 2015

	2014		% OF FINALISTS APPLYING TO SECTOR	APPLICANTS RATIO MEN:WOMEN	GRADUATE EMPLOYER OF CHOICE 2015
1.	2	CONSULTING	16.4%	56:44	PWC
2.	1	MARKETING	15.7%	32:68	UNILEVER
3.	3	MEDIA	12.7%	34:66	BBC
4.	6	CHARITY OR VOLUNTARY WORK	11.9%	24:76	OXFAM
5.	5	RESEARCH & DEVELOPMENT	11.9%	50:50	GLAXOSMITHKLINE
6.	4	TEACHING	11.9%	34:66	-
7.	7	INVESTMENT BANKING	10.8%	63:37	J.P. MORGAN
8.	9	FINANCE	10.2%	58:42	HSBC
9.	10	LAW	10.1%	39:61	ALLEN & OVERY
10.	8	ACCOUNTANCY	10.0%	55:45	PWC
11.	11	ENGINEERING	8.9%	79:21	ROLLS-ROYCE
12.	12	SALES	8.7%	43:57	JOHN LEWIS PARTNERSHIP
13.	13	HUMAN RESOURCES	8.5%	27:73	PWC
14.	14	GENERAL MANAGEMENT	6.8%	44:56	ALDI
15.	15	RETAILING	5.4%	34:66	JOHN LEWIS PARTNERSHIP
16.	17	IT	4.7%	75:25	GOOGLE
17.	16	BUYING OR PURCHASING	4.4%	35:65	-
18.	18	TRANSPORT OR LOGISTICS	2.9%	55:45	TRANSPORT FOR LONDON
19.	19	ARMED FORCES	2.5%	64:36	-
20.	20	PROPERTY	1.9%	48:52	SAVILLS

Source **High Fliers Research** 18,412 final year students leaving UK universities in the summer of 2015 were asked which sectors they had applied to for graduate jobs and which employers they would most like to join, during interviews for *The UK Graduate Careers Survey 2015*

SHAPE YOUR FUTURE

40% of our board joined us as graduates

Do you have what it takes?

Become the future of Savills.

@savillsgraduate
#careersinproperty

πεΔC̄hεr

There's no set formula for teaching, which means every day presents an opportunity to create your own fresh way of solving problems. Regardless of the subject you teach, you will start to really see the difference you're making in the minds of tomorrow. With a future in teaching you could be starting on a salary of £27k, after receiving a tax-free bursary while you train.* Inspire the next generation with your passion and knowledge and become a teacher. Start working out your future today at **education.gov.uk/teachtimes**

TEACHING
YOUR FUTURE | THEIR FUTURE

More than a quarter of graduates have got jobs

By Richard Garner
EDUCATION EDITOR

Graduate jobs boom

THE number of jobs for

This year's graduates go all out to find jobs to recoup £30,000 loan

Graduates are getting record salaries

Nicola Woolcock
Education Correspondent

The average graduate starting salary will reach £30,000 this year for the first tim. The numbers recruited at leading

More than a quarter of top gra programmes will pay new r more than £35,000 and four org tions are offering salaries highe £45,000. Aldi, the retailer, is one best payers outside the City, offe graduates £42,000, while the Eu

Students won't get out of bed for £23k

NEW graduates expect to earn at least £23,700 in their

9 per ce '98.

shows ving th s this career

One in three undergraduates takes finals with job waitir

HELEN WARRELL
— PUBLIC POLICY CORRE
High-flyin

Graduates 'now £30,000 in debt but more upbeat'

By Martin Evans

GRADUATES leaving u mer will have debts in but expect to receive l they start work, a surve
The cl o 2015 wh

Graduates eyeing higher salarie

NEW graduates may be facing an average debt of more than £30,000 after leaving university, but a sixth expect to be earning £100,000 by the age of 30, a survey reveals.
The Class of 2015 – among the first to pay the new £9,000-a-year university tuition fees

sharp rise in debt from averages of £20,400 in 2014, £20,300 in 2013 and £19,400 in 2012.
The UK Graduate Careers Survey 2015 also found that new graduates expect to earn £23,700 – a £700 rise in the salaries they expected in 20

one in six of the final students surveyed be they will be earning at £100,000 by age 30.
And the Class of 2 work experience and job applications seem

Grad jobs at a high

But work experience is more important than ever, recruiters wa

Graduate vacancies set to rise to highest level in a decade

SARAH O'CON
EMPLOYMENT

Leading emp most bullis plans in a de greater confic recovering.
Graduate v gest compani

More students securing jobs before finals

ago, implying there has been a sharp real-terms cut in graduates' pay as the supply of candidates h the demand f
That is sup Company dat year, which sh ates saw their ea

Median st offer this y

High Fliers, which specialises in graduate recruitment re rch said it

£9,000 uni fee push students toward caree

Job prospects and salaries set to soar for graduates in 2015

By Richard Garner
EDUCATION EDITOR

The class of 2015 will enjoy the best graduate recruitment prospects for more than a decade and higher starting salaries than their predecessors, says a report out today.
The Aldi supermarket chain comes

cies is expected to soar by 8.1 per cent this summer. In addition, starting salaries will rise to an average of £30,000 – after four years of stagnation at £29,000.
Martin Birchall, managing director of High Fliers Research, the graduate

ade, with a wider choice of ate vacancies at the country's sought-after employers an ter starting salaries
The research s employers were with vacancies year a 700 jobs

■ BY LAUREN FEDOR

A NEW study out today finds that the first graduates to pay £9,000 per year in university tuition fees are more career-oriented, organised and ambitious than their predecessors.

another quarter of gra said they intended to ate course following g
The researchers reco ic drop in the numbe students with "no def after university. Just r graduates are un

Understanding the Graduate Job Market

By **Martin Birchall**
Managing Director, High Fliers Research

New graduates leaving university in 2015, many of whom were the first to have paid annual tuition fees of £9,000 for their degrees, will have been relieved to be greeted by almost universally positive headlines about the graduate job market and the prospects for a successful career after university.

In part, this was due to the country's best-known employers stepping up their graduate vacancies by an impressive 8.3 per cent in 2015, taking entry-level recruitment at organisations in *The Times Top 100 Graduate Employers* to its highest level for more than a decade and surpassing the pre-recession peak in graduate jobs recorded in 2007.

But it was clear too that university-leavers from the 'Class of 2015' were among the most careers-motivated, organised and ambitious of their generation. Doubtless spurred on by the prospect of sky-high graduation debts, an unprecedented number had begun researching their options in the first year of their degree, many more had organised work experience alongside their studies, and a record proportion had secured a definite job offer before leaving university, often with increasingly generous starting salaries.

The outlook for graduates from the 'Class of 2016' is similarly encouraging – the latest analysis shows that vacancies at Britain's leading graduate employers are set to rise by a further 9.6 per cent in 2016, the fourth year running that graduate recruitment has increased.

Two-fifths of the organisations in *The Times Top 100 Graduate Employers* plan to hire more graduates than they did in 2015 and more than a third believe they will take on a similar number of new recruits in the next 12 months. Together, the employers featured in this year's *Top 100* are advertising 22,300 vacancies for 2016, compared to the 18,726 graduates hired in 2015.

The leading accountancy and professional services firms are set to dominate the graduate job market again this year, with an unprecedented intake of more than 5,600 new trainees in 2016, more than a quarter of the total number of graduate vacancies available at the *Top 100* employers.

Although general recruitment remains restricted within many parts of the public sector, the ten Government departments and agencies that appear in the latest *Top 100* rankings are planning to step up their graduate intake again in 2016 – making this the seventh time in eight years that recruitment of graduates has increased in the public sector.

" The typical graduate starting salary available at Britain's leading employers increased in 2015 to an average of £30,000. "

THE TOUGHEST JOB IN THE CITY. COMES WITH THE BIGGEST BONUS.

FRONTLINE

CHANGING LIVES

Frontline is a new initiative designed to recruit outstanding graduates to be leaders in social work and in broader society. Successful applicants will take part in an intensive and innovative two year leadership programme, and gain a masters degree. But most importantly, they'll be working to transform the lives of vulnerable children and young people.

Because there's no bigger bonus than changing a life for the better.
www.thefrontline.org.uk

The City's investment banks & fund managers and banking & financial services employers are set to take on at least 700 additional graduates in 2016 and for the seventh consecutive year, the number of graduate roles at the top engineering & industrial firms is expected to increase, taking recruitment in the sector more than 25 per cent higher than it was a decade ago.

In all, employers in twelve of the fifteen industries and business sectors represented within the *Top 100* expect to either maintain or step up their graduate recruitment in 2016 but there are likely to be fewer opportunities at media organisations, consulting firms and the leading law firms in the year ahead.

The rapid recent expansion of the popular Teach First programme means that for the fourth year running, its graduate recruitment targets are the largest of any organisation featured in *The Times Top 100 Graduate Employers*, with 1,860 places available in 2016.

Other substantial individual recruiters include the 'Big Four' professional services firms – PwC (1,500 vacancies), EY (1,400 vacancies), Deloitte (1,200 vacancies) and KPMG (1,000 vacancies).

Almost three-fifths of the employers featured in this year's *Top 100* have vacancies for graduates in IT, over half have opportunities in finance, two-fifths are recruiting for human resources roles, and a third are hiring general management,

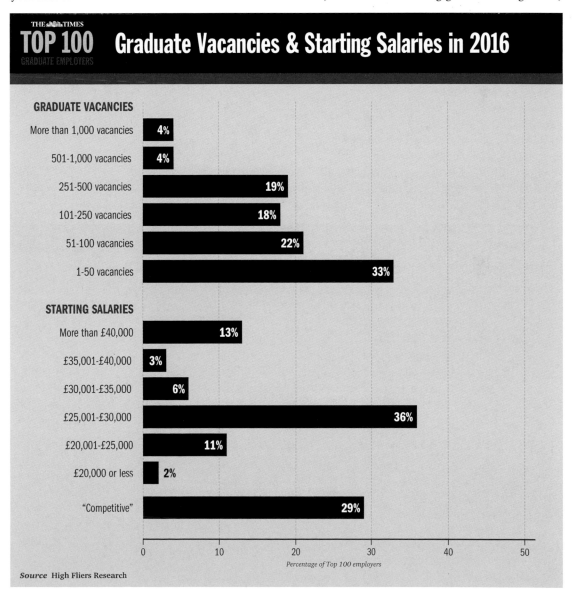

THE TIMES
TOP 100 Graduate Vacancies & Starting Salaries in 2016
GRADUATE EMPLOYERS

GRADUATE VACANCIES

More than 1,000 vacancies	4%
501-1,000 vacancies	4%
251-500 vacancies	19%
101-250 vacancies	18%
51-100 vacancies	22%
1-50 vacancies	33%

STARTING SALARIES

More than £40,000	13%
£35,001-£40,000	3%
£30,001-£35,000	6%
£25,001-£30,000	36%
£20,001-£25,000	11%
£20,000 or less	2%
"Competitive"	29%

Percentage of Top 100 employers

Source High Fliers Research

marketing or engineering graduates. A quarter are looking for recruits to work in sales, research & development or consulting, but fewer than a fifth want retail personnel or have roles in property or the media.

Over eighty of the *Top 100* employers have graduate vacancies in London in 2016 and half have posts available elsewhere in the south east of England. Up to half also have graduate roles in the south west of England, the north west and the Midlands. Northern Ireland, Wales and East Anglia have the fewest vacancies.

The typical graduate starting salary available at Britain's leading employers increased in 2015 to an average of £30,000. Up to half of the organisations featured in this year's edition of *The Times Top 100 Graduate Employers* have opted to leave their graduate starting salaries unchanged in 2016 but a number of major employers – including several leading law firms, banks and consulting firms – have announced increases to their graduate pay packages, typically of between £500 and £2,500 each.

More than a quarter of *Top 100* employers simply describe their salary packages for next year as "competitive" but one in six organisations, mainly investment banks, strategic consulting firms, City law firms, the leading oil & energy companies

and two well-known retailers, are planning to pay starting salaries in excess of £35,000. The most generous graduate packages publicised within this edition of the *Top 100* are again at the retailer Aldi which continues to offer its recruits a sector-leading graduate starting salary of £42,000 plus an Audi A4 company car, and the European Commission which offers new graduates a salary of at least £41,500.

Almost half the UK's leading employers now recruit graduates year-round, or in different phases during the year, and will accept applications throughout the 2015-2016 recruitment season, until all their vacancies are filled. For employers with a single application deadline, most are in either November, December or January, although several leading law firms have July closing dates for their training contracts.

Over two-thirds of *Top 100* employers insist that applicants for their graduate programmes should have a 2.1 degree or better and a quarter now specify a minimum UCAS tariff too, most in the range of 300 to 340 – the equivalent of 'BBB' to 'AAB' at A-level.

So for those who make the grade, there continues to be an excellent range of career opportunities and some great starting salaries on offer from *The Times Top 100 Graduate Employers* in 2016.

TOP 100 Graduate Vacancies at Top 100 Employers in 2016

	2015		NUMBER OF VACANCIES IN 2016	CHANGE SINCE 2015	MEDIAN STARTING SALARY IN 2015
1.	1	ACCOUNTANCY & PROFESSIONAL SERVICES FIRMS	5,650	▲ 8.7%	£30,000
2.	2	PUBLIC SECTOR EMPLOYERS	3,840	▲ 3.3%	£21,500
3.	4	ENGINEERING & INDUSTRIAL COMPANIES	2,475	▲ 5.2%	£27,500
4.	3	INVESTMENT BANKS & FUND MANAGERS	2,200	▲ 13.2%	£45,000
5.	6	BANKING & FINANCIAL SERVICES	1,830	▲ 41.1%	£28,000
6.	5	RETAILERS	1,175	▲ 34.8%	£26,000
7.	7	ARMED FORCES	1,050	▲ 34.8%	£30,000
8.	10	CONSULTING FIRMS	1,030	▼ 3.7%	£31,500
9.	8	IT & TELECOMMUNICATIONS COMPANIES	861	▲ 10.2%	£30,000
10.	9	LAW FIRMS	755	▼ 2.5%	£40,000
11.	12	MEDIA ORGANISATIONS	500	▼ 23.9%	£30,000
12.	13	CONSUMER GOODS MANUFACTURERS	390	NO CHANGE	£29,000
13.	11	OIL & ENERGY COMPANIES	320	▲ 7.7%	£32,500
14.	15	CHEMICAL & PHARMACEUTICAL COMPANIES	130	NO CHANGE	£28,000
15.	14	TRANSPORT COMPANIES	75	NO CHANGE	£29,500

Source High Fliers Research

Start today.
Change tomorrow.

Our work impacts at the highest level of global business. We advise some of the world's most important organisations on the issues that are shaping tomorrow.

It's the perfect environment for graduates who want to make an impact on business and their own careers.

Start thinking today about the impact you want to make tomorrow.

Find out more and apply **ey.com/uk/students**

EY
Building a better
working world

Anything but ordinary.

#LidlSurprises

www.lidlgraduatecareers.co.uk

There's nothing ordinary about
our graduate opportunities…

OR OUR GRADUATES!

Graduate Management Programme

NATIONWIDE FLEXIBILITY

Variety, responsibility and long-term career opportunities are on offer in our exciting new Graduate Management Programme. With a £36K salary our Programme will set you on a career path like no other.

We are anything but ordinary! Are you?

Not for the fainthearted, this two year comprehensive and intensive training programme covers all aspects of retail management; from Store Operations to Logistics, Property to Supply Chain; including various departments in our Head Office. This is a fantastic opportunity if you are a highly ambitious and talented graduate who wants to get right to the heart of how a retail business operates.

After two years of commitment and hard work, you will be in a perfect position to take on a permanent management role within the business and really kick-start your career with us.

If you're anything but ordinary, we want to know more!

To apply online please visit:
www.lidlgraduatecareers.co.uk

#LidlSurprises

Making the Most of Work Experience

By **Greg Hurst**
Education Editor, The Times

First, the good news for students who are about to turn their thoughts to job-hunting. Britain's top employers are offering more internships and work experience opportunities than ever before.

Now, the bad news. They can be very hard to get onto. Indeed competition for internships and work placements is so fierce that, in many industries, it can be tougher to get on these than it is to get full-time graduate job after university.

The explanation lies in the profound change that has taken place in the graduate recruitment market over the past decade. As competition between employers to find the best graduates has become more intense, particularly those with the most sought-after expertise and skills such as engineers, scientists and mathematicians, recruiters have moved to identify likely candidates earlier.

More and more employers have developed programmes aimed at penultimate-year students and, increasingly, even undergraduates in their first year. Until ten years ago work experience for students was something that graduate employers offered out of benevolence, to let them have a taste of working in an industry or sector and see if they liked it.

" A record 57 per cent of students graduating in 2015 had applied for internships or paid holiday placements while at university "

Now, these placements are usually part of the employers' graduate recruitment process. Internships are paid and used as an opportunity to assess a candidate's suitability for the business. Selection is therefore rigorous, usually using a similar process to that for screening applicants for graduate recruitment programmes.

The organisations featured in *The Times Top 100 Graduate Employers* have increased their work placements for students by more than 40 per cent since 2010, with a particularly big expansion for the 2015 recruiting cycle, when these rose by more than 10 per cent.

More than four-fifths of these employers now offer paid work experience places annually. In the last twelve months, two-thirds have provided internships, typically for penultimate year students during the summer holidays, whilst half of employers arranged longer-term industrial placements, usually lasting for six months or a year, organised as part of undergraduates' degree courses.

Many graduate recruiters also run work experience programmes for first year students – two fifths put on open days, taster sessions or introductory courses, often during the Easter holidays, and a quarter have short paid internships aimed specifically at first years.

Join the Institute of Physics

Apply for membership today, all details and application forms are available at **www.iop.org/students**

For physics • For physicists • For all

IOP Institute of Physics

The integral role these placements play in the recruitment process is illustrated by the fact that almost a third of the graduate vacancies at *Top 100* employers in 2015 – 31 per cent – were filled by candidates who had already worked for the organisation, either through an internship, degree course placement or a holiday job. And in a number of the most popular sectors, such as investment banking, financial services, consumer goods, oil & energy and law, more than half of all new graduates are now recruited through work experience schemes.

Can students who want to apply for a graduate programme afford to ignore the trend? Increasingly not – almost half the graduate recruiters working for *Top 100* employers, questioned recently, said they wouldn't hire an applicant who had done no previous work experience, or were very unlikely to do so.

Hence the stiff competition. A record 57 per cent of students graduating in 2015 had applied for internships or paid holiday placements with a graduate employer while at university, according to *The UK Graduate Careers Survey 2015*, the survey of 18,412 final year students at Britain's top thirty universities that provides the data for *The Times Top 100 Graduate Employers*. But despite

applying to an average of seven organisations, fewer than two-thirds of applicants were successful in securing a work placement with a graduate employer.

J.P. Morgan, the investment bank, is one of several well-known employers that runs work experience schemes for first year students. Over 200 undergraduates are invited to a "spring week" around Easter, either in London, Glasgow or Bournemouth, for taster sessions, group activities and internal speakers.

"It is a really good pipeline," says Phillip Paige, the bank's junior talent pipeline manager, "because if they are seen to engage really well whilst they are on that programme, then we will encourage them to apply for an internship and their application will be treated with favour if we can say, 'yes we saw you last year and here you are again'."

J.P. Morgan runs these paid internships over 10 weeks in the summer for penultimate year students, and year-long placements for students on a sandwich degree course.

While at the investment bank, interns are encouraged to integrate into the bank's culture and societies as well as the business.

"If they perform well with their internship they will be made a conditional graduate offer at the

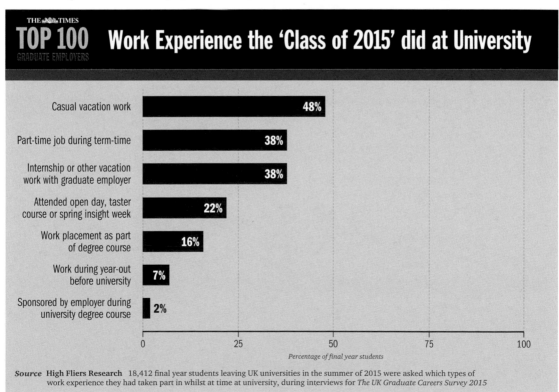

Work Experience the 'Class of 2015' did at University

Category	Percentage
Casual vacation work	48%
Part-time job during term-time	38%
Internship or other vacation work with graduate employer	38%
Attended open day, taster course or spring insight week	22%
Work placement as part of degree course	16%
Work during year-out before university	7%
Sponsored by employer during university degree course	2%

Percentage of final year students

Source **High Fliers Research** 18,412 final year students leaving UK universities in the summer of 2015 were asked which types of work experience they had taken part in whilst at time at university, during interviews for *The UK Graduate Careers Survey 2015*

end of the internship, which puts them in a great position because they are going back to university knowing they have the opportunity to secure a graduate job," Mr Paige says.

The majority of interns are offered a graduate position at the bank, which makes the application process highly competitive. J.P. Morgan does not disclose application figures but assesses candidates using a mix of tests, interviews and a day at an assessment centre.

A common mistake made by candidates at the bank's assessment centres, Mr Paige says, is to assume that they need to behave like a character out of an episode of *The Apprentice*. Not so, he says. He advises applicants to research the company carefully beforehand but, beyond that, to behave as naturally as possible.

"The tip that I tend to give people is don't go in there assuming we are looking only for leaders, that we only want the loudest voice at the table. That is

definitely not the case," he says. "It is very obvious when you are assessing students if someone is trying to fulfil a role that is not their natural one. Our strength is in the diversity of the people that we bring in so we will always be looking for 'who is the ideas person here?' and 'who is engaging members of the group?'. That's a great way to stand out. If you have a couple of quiet people and they say, 'what are your views on this?' then that puts you across as a really good candidate."

Shell, the energy company, has expanded its summer internship programme for penultimate year students from 25 to around 50 places and would like to increase it further.

Interns are given live projects to work on, which for engineering and other technical roles are based in Aberdeen, where they are offered pre-booked student accommodation, while roles such as human resources, IT and finance are based in London. Students at both locations are paid a

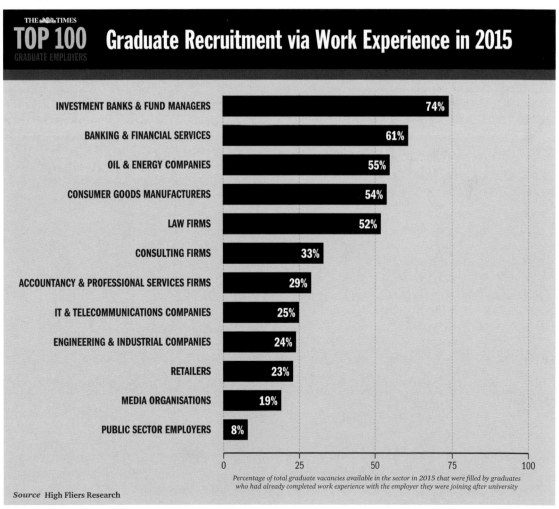

THE TIMES
TOP 100 Graduate Recruitment via Work Experience in 2015
GRADUATE EMPLOYERS

Sector	Percentage
INVESTMENT BANKS & FUND MANAGERS	74%
BANKING & FINANCIAL SERVICES	61%
OIL & ENERGY COMPANIES	55%
CONSUMER GOODS MANUFACTURERS	54%
LAW FIRMS	52%
CONSULTING FIRMS	33%
ACCOUNTANCY & PROFESSIONAL SERVICES FIRMS	29%
IT & TELECOMMUNICATIONS COMPANIES	25%
ENGINEERING & INDUSTRIAL COMPANIES	24%
RETAILERS	23%
MEDIA ORGANISATIONS	19%
PUBLIC SECTOR EMPLOYERS	8%

Percentage of total graduate vacancies available in the sector in 2015 that were filled by graduates who had already completed work experience with the employer they were joining after university

Source High Fliers Research

pro rata salary equivalent to around £20,000 a year, approximately two-thirds of the company's graduate starting salary.

It is highly competitive – Shell receives around 7,000 applications for internships, although these are not evenly spread, with fewer for human resources and specialist technology roles. Applications are made online with a CV, followed by an invitation to complete an online test and, if successful, a telephone interview.

"The selection process to that point is to exactly the same standard as if they were applying to us for a graduate role," says Beth Jenkins, recruitment marketing advisor with Shell. "It's just that their final assessment is via their internship rather than coming, if they were a final year student, to an assessment day."

Interns are assessed throughout their 10 or 12 week placement and make a final presentation but are also given an "e-tray exercise" – responding to an inbox into which emails are coming thick and fast, demanding an urgent response, with tasks such as retrieving data. It is deliberately impossible but tests applicants' ability to prioritise and cope under pressure. Typically three quarters are offered a graduate job.

While Shell has graduate roles that require specific engineering or technology-linked skills, it recruits, like many of the leading employers, according to core competencies – in its case capacity, achievement, and relationship building skills.

"Particularly on the corporate and commercial side we are far less interested in what someone's degree subject is or even what their predicted grades are. It's really about 'does someone have our competencies' and that is what they are assessed on," Ms Jenkins says.

"My top tip for students is really to quantify their experience as far as possible on the CV. Don't just say I did an internship with this employer – what did you do? How many people did you work with? What was the scope of your project? What was the impact of your project?"

Her ideal CV might run to two pages, tightly focused and relevant, with each entry accompanied by one example of how it developed the core skills Shell is looking for, she says.

IBM, the IT services and consulting company, is another graduate employer that recruits via its work placement programme. Its main focus is year-long placements, for which it takes around 300 penultimate year university students each year into roles across the business, such as marketing, finance, technical roles and software development. It also takes up to sixteen students

---

THE TIMES
TOP 100 Work Experience for First Year Students in 2016
GRADUATE EMPLOYERS

EMPLOYER, TYPE OF WORK EXPERIENCE, LENGTH	EMPLOYER, TYPE OF WORK EXPERIENCE, LENGTH
AECOM Summer Placements *6 weeks*	**HOGAN LOVELLS** Spring Vacation Scheme *1 week*
AIRBUS Internships *3 months*	**HSBC** First Year Summer Internships *8 weeks*, Insights Week *3 days*
BAE SYSTEMS Insight Programme *1 week*	**J.P. MORGAN** Spring Week *1 week*
BANK OF AMERICA MERRILL LYNCH Insight Programme *1 week*	**KPMG** First Year Insight Programme *2 days*
BARCLAYS Spring Programme *1 week*	**LINKLATERS** Pathfinder *2 days*
BDO Insight Day *1 day*	**MARS** Summer Internships *12 weeks*
BLACKROCK Insight Week *1 week*	**MORGAN STANLEY** Spring Insight Programme *1 week*
BLOOMBERG Bootcamp Insight Week *1 week*, Summer Internships *10 weeks*	**NORTON ROSE FULBRIGHT** Insight Scheme *1 week*
CENTRICA Insight Day *1 day*	**PWC** Talent Academies *2-5 days*, Insight Day *1 day*
CITI Work Experience Week *1 week*	**RBS** Spring Week *1 week*, Insight Day *1 day*
CIVIL SERVICE FAST STREAM Early Diversity Internship Programme *1 week*	**ROLLS-ROYCE** Summer Internships *10-12 weeks*
DELOITTE First Year Insight *2 days*	**SKY** Work Experience *1-2 weeks*
EY EY Leadership Academy *3 days*, Discover EY *2 days*, Insight Day *1 day*	**SLAUGHTER AND MAY** First Year Open Day *1 day*
FRESHFIELDS BRUCKHAUS DERINGER Freshers Meet Freshfields *1 day*	**UBS** Insights *1 week*, Horizons *8 weeks*
FRONTLINE Insight Day *1 day*	**UNILEVER** Spring Programme *3 days*
HERBERT SMITH FREEHILLS First Year Workshops *2 days*	**WELLCOME TRUST** Summer Internships *8 weeks*

Source **The Times Top 100 Graduate Employers** For full details of these work experience programmes for first year students in 2016 and other opportunities, see employers' individual graduate recruitment websites, as listed on page 240.

annually on summer holiday internships. They are paid £15,000 a year, or £18,000 with a London weighting.

The company gets around 8,000 applications a year for its longer placements although this is fewer than the 12,000 who apply annually for the 300 places on its graduate programme. Interns can go straight to a business interview for a graduate role, or may undergo a further assessment first if their placement has not matched the more specific roles for which IBM hires such as sales, consultancy or technical posts.

Applicants, who must be on track for a 2:1 degree or higher, complete an online test, are screened according to IBM's eight competency skills such as team-work, communication, leadership, drive and problem-solving, followed by an assessment day of group exercises and interviews.

While IBM recruits students studying a wide range of degrees, like many graduate employers it puts a premium on undergraduates with maths, engineering, science and other technology backgrounds. "Although we don't mind what degree background people have, we would love to be attracting students studying the STEM degrees – sciences, maths etc," says Kelly Markwick, IBM's UK schools and universities attraction manager. "Pretty much everyone is looking for very similar people."

In total, the employers featured within this edition of *The Times Top 100 Graduate Employers* offered a record 13,049 paid vacation placements, internships or other work experience opportunities during 2015 for university students and recent graduates, and that number is expected to rise further for 2016.

THE TIMES TOP 100 GRADUATE EMPLOYERS
Work Experience for Penultimate Year Students in 2016

EMPLOYER, TYPE OF WORK EXPERIENCE, LENGTH	EMPLOYER, TYPE OF WORK EXPERIENCE, LENGTH
ACCENTURE Summer Vacation Scheme *8 weeks*	**GOLDMAN SACHS** Summer Analyst Programme *10 weeks*
AECOM Summer Placements *6 weeks*	**GRANT THORNTON** Internships *4-6 weeks*
AIRBUS Internships *3 months*	**HERBERT SMITH FREEHILLS** Vacation Placements *2-3 weeks*
ALLEN & OVERY Summer Vacation Scheme *3 weeks*	**HOGAN LOVELLS** Summer Vacation Scheme *3 weeks*
BAE SYSTEMS Summer Internships *12 weeks*	**HSBC** Summer Internships *8-10 weeks*
BARCLAYS Summer Internships *9 weeks*	**IBM** Extreme Blue Summer Internships *3 months*
BDO Internships *6 weeks*	**J.P. MORGAN** Summer Internships *12 weeks*
BLACKROCK Summer Analyst Programme *10 weeks*	**KPMG** Summer Vacation Programme *4-6 weeks*
BLOOMBERG Summer Internships *10 weeks*	**LINKLATERS** Summer Vacation Scheme *4 weeks*
BOOTS Finance Internships *8 weeks*	**LLOYDS BANKING GROUP** Internships *10 weeks*
BOSTON CONSULTING GROUP Summer Internships *8 weeks*	**MARS** Summer Internships *12 weeks*
BP Summer Internships *11 weeks*	**MORGAN STANLEY** Summer Analyst Programme *10 weeks*
BT Summer Internships *12 weeks*	**MOTT MACDONALD** Summer Internships *8-12 weeks*
CENTRICA Insight Day *1 day*, Summer Placements *10 weeks*	**NESTLÉ** Summer Internships *10 weeks*
CITI Summer Analyst Programme *8-10 weeks*	**NORTON ROSE FULBRIGHT** Summer Vacation Scheme *3 weeks*
CIVIL SERVICE FAST STREAM Summer Diversity Internship Programme *6-9 weeks*	**P&G** Internships *8-12 weeks*
DANONE Summer Insight Week *1 week*	**PWC** Summer Internships *6-8 weeks*
DELOITTE Summer Internships *3-6 weeks*	**RBS** Summer Internships *10 weeks*
DIAGEO Summer Sales Internships *12 weeks*	**ROLLS-ROYCE** Summer Internships *10-12 weeks*
DLA PIPER Vacation Scheme *2 weeks*	**SHELL** Internships *12 weeks*
DYSON RDD Internships *3 months*	**SKY** Summer Placements *6-8 weeks*
EXXONMOBIL Summer Internships *8 weeks*	**SLAUGHTER AND MAY** Easter & Summer Work Experience *1-3 weeks*
EY Summer Internships *6 weeks*, Global Student Experience *11 weeks*	**TESCO** Summer Internships *10 weeks*
FRESHFIELDS BRUCKHAUS DERINGER Summer Vacation Scheme *3 weeks*	**UBS** Summer Internships *9 weeks*
FRONTLINE Insight Day *1 day*	**UNILEVER** Summer Placements *12 weeks*
GLAXOSMITHKLINE Summer Internships *10-12 weeks*	**WELLCOME TRUST** Summer Internships *8 weeks*

Source **The Times Top 100 Graduate Employers** For full details of these work experience programmes for penultimate year students in 2016 and other opportunities, see employers' individual graduate recruitment websites, as listed on page 240.

OUR BENEFITS PACKAGE CONTAINS SOMETHING OTHERS DON'T. PRIDE.

PUT YOUR MIND TO WORK AS A ROYAL NAVY OFFICER.
SEARCH .

LIFE
WITHOUT
LIMITS

ROYAL
NAVY

FOR THE STUDENT OF TODAY

AND THE CEO OF TOMORROW

The Student Membership

The latest news online and on your smartphone, plus sports highlights and exclusive student offers and events.

£20 a year (save 86%*)

thetimes.co.uk/studentmembership

VERIFIED BY
UNiDAYS®

THE TIMES
TOP 100
GRADUATE EMPLOYERS

Index

EMPLOYER	TOP 100 RANKING	ACCOUNTANCY	CONSULTING	ENGINEERING	FINANCE	GENERAL MANAGEMENT	HUMAN RESOURCES	INVESTMENT BANKING	IT	LAW	LOGISTICS	MARKETING	MEDIA	PROPERTY	PURCHASING	RESEARCH & DEVELOPMENT	RETAILING	SALES	NUMBER OF VACANCIES	PAGE
ACCENTURE	17		●						●										650+	56
AECOM	97		●	●	●	●								●					400	58
AIRBUS	62			●	●				●		●				●	●			50-60	60
ALDI	2				●												●		200	62
ALLEN & OVERY	39									●									90	64
ARMY	35	●	●	●	●	●	●		●	●	●	●	●	●	●	●			650	66
ARUP	31	●	●	●	●														250+	68
ASDA	77				●						●			●		●			No fixed quota	70
ASTRAZENECA	75		●		●				●		●			●	●				80+	72
ATKINS	42		●	●	●				●				●						300	74
BAE SYSTEMS	49	●	●	●	●		●		●		●				●				350+	76
BAIN & COMPANY	56		●																No fixed quota	78
BAKER & MCKENZIE	63									●									30	80
BANK OF AMERICA MERRILL LYNCH	84			●				●	●										200+	82
BANK OF ENGLAND	100	●			●	●	●	●	●										60+	84
BARCLAYS	16			●	●	●	●		●		●						●		300	86
BBC	10		●		●				●				●		●				50+	88
BDO	94	●																	250	90
BLACKROCK	79		●		●			●		●									100+	92
BLOOMBERG	65				●														300+	94
BOOTS	70			●	●				●		●	●		●		●			50	96
BOSTON CONSULTING GROUP	53		●																No fixed quota	98
BP	20	●		●	●	●	●	●	●		●			●	●	●	●		Around 100	100
BRITISH AIRWAYS	52		●	●		●	●				●			●	●				75+	102
BT	44				●	●			●	●		●			●		●		250	104
CANCER RESEARCH UK	46					●			●		●	●		●					8	106
CENTRICA	91		●	●	●	●	●		●		●	●							50+	108
CITI	48				●	●		●											180-220	110
CIVIL SERVICE FAST STREAM	5			●	●	●			●		●			●	●				900+	112
CREDIT SUISSE	99			●			●	●									●		150+	114
DANONE	66			●		●			●	●	●			●		●			25+	116
DELOITTE	6	●	●		●								●						1,200	118
DIAGEO	54		●	●	●					●						●			50+	120
DLA PIPER	60							●											85	122
DYSON	74		●	●	●				●		●			●	●	●			70+	124
EUROPEAN COMMISSION (EU CAREERS)	45			●	●	●		●	●		●	●		●					No fixed quota	126
EXXONMOBIL	64			●	●	●		●								●			No fixed quota	128
EY	8	●	●		●				●										1,400	130
FIRST DERIVATIVES	82	●	●	●	●			●											200	132
FRESHFIELDS BRUCKHAUS DERINGER	32								●										80	134
FRONTLINE	40				●	●	●		●						●				180	136
GLAXOSMITHKLINE	12		●	●		●			●		●				●				50+	138
GOLDMAN SACHS	15	●			●		●	●	●	●									Around 400	140
GOOGLE	3		●	●		●			●			●	●	●					No fixed quota	142
GRANT THORNTON	90	●																	300+	144
HERBERT SMITH FREEHILLS	96									●									70	146

EMPLOYER	TOP 100 RANKING	ACCOUNTANCY	CONSULTING	ENGINEERING	FINANCE	GENERAL MANAGEMENT	HUMAN RESOURCES	INVESTMENT BANKING	IT	LAW	LOGISTICS	MARKETING	MEDIA	PROPERTY	PURCHASING	RESEARCH & DEVELOPMENT	RETAILING	SALES	NUMBER OF VACANCIES	PAGE
HOGAN LOVELLS	61									●									60	148
HSBC	18				●		●										●	●	500+	150
IBM	21		●						●									●	300+	152
JAGUAR LAND ROVER	19			●	●	●			●		●	●		●	●	●			270	154
JOHN LEWIS PARTNERSHIP	11				●	●									●		●		40+	156
J.P. MORGAN	14				●		●	●											No fixed quota	158
KPMG	9	●	●		●	●			●	●									1,000	160
L'ORÉAL	28				●							●	●				●		40	162
LIDL	25					●					●			●			●		100	164
LINKLATERS	41									●									110	166
LLOYD'S	93				●														15-20	168
LLOYDS BANKING GROUP	30	●	●		●	●	●		●								●		Around 450	170
M&S	34				●	●			●		●	●		●	●		●		200	172
MARS	38		●	●	●				●		●	●		●	●				50	174
MCDONALD'S	68					●											●		250-350	176
MCKINSEY & COMPANY	22		●																No fixed quota	178
METROPOLITAN POLICE	58																		To be confirmed	180
MI5 – THE SECURITY SERVICE	83					●			●										80+	182
MICROSOFT	29		●															●	36	184
MONDELĒZ INTERNATIONAL	80		●	●		●					●	●			●			●	Around 40	186
MORGAN STANLEY	36				●	●		●	●										No fixed quota	188
MOTT MACDONALD	71		●	●									●						300	190
NESTLÉ	78		●	●	●	●						●					●		30-35	192
NETWORK RAIL	76		●	●	●	●			●		●		●						Around 200	194
NEWTON EUROPE	55		●																60	196
NGDP FOR LOCAL GOVERNMENT	67					●													120	198
NHS	7				●	●	●		●										100+	200
NORTON ROSE FULBRIGHT	87									●									Up to 50	202
OXFAM	86					●						●	●		●	●			50+ (voluntary)	204
P&G	27			●	●	●			●		●	●			●			●	100	206
PENGUIN RANDOM HOUSE	85	●			●	●						●	●					●	50+	208
PWC	1	●	●		●				●	●									1,500	210
RBS	51	●			●	●	●	●											500+	212
ROLLS-ROYCE	23			●	●	●								●			●		350+	214
ROYAL NAVY	47		●	●	●	●			●	●	●			●					No fixed quota	216
SHELL	26		●	●	●				●			●		●					80-100	218
SIEMENS	73		●	●	●				●					●			●		80	220
SKY	43	●	●	●	●	●			●			●	●	●					90+	222
SLAUGHTER AND MAY	50									●									80	224
TEACH FIRST	4	●	●	●	●	●	●	●	●	●	●	●	●	●	●	●	●	●	1,860	226
TESCO	24			●	●	●			●		●	●	●	●	●		●		200+	228
TRANSPORT FOR LONDON	69	●		●		●			●					●					150	230
UBS	92				●	●	●	●	●									●	300	232
UNILEVER	13			●	●	●			●			●			●		●		50	234
WELLCOME TRUST	95			●	●	●	●		●	●				●	●				10-12	236
WPP	72											●	●						1-10	238

accenture.com/timestop100

More than a consultancy firm, Accenture is the perfect mix of strategy, digital, technology, consulting and operations expertise. Through these areas Accenture is able to create end-to-end solutions that transform the way organisations work and offer a great environment for any graduate to thrive.

Every year, Accenture's diversity of work, expertise, people, clients and training turns talented students into successful professionals. Whether they are helping to develop a commercially available app, like the RBS 6 Nations Official Championship app; advising organisations on their people and processes; or creating technology that changes millions of lives, such as biometric passport readers, Accenture's graduate prorgammes allow people to make a real impact across a spectrum of industries and work with clients that span more than three-quarters of the Fortune Global 500.

Graduates who join the Consulting Programme will work with clients to identify market opportunities and shape the strategies that solve the most complex business challenges. Accenture's Client Delivery Programme is all about delivering solutions that really work. Using a deep understanding of technology, graduates will work to assess which innovations are right for clients – then work to implement them. Our Software Engineering Programme offers graduates with practical programming knowledge the chance to design, build, and support cutting-edge technical solutions – advising on which technologies should be used and making sure they're delivered in the best way.

Of course, wherever graduates join Accenture, they can look forward to fantastic support, as well as a structured and tailored training programme, which provides the key practical (and technical) knowledge to do the role, but also the all-round business skills that make Accenture people so highly regarded in the industry.

GRADUATE VACANCIES IN 2016
CONSULTING
IT

NUMBER OF VACANCIES
650+ graduate jobs

LOCATIONS OF VACANCIES

STARTING SALARY FOR 2016
£Competitive

UNIVERSITY VISITS IN 2015-16
ASTON, BATH, BIRMINGHAM, BRISTOL, CAMBRIDGE, CITY, DURHAM, EDINBURGH, EXETER, IMPERIAL COLLEGE LONDON, KENT, LANCASTER, LEEDS, LONDON SCHOOL OF ECONOMICS, LOUGHBOROUGH, MANCHESTER, NEWCASTLE, NOTTINGHAM, OXFORD, QUEEN MARY LONDON, SHEFFIELD, SOUTHAMPTON, ST ANDREWS, UNIVERSITY COLLEGE LONDON, WARWICK
Please check with your university careers service for full details of local events.

MINIMUM ENTRY REQUIREMENTS
Dependent on scheme
Please see website for full details.

APPLICATION DEADLINE
Year-round recruitment
Early application advised.

FURTHER INFORMATION
www.Top100GraduateEmployers.com
Register now for the latest news, events information and graduate recruitment details for Britain's leading employers.

be  you
imagined

Bring your talent and passion to a global
organisation at the forefront of business, technology
and innovation. Collaborate with diverse, talented
colleagues and leaders who support your success.
Help transform organisations and communities
around the world. Sharpen your skills through
industry leading training and development, as you
build an extraordinary career. Discover how great
you can be. Visit **accenture.com/gradfutures**

Be greater than.

Strategy | Consulting | Digital | Technology | Operations

accenture
High performance. Delivered.

With nearly 100,000 employees worldwide – including engineers, designers, planners, scientists, surveyors, architects, and management and construction services professionals – serving clients in more than 150 countries, AECOM is a premier, fully integrated infrastructure and support services firm.

AECOM is ranked as the number 1 engineering design firm by revenue in Engineering News-Record magazine's annual industry rankings. The company is a leader in all of the key markets that it serves, including transportation, facilities, environmental, energy, oil and gas, water, high-rise buildings and government. AECOM provides a blend of global reach, local knowledge, innovation and technical excellence in delivering solutions that create, enhance and sustain the world's built, natural and social environments. A Fortune 500 company, AECOM companies, including URS, had revenue of $19.2 billion during the 12 months ended June 30, 2014.

AECOM invests heavily in the quality of their graduate programme and the opportunities it provides. Of course they do – it is designed to equip their future leaders and technical experts. AECOM currently has more than 1,100 graduates across the UK & Ireland, learning from some of the most talented and renowned experts in their field, bringing fresh approaches and further diversifying their workforce.

As a company AECOM are responding fast to the fact that since this is an increasingly interconnected and challenging world, new thinking is called for. The global population is growing, yet resources are finite and carbon emissions are already way too high. AECOM gets the bigger picture, uniting clever ingenuity with global experience. Their focus is to realise their clients' boldest ambitions.

GRADUATE VACANCIES IN 2016
CONSULTING
ENGINEERING
FINANCE
GENERAL MANAGEMENT
PROPERTY

NUMBER OF VACANCIES
400 graduate jobs

LOCATIONS OF VACANCIES

STARTING SALARY FOR 2016
£23,000-£26,000

UNIVERSITY VISITS IN 2015-16
BATH, BELFAST, BIRMINGHAM, BRISTOL, CAMBRIDGE, CARDIFF, DURHAM, EDINBURGH, EXETER, GLASGOW, HERIOT-WATT, IMPERIAL COLLEGE LONDON, KING'S COLLEGE LONDON, LEEDS, LIVERPOOL, LOUGHBOROUGH, MANCHESTER, NEWCASTLE, NORTHUMBRIA, NOTTINGHAM, NOTTINGHAM TRENT, OXFORD, OXFORD BROOKES, PLYMOUTH, READING, SHEFFIELD, SOUTHAMPTON, STRATHCLYDE, SURREY, TRINITY COLLEGE DUBLIN, ULSTER, UNIVERSITY COLLEGE DUBLIN, UNIVERSITY COLLEGE LONDON, WARWICK, YORK
Please check with your university careers service for full details of local events.

MINIMUM ENTRY REQUIREMENTS
2.2 Degree

APPLICATION DEADLINE
Year-round recruitment
Early application advised.

FURTHER INFORMATION
www.Top100GraduateEmployers.com
Register now for the latest news, events information and graduate recruitment details for Britain's leading employers.

AIRBUS
GROUP

www.jobs.airbusgroup.com

graduates@airbus.com

twitter.com/AirbusGroup   facebook.com/AirbusGroupCareers

youtube.com/AirbusGroup   linkedin.com/company/airbusgroup

Airbus Group is a global pioneer in aeronautics, space and related services. Uniting the capabilities of three market leaders – Airbus, Airbus Defence and Space, and Airbus Helicopters – it strives towards amazing innovation, from the double-deck Airbus A380, to the comet explorer Rosetta.

Airbus is a leading aircraft manufacturer, offering a complete range of aircraft families, from 100 to over 500 passenger seats. Responsible for around half of the world's commercial airline orders, Airbus takes pride in quality, in expertise, and in learning together.

Airbus Defence and Space is No.1 in Europe and No.2 in the world's space industry. That's because their people are driven to find new and better ways to protect the world, and to explore beyond it, for everyone's benefit.

Airbus Group looks for graduates with passionate drive and sound commercial awareness to join the Airbus and Airbus Defence and Space UK Graduate Programmes. These programmes offer unrivalled opportunities for graduates to learn and hone their talents, providing the support they need to grow.

The two/three-year programmes consist of structured rotational placements, so graduates will learn and develop technical and management skills, gaining a rounded picture of their division's work. With the training and support of Airbus Group, graduates will drive their development in the direction they choose, building a career of outstanding opportunities. For those looking for a direct role, there are also graduate openings available within Airbus Defence and Space.

Whatever their chosen path, successful applicants will join a team dedicated to creating a better future for everyone. They'll explore new ideas, think innovatively, and help Airbus Group achieve incredible things on the ground, in the air, and in space.

GRADUATE VACANCIES IN 2016
ENGINEERING
FINANCE
IT
LOGISTICS
PURCHASING
RESEARCH & DEVELOPMENT

NUMBER OF VACANCIES
50-60 graduate jobs

LOCATIONS OF VACANCIES

STARTING SALARY FOR 2016
£26,000+
Plus a welcome payment for graduates.

UNIVERSITY VISITS IN 2015-16
ASTON, BATH, BIRMINGHAM, BRISTOL, CAMBRIDGE, DURHAM, IMPERIAL COLLEGE LONDON, KENT, LEEDS, LEICESTER, LIVERPOOL, LOUGHBOROUGH, MANCHESTER, READING, SHEFFIELD, SOUTHAMPTON, SWANSEA, UNIVERSITY COLLEGE LONDON, WARWICK
Please check with your university careers service for full details of local events.

MINIMUM ENTRY REQUIREMENTS
2.2 Degree

APPLICATION DEADLINE
30th November 2015

FURTHER INFORMATION
www.Top100GraduateEmployers.com
Register now for the latest news, events information and graduate recruitment details for Britain's leading employers.

MAKE IT POSSIBLE.
MAKE IT HAPPEN.
MAKE IT FLY.

LAUNCH
YOUR CAREER
INTO ORBIT!

Airbus Group is a global leader in aeronautics, space and related services. Our people work with passion and determination to make the world safer, smarter and more connected. If you share that passion, then start an incredible career with our UK Airbus or Airbus Defence and Space Graduate Programmes.

See the full picture at
www.jobs.airbusgroup.com

AIRBUS
GROUP

www.aldirecruitment.co.uk/graduate

With roots dating back to 1913, Aldi (short for Albrecht Discount) came to the UK in 1990 and customers were amazed to see a fantastic example of 'no frills' shopping. Aldi are now the UK's fastest-growing supermarket and one of the world's most successful retailers.

All graduates enter the business on their Area Manager Training Programme. It's gained a reputation for being tough, and rightly so. Graduates have an enormous amount of responsibility very early on. By week 14, they'll take the keys to at least one store. After 12 months, they'll take control of a multi-million pound area of three to four stores. Graduates receive incredible support throughout their training, with a dedicated mentor and regular one-to-one sessions with talented colleagues.

It's the perfect introduction to Aldi and a superb foundation for future success. It gives graduates a wider lens to make critical business decisions later on in their journey. One or two years into the programme, secondments are available with many graduates having the chance to spend time in other parts of the UK, the US or even Australia. After five or so years as an Area Manager, high-performing graduates can then move into a Director role within (for example) Buying, Finance or Operations.

Aldi is built on an attitude. It's about never giving up; always striving for smarter, simpler ways of doing things. They're a business with integrity: they're fair to their partners and suppliers, and everything they do is for the benefit of their customers and their people. They look for graduates who are incredibly hardworking with a positive, 'roll their sleeves up' attitude. Those who join Aldi will blend intellect with a practical, business-focused mindset as they achieve impressive results with a world-class team.

GRADUATE VACANCIES IN 2016
GENERAL MANAGEMENT
RETAILING

NUMBER OF VACANCIES
200 graduate jobs

LOCATIONS OF VACANCIES

STARTING SALARY FOR 2016
£42,000

UNIVERSITY VISITS IN 2015-16
ABERDEEN, ASTON, BATH, BIRMINGHAM, CARDIFF, DURHAM, EAST ANGLIA, EDINBURGH, EXETER, GLASGOW, LANCASTER, LEEDS, LEICESTER, LIVERPOOL, LONDON SCHOOL OF ECONOMICS, LOUGHBOROUGH, MANCHESTER, NEWCASTLE, NORTHUMBRIA, NOTTINGHAM, READING, SHEFFIELD, SOUTHAMPTON, ST ANDREWS, STRATHCLYDE, SWANSEA, WARWICK, YORK
Please check with your university careers service for full details of local events.

MINIMUM ENTRY REQUIREMENTS
2.1 Degree
240 UCAS points

APPLICATION DEADLINE
Year-round recruitment
Early application advised.

FURTHER INFORMATION
www.Top100GraduateEmployers.com
Register now for the latest news, events information and graduate recruitment details for Britain's leading employers.

It's tougher than you think.

Turns out I'm tougher than I thought.

Graduate Area Manager Programme

- **£42,000 starting salary (rising to £70,000 after four years) • Pension • Healthcare • Audi A4**
- **All-year recruitment but spaces go quickly**

Not many employers would ask you to run a multi-million pound business after 14 weeks. But that's the beauty of Aldi. They trust you. They listen to you. You feel like the 'newbie' at the start but you just roll your sleeves up and get stuck in. It's tough. Tougher than I thought it would be. You're often managing people who have been there for years. You're organising store openings at breathtaking speed. You're taken out of your comfort zone on a daily basis and given a million things to juggle. But helping to drive the UK's fastest-growing supermarket? It feels utterly amazing.

aldirecruitment.co.uk/graduates

BECAUSE I'M ALDI. AND I'M LIKE NO OTHER.

aograduate.com
graduate.recruitment@allenovery.com
twitter.com/AllenOveryGrads facebook.com/allenoverygrads

ALLEN & OVERY

Allen & Overy is a pioneering legal practice operating around the world at the frontline of developing business. By helping companies, institutions and governments tackle ever more complex issues and transactions on a global stage, it is leading the way and extending what is possible in law.

With 45 offices in 32 countries, plus a network of relationship firms in other locations, Allen & Overy is one of the few legal practices that can genuinely claim to be global, covering 99% of the world's economy.

For the firm's clients this means global reach and access to high-calibre, local expertise with an international outlook, while for trainees, it means exposure to multinational work, collaboration with global colleagues and, in many cases, the opportunity to travel. In 2015, 71% of its transactional work involved two or more countries, 52% involved three or more, and 25% involved five or more.

Trainee lawyers joining the firm enter an environment characterised by innovative thinking and a global vision. They are exposed to challenging and meaningful work from the outset, supporting a Partner or Senior Associate in each of their training 'seats'. In addition, they are encouraged to spend six months in one of the firm's overseas offices, or on secondment to one of its corporate clients – currently approximately 80% of its trainees take up this opportunity.

Alongside a rich and exciting experience as a trainee, graduates can also look forward to world-class training and working in a uniquely open and supportive culture. Allen & Overy has established a reputation for combining the very highest professional standards with warmth and approachability.

Regardless of their degree discipline – and around half of the firm's trainees study subjects other than law – joining Allen & Overy puts graduates at the forefront of the rapidly-evolving global market for legal services.

GRADUATE VACANCIES IN 2016

LAW

NUMBER OF VACANCIES
90 graduate jobs
For training contracts starting in 2018.

LOCATIONS OF VACANCIES

STARTING SALARY FOR 2016
£42,000

UNIVERSITY VISITS IN 2015-16
BATH, BELFAST, BIRMINGHAM, BRISTOL, CAMBRIDGE, CARDIFF, DURHAM, EDINBURGH, EXETER, IMPERIAL COLLEGE LONDON, LANCASTER, LEEDS, LONDON SCHOOL OF ECONOMICS, MANCHESTER, NEWCASTLE, NOTTINGHAM, OXFORD, SHEFFIELD, SOUTHAMPTON, ST ANDREWS, TRINITY COLLEGE DUBLIN, UNIVERSITY COLLEGE DUBLIN, UNIVERSITY COLLEGE LONDON, WARWICK, YORK
Please check with your university careers service for full details of local events.

MINIMUM ENTRY REQUIREMENTS
2.1 Degree
340 UCAS points

APPLICATION DEADLINE
Please see website for full details.

FURTHER INFORMATION
www.Top100GraduateEmployers.com
Register now for the latest news, events information and graduate recruitment details for Britain's leading employers.

ALLEN & OVERY

A career in law

Setting precedents, not following them...
because tomorrow will not be like today.

Being a lawyer at Allen & Overy means having an international outlook. When Alibaba, China's answer to eBay and Amazon combined, staged the largest-ever private financing deal for a Chinese company, teams from Allen & Overy in Beijing, Hong Kong and New York ensured the Chinese debt funding for the $7.1bn share buy-back ran smoothly. And when Oracle and Sun Microsystems merged, we ensured the deal was watertight across 28 countries.

Our clients are doing deals around the globe. To support them you'll need teamwork and a mindset that embraces the challenges of international business.

Find out more at **aograduate.com**

Follow the conversation **@AllenOveryGrads | facebook.com/allenoverygrads**

ARMY
BE THE BEST

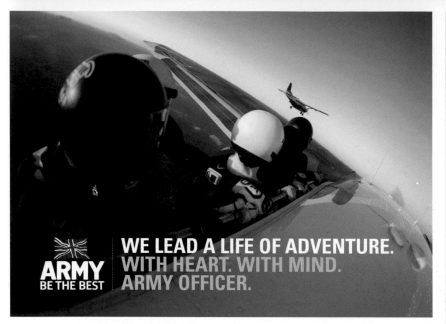

WE LEAD A LIFE OF ADVENTURE.
WITH HEART. WITH MIND.
ARMY OFFICER.

ARMY BE THE BEST

Becoming an Army Officer can teach graduates many things. It teaches them to work harder, see further, stand taller. It teaches them skills in leadership, management and communication. Professional skills and skills for life. A life of achievement, purpose and opportunity. A life full of adventure.

The route from university to becoming an Army Officer starts at the Royal Military Academy Sandhurst. This elite training academy has welcomed graduates in Geography, French, IT, Engineering, Law, Management Accounting and many other subjects. The 44 weeks of Officer training provided there, prepares graduates to apply their knowledge in ways they never imagined: leading projects of incredible scope and scale; leading humanitarian relief efforts; and leading life-saving missions.

Sandhurst is also the place where graduates get their first taste of Army Adventurous Training. This is an opportunity to participate in, and gain qualifications in, a broad range of outdoor activities from skiing in Canada to skydiving in the Bahamas.

When graduates complete their Officer training, they are commissioned as a Second Lieutenant. They then move to their chosen Regiment or Corps for further specialist training and to take immediate responsibility for leading a team of around 30 soldiers.

The best leadership training in the world together with the support needed to make the most of it, a clear path for promotion, and challenge and adventure all the way. Life as an Army Officer offers everything people with leadership potential, a strong sense of moral direction and focused ambition could want.

Bring people together. Bring a nation to its feet. With heart. With mind. Army Officer.

GRADUATE VACANCIES IN 2016
ALL SECTORS

NUMBER OF VACANCIES
650 graduate jobs

LOCATIONS OF VACANCIES

STARTING SALARY FOR 2016
£25,472
Rising to £30,617 upon completion of training.

UNIVERSITY VISITS IN 2015-16
ABERYSTWYTH, BELFAST, BIRMINGHAM, BRISTOL, CARDIFF, DUNDEE, DURHAM, EAST ANGLIA, EDINBURGH, EXETER, LEEDS, LOUGHBOROUGH, MANCHESTER, NEWCASTLE, NOTTINGHAM, NOTTINGHAM TRENT, OXFORD BROOKES, SHEFFIELD, SOUTHAMPTON
Please check with your university careers service for full details of local events.

MINIMUM ENTRY REQUIREMENTS
180 UCAS points

APPLICATION DEADLINE
30th November 2015
The deadline for January 2017 entry is 31st March 2016.

FURTHER INFORMATION
www.Top100GraduateEmployers.com
Register now for the latest news, events information and graduate recruitment details for Britain's leading employers.

**WE ARRIVE.
THE TEAM IS HUNGRY,
THIRSTY, EXHAUSTED.
BUT WE CARRY ON.
WE SEARCH, WE CLEAR.
WE SAVE, WE SERVE.
WE LEAD A LIFE OF PURPOSE.
WITH HEART. WITH MIND.
ARMY OFFICER.**

For an Army Officer, it's more than just work. It's a life-saving mission. It's thinking clearly and acting quickly. It's always looking for the most effective way to apply their knowledge and experience. It's what they've been trained for. It's how you could serve. Lead a life with purpose. **army.mod.uk/officer**

ARMY
BE THE BEST

ARUP

An independent firm offering a broad range of professional services, Arup believes that by bringing great people together, there are infinite possibilities. With experts in design, engineering, planning, business consultancy, project management and much more, Arup people work together to shape a better world.

Arup has offices in more than 30 countries across the world, making international team-working part of everyday life and bringing together professionals from diverse disciplines and with complementary skills on a uniquely global scale.

The firm is owned in trust for Arup's employees and this independence translates through the thoughts and actions of its people. Commitment to sustainability is paramount and Arup strives not only to embrace this in projects, but also to embed it into everyday thinking and working.

Graduate opportunities span a wide range of disciplines and offer exceptional experience for individuals who are ambitious, friendly and approach work with fresh eyes and enthusiasm. Arup's diversity helps to foster the creativity that is its hallmark; and the support and freedom for innovation that is encouraged has made Arup the driving force behind some of the most iconic and sustainable designs in the world.

Arup offers competitive benefits and continuous professional development built around employees and their ambitions. Graduates can undertake a professional training programme, accredited by leading organisations such as the Institution of Civil Engineers and the Association for Project Management. As a firm, Arup seeks exceptional people with innovative ideas and curious minds who want to make a real difference to the environment; passion, drive and creativity are a must.

GRADUATE VACANCIES IN 2016
ACCOUNTANCY
CONSULTING
ENGINEERING
FINANCE

NUMBER OF VACANCIES
250+ graduate jobs

LOCATIONS OF VACANCIES

Vacancies also available in Europe, Asia, the USA and elsewhere in the world.

STARTING SALARY FOR 2016
£22,000-£26,500
Plus, up to a £4,000 welcome bonus, and a bi-annual profit share scheme.

UNIVERSITY VISITS IN 2015-16
ABERDEEN, ASTON, BATH, BELFAST, BIRMINGHAM, BRISTOL, CAMBRIDGE, CARDIFF, DURHAM, EXETER, GLASGOW, HERIOT-WATT, IMPERIAL COLLEGE LONDON, LEEDS, LIVERPOOL, LOUGHBOROUGH, MANCHESTER, NEWCASTLE, NOTTINGHAM, OXFORD, SHEFFIELD, SOUTHAMPTON, STRATHCLYDE, SWANSEA, UNIVERSITY COLLEGE LONDON, WARWICK, YORK
Please check with your university careers service for full details of local events.

MINIMUM ENTRY REQUIREMENTS
2.1 Degree
Relevant degree required for some roles.

APPLICATION DEADLINE
Varies by function

FURTHER INFORMATION
www.Top100GraduateEmployers.com
Register now for the latest news, events information and graduate recruitment details for Britain's leading employers.

Infinite possibilities.

At Arup our people are always on the lookout for new and innovative ways to transform the world's infrastructure and built environment. We help to turn the challenges and obstacles of the past into the achievements of the future. We approach our work with fresh eyes and enthusiasm – working to take our industry in exciting directions. This philosophy has helped us design and deliver groundbreaking and iconic work across the world. Involving everyone from design teams and engineers, through consultants, project managers and a myriad of other professions and disciplines.

Early exposure and responsibility is a given. Work life balance is a reality, not an aspiration. And we share our success with everyone – we deliver results collaboratively and we all benefit from those results. It's about making the impossible happen, making a real difference to the world around us. It's about infinite possibilities.

Explore an opportunity where the possibilities are endless...

www.arup.com/ukmeagrads

We are committed to equal opportunities.

Save money. Live better.

CELEBRATING
1965 **50** 2015
YEARS OF
ASDA
Save money. Live better.

GRADUATE VACANCIES IN 2016
GENERAL MANAGEMENT
LOGISTICS
PURCHASING
RETAILING

NUMBER OF VACANCIES
No fixed quota

LOCATIONS OF VACANCIES

Celebrating their 50th birthday, Asda is one of Britain's most successful supermarket chains, with 600 stores, 26 depots and over 175,000 colleagues. The £multi-million business is a major graduate employer offering ambitious individuals opportunities across retail, logistics and head office.

Part of the world's largest retailer family in Walmart, Asda has created a successful and long-lasting business by selling quality products at affordable prices. Since opening, the retailer has added George Clothing, Asda Money and Asda Mobile to its list of services that promises to help customers save money so they can live better.

On the graduate scheme, candidates will experience fast progression as they contribute to helping the organisation become Britain's most trusted retailer. With a high level of responsibility and access to influential leaders in the industry, the programme is known for producing some of Asda's most successful colleagues. The scheme's notable alumni include the Project Manager to CEO Andy Clarke, and the Senior Vice President of Merchandising of Walmart, Canada.

Throughout the development period, graduates can expect to receive first-class training to take on exciting challenges across the business. It's a great opportunity for graduates with an entrepreneurial mindset to see their ideas become reality, providing innovative solutions to shape the Asda of tomorrow.

Due to the rapid pace of retail, Asda looks for ambitious graduates who can demonstrate an inspirational way with people. Ultimately, applicants will need to embody the same collaborative, fun and caring personality the supermarket has become famous for.

STARTING SALARY FOR 2016
£Competitive

UNIVERSITY VISITS IN 2015-16
BIRMINGHAM, HULL, LEEDS, MANCHESTER,
NEWCASTLE, SHEFFIELD, YORK
Please check with your university careers service for full details of local events.

APPLICATION DEADLINE
Please see website for full details.

FURTHER INFORMATION
www.Top100GraduateEmployers.com
Register now for the latest news, events information and graduate recruitment details for Britain's leading employers.

When
FRESH THINKING
builds
TRUST

We've got 600 stores and counting. More than
175,000 colleagues. Over 18 million customers.
And we're part of Walmart, one of the world's
most successful retailers. But success is more than
just numbers. It's about possibilities. Not changing
who you are. Stretching ambitions. Senior-level
exposure. Individual coaching. And meaningful
work that makes our local communities a healthier,
happier and better place to live. We want to be
the country's most trusted retailer, and Graduates
like you are already leading the way.

ASDA
Save money. Live better.

asdagraduates.com

AstraZeneca

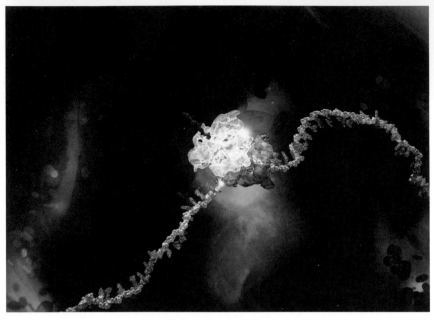

AstraZeneca pushes the boundaries of science to deliver life-changing medicines. A global, innovation-driven biopharmaceutical business, they invest very heavily in their scientific & clinical capabilities, and are proud to have a unique workplace culture that inspires innovation and collaboration.

AstraZeneca offers graduates the opportunity to thrive in an international and diverse organisation with numerous stakeholders, and take real responsibility from day one. Throughout the graduate programme, graduates will have frequent opportunities to review their progress as they train, experience groundbreaking projects, and build a strong support network, gaining an extensive understanding of the pharmaceutical industry whatever their degree. The company provides many paths towards the achievement of graduates' career objectives, and outstanding personal development plans, devised with managers, and incorporating a formal performance management process.

Some programmes will give graduates the chance to work abroad, and whichever excellent learning and development route they take, they'll find this is a company with a diverse range of perspectives, challenges and ideas.

Proud to have gained a host of awards for their progressive and diverse working practices, AstraZeneca is always reaching for more. Each award pushes them further, and strengthens the connections between fellow employees, patients, stakeholders and the communities in which they work.

At AstraZeneca, graduates find an energised, supportive environment, stoked by innovation and exemplary leaders at every level. This is the chance to collaborate with people whose ideas are as diverse as the cultures that have helped shape them.

GRADUATE VACANCIES IN 2016
ENGINEERING
GENERAL MANAGEMENT
IT
LOGISTICS
PURCHASING
RESEARCH & DEVELOPMENT

NUMBER OF VACANCIES
80+ graduate jobs

LOCATIONS OF VACANCIES

Vacancies also available in Europe, Asia, the USA and elsewhere in the world.

STARTING SALARY FOR 2016
£28,000
Plus potential for bonus, benefits and relocation (if applicable).

UNIVERSITY VISITS IN 2015-16
BRISTOL, CAMBRIDGE, DURHAM, IMPERIAL COLLEGE LONDON, KING'S COLLEGE LONDON, LEEDS, LONDON SCHOOL OF ECONOMICS, MANCHESTER, OXFORD, UNIVERSITY COLLEGE LONDON, SHEFFIELD, WARWICK, YORK
Please check with your university careers service for full details of local events.

MINIMUM ENTRY REQUIREMENTS
2.1 Degree

APPLICATION DEADLINE
Varies by function

FURTHER INFORMATION
www.Top100GraduateEmployers.com
Register now for the latest news, events information and graduate recruitment details for Britain's leading employers.

Exciting challenges on a global scale.
How will you make a difference?

AstraZeneca

Active in over 100 countries, AstraZeneca pushes the boundaries of science to deliver life-changing medicines which are already used by millions of patients worldwide. Our ambition is to improve the lives of 200 million people, and be a $50 billion company, by 2025. Right now we have opportunities for high-calibre graduates to join our Graduate Programmes in 2016.

These programmes offer you myriad possibilities for development, enabling you to excel as a graduate in your chosen field. You'll find AstraZeneca is ideally placed to help you build a satisfying career, where learning, growing and meeting exciting challenges are all in a day's work.

We offer programmes within:

- **Global Operations**
- **Information Technology**
- **Innovative Medicines and Early Development**
- **Pharmaceutical Development**

As we build on our strengths, to continue to meet the needs of a changing world, you'll also find we have a diverse workforce, with employees drawn from all backgrounds and cultures. This helps us to better reflect and understand our patients and the healthcare professionals we serve, in increasingly global markets - and ultimately, develop the medicines the world needs.

AstraZeneca welcomes applications from all sections of the community.

An Equal Opportunity Employer Minorities/ Women/Protected Veterans/Disabled/ Sexual Orientation/Gender Identity.

To find out more, please visit: **www.astrazenecacareers.com/students**

What science can do

Oncology combination therapies
AstraZeneca is investigating combinations of biologic and small molecule therapies for the treatment of cancer. These combinations target the tumour directly and some help boost the body's own immune system to induce tumour cell death.

As one of the world's most respected design, engineering and project management consultancies, Atkins is well placed to invest in the development of its graduates and support them in becoming experts in whatever inspires them most. Their imaginations could help to transform the future.

With Atkins, graduates join teams who help to create a world where lives are enriched through the implementation of the organisation's ideas, from moving people across London faster on Crossrail through to solving the energy challenges of the future.

Atkins's work covers a range of sectors including Transportation, Water, Defence, Energy and the Built Environment. They're looking for talented engineering graduates from civil, structural, mechanical, electrical, chemical, aerospace and aeronautical, systems and communications as well as IT, physics, geography and maths.

Atkins is looking for bright and ambitious graduates to join their award-winning Graduate Development Programme. Applicants will be passionate about addressing challenges with creative thinking, and be able to demonstrate flexibility, resilience and drive. Atkins offers an environment in which engineers, planners, architects and a myriad of related professionals flourish. Graduates on the scheme will have access to extensive opportunities across a range of geographical locations, functional disciplines and business areas. They will be responsible for driving their own development, but with plenty of support.

Atkins also offers a range of undergraduate opportunities too. Year-long placements and summer internships to help explore career ideas and focus on future plans, so undergraduates can spend some time with Atkins and get valuable experience and ideas.

GRADUATE VACANCIES IN 2016

CONSULTING
ENGINEERING
GENERAL MANAGEMENT
IT
PROPERTY

NUMBER OF VACANCIES
300 graduate jobs

LOCATIONS OF VACANCIES

STARTING SALARY FOR 2016
£23,000-£30,000
Plus a settling-in payment and qualification bonus of £5,000.

UNIVERSITY VISITS IN 2015-16
ABERDEEN, BATH, BIRMINGHAM, BRISTOL, CAMBRIDGE, CARDIFF, DURHAM, HERIOT-WATT, IMPERIAL COLLEGE LONDON, LEEDS, LIVERPOOL, LOUGHBOROUGH, MANCHESTER, NEWCASTLE, NOTTINGHAM TRENT, OXFORD, SHEFFIELD, SOUTHAMPTON, STRATHCLYDE, SURREY, UNIVERSITY COLLEGE LONDON, TRINITY COLLEGE DUBLIN, WARWICK
Please check with your university careers service for full details of local events.

MINIMUM ENTRY REQUIREMENTS
2.1 Degree

APPLICATION DEADLINE
Year-round recruitment
Early application advised.

FURTHER INFORMATION
www.Top100GraduateEmployers.com
Register now for the latest news, events information and graduate recruitment details for Britain's leading employers.

ATKINS

"I'm helping to power our world."

Michael, graduate

Graduate and undergraduate opportunities
£competitive pay | Opportunities across the UK

At Atkins we're taking on the most exciting engineering challenges of our time. From London to Qatar, our team of 17,000 people are designing, engineering and project managing bridges, skyscrapers, roads, airports, power stations, tidal lagoons and more.

Join us on a placement or as a graduate and you'll take your skills to the next level, working on amazing projects and achieving great things.

So, discover more about Atkins, our projects and our opportunities.

The future is in your hands.

Visit careers.atkinsglobal.com

BAE SYSTEMS

"THERE'S SUPPORT FROM MANAGERS, SENIOR MENTORS AND COLLEAGUES, WHICH MEANS THERE'S A LOT OF OPPORTUNITY TO REACH MY CAREER GOALS"

BAE Systems is one of the world's most innovative companies. Their customers span a range of sectors, from technology-led defence and security to aerospace systems and security solutions. The Graduate Development Framework (GDF) enables talented graduates to develop their potential.

Innovative, inspired engineering is the bedrock of BAE Systems. With over 18,000 engineers in the UK, it supports professional accreditation and offers opportunities across a wide range of engineering disciplines. Openings encompass everything from civil, electrical, manufacturing and naval architecture, to research, software and systems. However, it takes more than engineering excellence to deliver its customer commitments. That's why it has a continual need for people who can add real value to the business; be that in Business Development, Commercial, Human Resources, Information Technology, Procurement and Project Management.

Along-side this, BAE Systems Applied Intelligence offers more than 120 positions each year in a range of programming, data analytics, electronic engineering and consultancy roles. Over the course of 18 months, it equips people to contribute to driving a world-class reputation in developing innovative, cutting edge solutions.

Then there's the five-year, fast-track finance graduate scheme. This prepares individuals to become Finance Directors of the future. The programme includes a structured and fully supported route to the highly respected Chartered Institute of Management Accountants (CIMA) qualification.

Finally, Sigma is a three-year, fast-track leadership programme created for people with the very highest potential. With only a few places available each year, it's unique, fast-paced and aimed at giving individuals a breadth and depth of knowledge across multiple business areas in business or engineering.

GRADUATE VACANCIES IN 2016

ACCOUNTANCY
CONSULTING
ENGINEERING
FINANCE
HUMAN RESOURCES
IT
MARKETING
RESEARCH & DEVELOPMENT

NUMBER OF VACANCIES
350+ graduate jobs

LOCATIONS OF VACANCIES

STARTING SALARY FOR 2016
£25,000+
Plus a £2,000 welcome payment.

UNIVERSITY VISITS IN 2015-16
BATH, BIRMINGHAM, BRISTOL, BRUNEL, CAMBRIDGE, CARDIFF, DURHAM, EDINBURGH, GLASGOW, HERIOT-WATT, IMPERIAL COLLEGE LONDON, KENT, LANCASTER, LEEDS, LIVERPOOL, LOUGHBOROUGH, MANCHESTER, NEWCASTLE, NOTTINGHAM, OXFORD, SHEFFIELD, SOUTHAMPTON, STRATHCLYDE, SURREY, UNIVERSITY COLLEGE LONDON, WARWICK, YORK
Please check with your university careers service for full details of local events.

MINIMUM ENTRY REQUIREMENTS
2.1 Degree
Relevant degree required for some roles.

APPLICATION DEADLINE
Year-round recruitment
Early application advised.

FURTHER INFORMATION
www.Top100GraduateEmployers.com
Register now for the latest news, events information and graduate recruitment details for Britain's leading employers.

HOW DO YOU SEE YOUR CAREER LIGHTING UP?

WELCOME TO SUCCESS IN THE REAL WORLD.

At BAE Systems, we provide some of the world's most advanced, technology-led defence, aerospace and security solutions and employ a skilled workforce of some 83,400 people in over 40 countries. Working with customers and local partners, we develop, engineer, manufacture and support products and systems to deliver military capability, protect national security and people and keep critical information and infrastructure secure. That's work that inspires us. That's BAE Systems.

To do that, we're constantly innovating and looking out for people who can add real value to our business. That's why we offer exciting and challenging career opportunities to enthusiastic, driven graduates and undergraduates.

If you're aspiring to develop professional excellence, you can join our Graduate Development Framework in a business or engineering role, ranging from human resources to naval architecture. For those who want to be part of a team that builds solutions of the future there's Applied Intelligence, with roles ranging from cyber security to software engineering. For individuals with the capability and determination to take up a senior finance role in the future, there's the Finance Leader Development Programme. Or, there's the Sigma Leadership Programme designed to develop those with the highest leadership potential into a business or engineering leader of the future. We also welcome undergraduates with bold ambitions to take up an Industrial Placement or Summer Internship.

If you're ready to work on projects that make a real difference, visit
baesystems.com/graduates

BAE SYSTEMS
INSPIRED WORK

BAIN & COMPANY

www.joinbain.com

GraduateRecruiting.London@Bain.com

twitter.com/joinbain
facebook.com/bainandcompanyUK
youtube.com/baincareers
linkedin.com/company/bain-and-company

Bain & Company is one of the world's leading management consulting firms. Bain advises top businesses on their most critical issues and opportunities: Strategy, marketing, organization, operations, technology and mergers & acquisitions, across all industries and geographies.

Every case begins by looking at the business from a chief executive's perspective, asking the right questions, and then digging deep into the numbers to unearth the right solutions. It is not about off-the-shelf solutions. The approach and recommendations are highly customized - Bain helps clients decide where they want to go, and how to get there.

From the first day, an associate consultant (AC) at Bain will work in teams of passionate and talented professionals to understand new markets, frame new business models and help clients transform their organisations. Exposure to a variety of business challenges across multiple industries quickly accelerates an AC's career development and builds a valuable toolkit of business and management experience.

Bain seeks to attract, develop, and retain talented individuals who are passionate about making a difference. Bain's supportive culture and mentorship model ensures that each graduate has the opportunity to reach their full potential. Bain invests heavily in professional development – ranging from formal training around the world, personalized coaching on every project, and a mentor to help guide a graduate through their career. These intangibles are part of why Bain is consistently ranked as one of the best firms to work for by many leading publications, including Consulting Magazine (number 1 for 11 years' running), Vault Magazine (number 1 or 2 for 7 years' running) and Glassdoor (in the top 5 for 7 years' running).

GRADUATE VACANCIES IN 2016
CONSULTING

NUMBER OF VACANCIES
No fixed quota

LOCATIONS OF VACANCIES

Vacancies also available in Europe, the USA, Asia and elsewhere in the world.

STARTING SALARY FOR 2016
£Competitive
Plus a starting bonus and performance related annual bonus.

UNIVERSITY VISITS IN 2015-16
BATH, BRISTOL, CAMBRIDGE, IMPERIAL COLLEGE LONDON, LONDON SCHOOL OF ECONOMICS, OXFORD, UNIVERSITY COLLEGE LONDON, WARWICK
Please check with your university careers service for full details of local events.

MINIMUM ENTRY REQUIREMENTS
2.1 Degree

APPLICATION DEADLINE
1st November 2015

FURTHER INFORMATION
www.Top100GraduateEmployers.com
Register now for the latest news, events information and graduate recruitment details for Britain's leading employers.

WORLD-CHANGERS WANTED.

We have a proud 40+ year track record of helping the world's most influential organizations solve their toughest challenges. Our success is simple – we hire immensely talented people and give them everything they could possibly need to be brilliant at what they do. Introduce yourself to us at **joinbain.com** – we'd love to chat with you.

BAIN & COMPANY

joinbain.com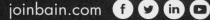

BAKER & MCKENZIE

Go
–places–

Baker & McKenzie prides itself on being the global law firm that offers a personal and professional approach to its graduates and clients alike. It's this approach that ensures the firm is ideally placed to offer graduates the best possible start to their legal career.

The firm currently operates in over 75 locations in nearly 50 countries and has a presence in all of the world's leading financial centres. The London office, which has been established for over 50 years, is the largest. From here over 400 legal professionals serve a wide and varied network of clients, both in the UK and across the globe.

The global nature of the firm means it offers a great deal of variety to its graduates. It works hard to combine its local legal expertise with the wider experience of its international offices, providing clients with a consistent service and legal professionals the opportunity to interact with colleagues from across the world.

In terms of its client base, Baker & McKenzie works principally with multinational corporations and large financial institutions. Its international scope and client list mean the firm is well equipped to act on cross-border transactions and disputes. Baker & McKenzie in London provides the practices that one would expect from one of the world's leading law firms, and is the recognised market leader in many of these.

The firm thrives on new talent. So it makes a significant investment in its graduates' potential through tailored training and development. Those who enjoy intellectual challenge, are problem solvers and team players with a personable approach will feel at home at this friendly and supportive firm. A career with Baker & McKenzie can really go places.

GRADUATE VACANCIES IN 2016

LAW

NUMBER OF VACANCIES
30 graduate jobs
For training contracts starting in 2018.

LOCATIONS OF VACANCIES

STARTING SALARY FOR 2016
£42,000

UNIVERSITY VISITS IN 2015-16
BELFAST, BIRMINGHAM, BRISTOL, CAMBRIDGE, EDINBURGH, EXETER, KING'S COLLEGE LONDON, LEEDS, LEICESTER, LONDON SCHOOL OF ECONOMICS, MANCHESTER, NOTTINGHAM, OXFORD, SOUTHAMPTON, ST ANDREWS, UNIVERSITY COLLEGE LONDON, WARWICK, YORK
Please check with your university careers service for full details of local events.

MINIMUM ENTRY REQUIREMENTS
2.1 Degree

APPLICATION DEADLINE
Varies by function

FURTHER INFORMATION
www.Top100GraduateEmployers.com
Register now for the latest news, events information and graduate recruitment details for Britain's leading employers.

BAKER & McKENZIE

Go –places–

Graduate careers in Law

Journeys can begin anywhere. With a meeting of minds. A desire to learn. Or simply the ambition to be the best you possibly can be. We're looking for all of these things and more at Baker & McKenzie. We pride ourselves on being a global law firm with a personal touch, and a friendly approach that will make your career really go places. Begin your journey with us and we'll invest in your potential through tailored training and development. Begin your journey with us and we'll give you early responsibility and the opportunity to make your mark. Begin your journey with us and we'll give you the opportunity to explore your potential, the means to achieve it and all the support that driven people demand.

Journeys can begin anywhere. Yours begins at Baker & McKenzie.

bakermckenzie.com/londongraduates

Bank of America Merrill Lynch

www.baml.com/campusEMEA

linkedin.com/company/bank-of-america-merrill-lynch **in**   twitter.com/BofAML_Careers **y**

Bank of America is one of the world's leading financial institutions, serving individual consumers, small- and middle-market businesses, large corporations and governments with a full range of financial and risk management products and services. Their purpose is to make financial lives better.

Bank of America Merrill Lynch is the marketing name for the Global Banking and Markets businesses. Combining local knowledge and global expertise, the company offers products and services across Global Corporate and Investment Banking, Global Markets and Consumer Card. In Europe, the Middle East and Africa it has offices in 21 countries serving the needs of individual, corporate, institutional and government clients.

Being a responsible business is integral to the success of Bank of America Merrill Lynch's employees, clients and stakeholders, which is why the company is committed to making a difference in the communities where its employees live and work. Its efforts focus on youth employment, environmental sustainability, arts and cultural investments and responsible business practices.

Bank of America Merrill Lynch's goal is for each employee to have the best possible experience with them throughout their career. The company offers everyone the highest level of training and mentoring support. Furthermore, its commitment to diversity, the communities and the wellbeing of its employees, brings numerous opportunities for all employees to participate in initiatives that help make Bank of America Merrill Lynch a great place to work.

Full-time and internship programmes are available in the following areas: Compliance, Corporate Audit, Global Corporate & Investment Banking, Global Loan Products, Global Markets, Global Transaction Services, Quantitative Management, Research, Risk and Technology.

GRADUATE VACANCIES IN 2016

FINANCE

INVESTMENT BANKING

IT

NUMBER OF VACANCIES
200+ graduate jobs

LOCATIONS OF VACANCIES

Vacancies also available in Europe.

STARTING SALARY FOR 2016
£Competitive

UNIVERSITY VISITS IN 2015-16
BRISTOL, CAMBRIDGE, DURHAM, EDINBURGH, IMPERIAL COLLEGE LONDON, LIVERPOOL, LONDON SCHOOL OF ECONOMICS, LOUGHBOROUGH, MANCHESTER, OXFORD, ST ANDREWS, UNIVERSITY COLLEGE DUBLIN, UNIVERSITY COLLEGE LONDON, WARWICK, YORK
Please check with your university careers service for full details of local events.

MINIMUM ENTRY REQUIREMENTS
2.1 Degree

APPLICATION DEADLINE
Varies by function
Please see website for full details.

FURTHER INFORMATION
www.Top100GraduateEmployers.com
Register now for the latest news, events information and graduate recruitment details for Britain's leading employers.

Where your potential becomes greatness.

At Bank of America Merrill Lynch, we'll match your drive and ambition to where you can make a real impact.

As one of the world's largest financial institutions, our global connections allow you to create a career on your own terms.

We're currently running a range of schemes, including insight programmes, analyst programmes, associate programmes, internships and placements. Discover your potential.

Real Connections. Global Reach.

Get started. Apply today at:
baml.com/campusEMEA

 bankofenglandearlycareers.co.uk

linkedin.com/company/bank-of-england **in**   early.careers@bankfoengland.co.uk ✉

The impact of the Bank of England's work is uniquely far-reaching. As the country's central bank, they promote the good of the people of the UK by maintaining monetary and financial stability. The work they do, and the decisions they make, influences the daily lives of millions of people.

Their primary role hasn't changed for over 300 years. But the range of work they do, and the ways in which they deliver it, is changing all the time. Today, driven by new leadership and a fresh vision, it's changing quicker than ever before. And their graduates are a key part of this progress.

Wherever they work – from Regulation and Policy Analysis to Economics, Project Management, Technology and Communications – graduates at the Bank take on complex work that they can be proud of. They take on projects that support, shape and challenge the biggest ideas in the economy. And the work they do benefits every single person in the UK.

Despite the nature of the Bank's work, economics is not the only way in. Graduates are welcome from all disciplines, because quality of thinking is what counts there. The culture at the Bank is open and collaborative, where ideas are shared freely and people at every level are empowered to speak up. It is refreshingly diverse too. The Bank is open to people from all backgrounds and degree disciplines, and individual perspectives are embraced. Graduates will also find a wide range of societies, clubs and employee networks open to them.

Training is at the heart of the programme, enabling graduates to grow into real experts in their field. Equally, the support is also there to explore other parts of the Bank, there are many and varied pathways available. For graduates keen to broaden their horizons, there are plenty of opportunities to define their own future as the Bank itself moves forward.

GRADUATE VACANCIES IN 2016
ACCOUNTANCY
FINANCE
GENERAL MANAGEMENT
HUMAN RESOURCES
INVESTMENT BANKING
IT

NUMBER OF VACANCIES
60+ graduate jobs

LOCATIONS OF VACANCIES

STARTING SALARY FOR 2016
£Competitive
Plus benefits.

UNIVERSITY VISITS IN 2015-16
ASTON, BATH, BIRMINGHAM, CAMBRIDGE, CARDIFF, CITY, DURHAM, EAST ANGLIA, EDINBURGH, EXETER, KENT, LANCASTER, LEICESTER, LIVERPOOL, LONDON SCHOOL OF ECONOMICS, LOUGHBOROUGH, MANCHESTER, NEWCASTLE, NORTHUMBRIA, NOTTINGHAM, OXFORD, QUEEN MARY LONDON, SHEFFIELD, SURREY, UNIVERSITY COLLEGE LONDON, WARWICK, YORK
Please check with your university careers service for full details of local events.

MINIMUM ENTRY REQUIREMENTS
2.1 Degree
300 UCAS points

APPLICATION DEADLINE
Varies by function

FURTHER INFORMATION
www.Top100GraduateEmployers.com
Register now for the latest news, events information and graduate recruitment details for Britain's leading employers.

BANK OF ENGLAND

CHOOSE A PATH THAT FASCINATES YOU THEN FOLLOW IT

We have one clear aim – to ensure stability at the heart of the UK's economy. But there are countless ways in which you could help us achieve this. From HR and Technology to Economics and Risk, you'll be encouraged and supported to follow the path that inspires you the most. And you'll enjoy real influence – not just over the projects you're involved in, but also over where your future with us goes next.

The Bank of England is changing today. **You define tomorrow.**

bankofenglandearlycareers.co.uk

BARCLAYS

twitter.com/barclaysgrads 🐦 facebook.com/BarclaysGraduates f
youtube.com/barclaysgrads ▶ linkedin.com/company/barclays-bank in

GRADUATE VACANCIES IN 2016
FINANCE
GENERAL MANAGEMENT
HUMAN RESOURCES
INVESTMENT BANKING
IT
MARKETING
SALES

NUMBER OF VACANCIES
300 graduate jobs

LOCATIONS OF VACANCIES

Vacancies also available in Europe, Asia, the USA and elsewhere in the world.

STARTING SALARY FOR 2016
£Competitive

UNIVERSITY VISITS IN 2015-16
BATH, BIRMINGHAM, BRISTOL, CAMBRIDGE, DURHAM, EDINBURGH, EXETER, IMPERIAL COLLEGE LONDON, LEEDS, LONDON SCHOOL OF ECONOMICS, LOUGHBOROUGH, MANCHESTER, NOTTINGHAM, OXFORD, SHEFFIELD, SOUTHAMPTON, ST ANDREWS, STRATHCLYDE, UNIVERSITY COLLEGE LONDON, WARWICK
Please check with your university careers service for full details of local events.

MINIMUM ENTRY REQUIREMENTS
2.1 Degree

APPLICATION DEADLINE
Varies by function

FURTHER INFORMATION
www.Top100GraduateEmployers.com
Register now for the latest news, events information and graduate recruitment details for Britain's leading employers.

Barclays is a bank with strong values and a clear vision: to help people achieve their ambitions in the right way. It starts with their graduates, from day one. Right across Barclays, they play a critical part in maintaining its momentum and in so doing, driving their own careers too.

Those joining can expect immediate responsibility, whichever part of the bank they're in. Their development will focus on building their strengths through challenging work, collaborative projects, and looking at things from a new perspective. Supported by colleagues and outstanding training, they will also feel encouraged to take the initiative, be flexible and own the work they do.

Barclays offers a remarkable breadth of career opportunities for undergraduates, graduates and postgraduates from all backgrounds and degree disciplines. As well as a strong academic record and a commercial outlook, new graduates coming into Barclays need to be ready to express their ideas and learn quickly.

As an organisation, Barclays has a long tradition of innovation and firsts. They were the first bank to have a female bank manager, introduce ATMs, debit cards and contactless payment. Digital remains at the heart of the business today, with significant investment in new products and technologies that are cementing their position as the digital market leader. This is not the only progress they're making. Already a major international financial services provider, with 130,000 people working in more than 50 countries, Barclays is reshaping to build on its strengths. Across Investment Banking, Personal and Corporate Banking, Barclaycard, Technology and all functional businesses, this has created solid foundations upon which to grow and flourish.

The result is impressive momentum and a positive and forward-looking work environment – the perfect place for graduates to build their careers.

It's the deal of the year. And it's all wrapping up, while the rest of Europe is gearing up for the holidays.

Graduate and internship opportunities

There's a certain thrill that's hard to describe when a deal comes together. This was a landmark telecoms deal – one that would become a defining moment for us. And it's exactly this kind of moment when our character shows through: teams across Europe pulled together, and with the holidays fast approaching, we worked tirelessly to complete the deal. This is what momentum feels like: being part of a collaborative team, working on landmark projects, and delivering results whilst continuously developing your career.

Explore how you can be part of career-defining moments like this at joinus.barclays.com

BBC

The BBC is one of the world's best-known broadcasting brands. Roughly 97% of UK adults use its services each week – not to mention millions more around the globe. The BBC would like to offer everyone a future that is truly interactive, on-demand and online and so needs the best graduates to help make it happen.

There are graduate opportunities in everything from digital through to journalism and production.

In BBC Digital and Engineering graduates will have the unique chance to work on some of the nation's most innovative and popular digital products including BBC News, Weather and Sport apps and BBC iPlayer. Or why not join Research & Development's Trainee scheme and work in areas such as audio and video signal processing, computer vision and coding. With the BBC's User Experience Design scheme, graduates will work alongside the BBC's technical and editorial teams to research and design experiences for their audiences across all of their products from BBC Sport to Children's CBeebies.

Journalism graduates could be writing for BBC News or join Production and work on BBC One's Poldark, BBC Two's The Fall or the award-winning BBC Three drama Murdered By My Boyfriend.

Graduates who join the BBC on any of these schemes will spend one to two years receiving some of the best training in the industry whilst working alongside global leading experts. Joining the Engineering scheme will even allow graduates to earn a Master's in Digital Broadcast Technology along the way.

And that's just a taste…no matter which scheme is chosen, BBC graduates have the opportunity to work on some of the UK's highly recognised, world-class products and services and will come away from the schemes with the expertise and knowledge to succeed in their chosen career.

GRADUATE VACANCIES IN 2016
ENGINEERING
GENERAL MANAGEMENT
IT
MEDIA
RESEARCH & DEVELOPMENT

NUMBER OF VACANCIES
50+ graduate jobs

LOCATIONS OF VACANCIES

STARTING SALARY FOR 2016
£22,000-£26,000

UNIVERSITY VISITS IN 2015-16
Please check with your university careers service for full details of local events.

MINIMUM ENTRY REQUIREMENTS
Relevant degree required for some roles.

APPLICATION DEADLINE
Varies by function

FURTHER INFORMATION
www.Top100GraduateEmployers.com
Register now for the latest news, events information and graduate recruitment details for Britain's leading employers.

Help create the future of the BBC
Graduate Opportunities | UK Wide | £22,000 – £26,000 pa

The BBC is one of the world's best-known broadcasting brands. 97% of UK adults use its services each week – not to mention millions more around the globe. The BBC would like to offer everyone a future that is interactive, on-demand and online, and so needs the best graduates to help make it happen – from digital and engineering to journalism and production teams.

As a Digital or Engineering graduate, you'll have the unique chance to be a part of some of the nation's most innovative and popular products, such as the BBC News, Weather and Sport apps, BBC iPlayer and the new BBC Taster.

As a Production or Journalism graduate, you can help shape the future of the BBC's news programming or maybe help to create the next Doctor Who or Poldark.

No matter which scheme is chosen, BBC graduates have the opportunity to work on some of the UK's highly recognised, world-class products and services and will come away from the schemes with the expertise and knowledge to succeed in their chosen career.

To find out more visit **www.bbc.co.uk/careers/trainee-schemes**

The world's watching

www.bdo.co.uk/careers

SHOW YOUR TRUE COLOURS

BDO are a leading accountancy and business advisory firm, aimed at mid-market businesses. They work with retail brands, manufacturing companies, growing technology and media companies, hotel and restaurant chains and many more, both in the UK and internationally.

BDO know how to make sure their people give their best. Quite simply, they let them. They hire those who show potential and then help them put it to work, turning business dreams into realities.

BDO is about exceptional client service. This means getting to know their clients well and understanding what they want to achieve. So the company chooses people who can rise to this challenge, who have colourful personalities as well as brilliant skills, and who can take the initiative and be creative.

If graduates want to work in a firm where they can make real progress, then BDO is the ideal size – combining nationwide presence with local expertise and a personal touch. They have 18 regional offices across the British Isles, and their international network is the world's fifth largest, with 1,300 offices in 152 countries.

BDO offer a whole spectrum of different services, and they'll encourage graduates to find their specialist area. Possible choices include audit, tax advice, corporate finance work, business restructuring, forensic accounting, management consulting, and specialist work for the financial services sector. BDO are experts in a huge variety of other sectors too, with clients ranging from family businesses to multi-national companies, to public sector organisations and charities.

BDO gives graduates all the training they need to attain their professional qualifications, along with extensive practical experience that includes on-site client work. The firm also offers constant support to make sure graduates are never out of their depth. It all adds up to a colourful world of choice.

GRADUATE VACANCIES IN 2016
ACCOUNTANCY

NUMBER OF VACANCIES
250 graduate jobs

LOCATIONS OF VACANCIES

STARTING SALARY FOR 2016
£26,750+

UNIVERSITY VISITS IN 2015-16
ASTON, BATH, BIRMINGHAM, BRISTOL, CAMBRIDGE, CARDIFF, CITY, DURHAM, EAST ANGLIA, EDINBURGH, EXETER, GLASGOW, HERIOT-WATT, IMPERIAL COLLEGE LONDON, KING'S COLLEGE LONDON, LANCASTER, LEEDS, LEICESTER, LIVERPOOL, LONDON SCHOOL OF ECONOMICS, LOUGHBOROUGH, MANCHESTER, NEWCASTLE, NOTTINGHAM, OXFORD, QUEEN MARY LONDON, READING, ROYAL HOLLOWAY, SHEFFIELD, SOUTHAMPTON, STRATHCLYDE, SURREY, SUSSEX, UNIVERSITY COLLEGE LONDON, WARWICK, YORK
Please check with your university careers service for full details of local events.

MINIMUM ENTRY REQUIREMENTS
2.1 Degree
280 UCAS points

APPLICATION DEADLINE
Year-round recruitment
Early application advised.

FURTHER INFORMATION
www.Top100GraduateEmployers.com
Register now for the latest news, events information and graduate recruitment details for Britain's leading employers.

SHOW YOUR
TRUE COLOURS

We're BDO. Welcome to our world.

It's a world where the only predictable thing is that today will be different. It's bright people turning professional solutions into an art form. It's a place to be yourself and give your best.

We give you all the training you need to attain your professional qualifications, along with extensive practical experience that includes on-site client work. And given the size of our firm, the rewards and benefits are of course highly competitive.

COLOURFUL CAREERS | COLOURFUL CHARACTERS

BLACKROCK®

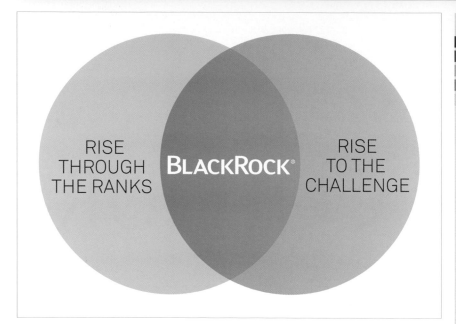

RISE THROUGH THE RANKS | **BLACKROCK®** | RISE TO THE CHALLENGE

As the world's largest asset manager, BlackRock brings together financial leadership, worldwide reach and state-of-the-art technology to provide answers to the millions of investors from across the globe who entrust their financial futures to the company.

At BlackRock a collaborative culture unites all the business groups – as does a common focus on helping the firm's clients and the communities in which BlackRock employees work and live. BlackRock seeks the best and brightest talent to join a dynamic and diverse environment that inspires high performance.

The Graduate Programme at BlackRock is an ideal opportunity for naturalborn problem solvers, innovators and future leaders to work for a firm that has been called in by some of the world's largest companies and governments to find solutions for their most pressing financial challenges.

BlackRock is committed to harnessing every graduate's potential, developing their expertise and advancing their career. All members of the Graduate Programme begin their BlackRock career with a two-week orientation in New York. Following this, graduates benefit from a structured curriculum of ongoing training throughout the first year and beyond, all designed to maximise their business knowledge and individual effectiveness.

Over the last 27 years BlackRock has built up a network of more than 60 offices worldwide, including London, Edinburgh, Paris, Frankfurt, Zurich, Milan, New York, San Francisco and Hong Kong, which gives graduates ample room to move across businesses and boarders. As a global firm, the work is diverse and the opportunities are limitless, with positions in Advisory, Analytics & Risk, Client Businesses, Corporate Operations, Investments and Technology.

GRADUATE VACANCIES IN 2016

CONSULTING
FINANCE
IT
MARKETING
SALES

NUMBER OF VACANCIES
100+ graduate jobs

LOCATIONS OF VACANCIES

Vacancies also available in Europe, the USA and Asia.

STARTING SALARY FOR 2016
£Competitive
Plus a sign-on bonus.

UNIVERSITY VISITS IN 2015-16
BATH, BRISTOL, CAMBRIDGE, CITY, EDINBURGH, GLASGOW, HERIOT-WATT, IMPERIAL COLLEGE LONDON, KING'S COLLEGE LONDON, LONDON SCHOOL OF ECONOMICS, MANCHESTER, NOTTINGHAM, OXFORD, ST ANDREWS, UNIVERSITY COLLEGE LONDON, WARWICK
Please check with your university careers service for full details of local events.

MINIMUM ENTRY REQUIREMENTS
2.1 Degree

APPLICATION DEADLINE
Varies by function

FURTHER INFORMATION
www.Top100GraduateEmployers.com
Register now for the latest news, events information and graduate recruitment details for Britain's leading employers.

MAKE A
LIVING

BlackRock®

MAKE A
DIFFERENCE

The world is more complex than ever before. And with the financial futures of millions in our hands, we're looking for the best and brightest talent – the future leaders that will help make a difference for our clients and the larger world around us. From Advisory and Client Support to Investment Management and Technology – no matter what you're looking to do, there are many exciting challenges waiting for you at BlackRock.

Meet our people and find out how you can make a difference at BlackRock at **blackrockoncampus.com**

BlackRock®
INVESTING FOR A NEW WORLD™

Bloomberg

Bloomberg unleashes the power of information to inspire people who want to change the world. Well-established yet dynamic and disruptive at heart, Bloomberg is truly global, connecting influential decision-makers to a network of news, people and ideas.

It all starts with data. Anchored by the Bloomberg Professional® service (the Terminal), which offers real-time financial information to more than 325,000 subscribers globally, Bloomberg solves a variety of challenges for clients through an ever-expanding array of technology, data, news and media services that add value to information. Global Data provides the foundation for innovation as the company continues to evolve beyond traditional data analysis to provide clients with unique, meaningful and actionable information delivered through a variety of technologies and platforms.

The Enterprise Solutions business delivers the tools companies need to improve efficiency, minimise operational costs, comply with mounting regulations and achieve meaningful transparency. Bloomberg's approach helps clients not just access data, but capitalize on it in the most agile ways possible.

Bloomberg Media – digital, television, print, mobile and radio – is a critical input that reaches influential business decision makers around the world in over 150 bureaus across 73 countries. Through Bloomberg Government (BGOV), Bloomberg New Energy Finance (BNEF) and Bloomberg Bureau of National Affairs (BNA), Bloomberg provides data, news and analytics to decision makers in government, clean energy and legal markets.

Bloomberg takes care to foster a culture of community, and are dedicated to employees' well-being, offering generous benefits, training and opportunities for meaningful volunteerism.

GRADUATE VACANCIES IN 2016

FINANCE

IT

SALES

NUMBER OF VACANCIES
300+ graduate jobs

LOCATIONS OF VACANCIES

STARTING SALARY FOR 2016
£Competitive
Plus benefits.

UNIVERSITY VISITS IN 2015-16
ASTON, BATH, BIRMINGHAM, BRISTOL, CAMBRIDGE, CARDIFF, CITY, DURHAM, EDINBURGH, GLASGOW, IMPERIAL COLLEGE LONDON, KING'S COLLEGE LONDON, LEEDS, LONDON SCHOOL OF ECONOMICS, MANCHESTER, NOTTINGHAM, OXFORD, QUEEN MARY LONDON, SOUTHAMPTON, TRINITY COLLEGE DUBLIN, UNIVERSITY COLLEGE DUBLIN, UNIVERSITY COLLEGE LONDON, WARWICK, YORK
Please check with your university careers service for full details of local events.

APPLICATION DEADLINE
Year-round recruitment

FURTHER INFORMATION
www.Top100GraduateEmployers.com
Register now for the latest news, events information and graduate recruitment details for Britain's leading employers.

MY SKILLS ARE
MOVING FORWARD,
NOT STANDING STILL.

Make your mark.

The world's top investors,
traders and leaders depend
on our information and news.
We need your ideas and passion
to help us meet some of the
biggest challenges around.
How will you make your mark?

bloomberg.com/careers

Bloomberg

/company/bloomberg-lp/careers

SO MANY REASONS WHY BOOTS IS #Good4Grads

As the UK's leading pharmacy-led health and beauty retailer and one of the country's most trusted household names, Boots is evolving in the changing world of retail and our future looks very bright. The company needs to develop future leaders who genuinely love driving business performance by creating "feel good" moments for customers.

On the Boots Graduate Programme there are six exciting, involving and evolving areas of the business to choose from.

The Retail Management Programme develops graduates as store leaders capable of offering Boots customers the legendary experience they expect. On the Commercial Programme, candidates will explore how to develop, source and market Boots' renowned brands, as well as a range of external brands.

The Finance Programme offers graduates more than just experience in financial accounting, management information and business partnering. They'll be part of the department creating the business framework for now and the future. Boots also fund a relevant qualification and offer the opportunity to work in an international role. On the Technology Leadership Programme, graduates will be driving IT solutions to meet the demands of this fast growing business now and in the future.

This year Boots also have programmes in Supply Chain and Operations. Graduates will see how the business responds to the ever-changing customer needs and drives loyalty & sales to increase market share. It's a big operation and this is a big opportunity.

What's really important for all the programmes is a passion for retail and a desire to drive the business into the future. Develop an amazing career with Boots and realise why the company is #Good4Grads.

GRADUATE VACANCIES IN 2016
FINANCE
GENERAL MANAGEMENT
IT
LOGISTICS
MARKETING
PURCHASING
RETAILING

NUMBER OF VACANCIES
50 graduate jobs

LOCATIONS OF VACANCIES

Vacancies also available in Europe, the USA and Asia.

STARTING SALARY FOR 2016
£25,000
Plus a £1,000 welcome payment.

UNIVERSITY VISITS IN 2015-16
NOTTINGHAM, NOTTINGHAM TRENT
Please check with your university careers service for full details of local events.

MINIMUM ENTRY REQUIREMENTS
2.1 Degree
280 UCAS points

APPLICATION DEADLINE
Year-round recruitment
Early application advised.

FURTHER INFORMATION
www.Top100GraduateEmployers.com
Register now for the latest news, events information and graduate recruitment details for Britain's leading employers.

#Good4Grads

hello
The Grads
are all here
#Good4Grads

THE BOOTS FINANCE PROGRAMME HAS ENABLED ME TO EXPERIENCE SO MUCH
#Good4Grads

I'LL BE TELLING ALL ABOUT OUR RETAIL MANAGEMENT PROGRAMME
#Good4Grads

WHY IS NOTTINGHAM A GREAT PLACE TO BE ON THE BOOTS TECHNOLOGY PROGRAMME?
#Good4Grads

SO THIS IS CHRISTMAS ON MY COMMERCIAL STORE PLACEMENT
#Good4Grads

WEEK FOUR LAUNCH OF 'AMAZE ME' BY UNION J
#Good4Grads

HOW YOUR TIME IN STORE PREPARES YOU FOR THE OPERATIONS PROGRAMME
#Good4Grads

Why our Self Experiential days are
#Good4Grads

#Good4Grads AND I'D LIKE TO THANK THE BOOTS GRADUATE TECHNOLOGY PROGRAMME...

HELLO
FROM RETAIL MANAGEMENT
#Good4Grads

I'LL BE AT LEEDS UNI TALKING IN SEMINARS TOMORROW ABOUT WHY BOOTS IS
#Good4Grads

good luck
everyone
#Good4Grads

BUILD. CONNECT. GROW.

The Boston Consulting Group (BCG) is a global management consulting firm and the world's leading advisor on business strategy and transformation. BCG partners with clients in all sectors to identify their highest-value opportunities, address their most critical challenges, and transform their businesses.

BCG hires talented graduates from diverse academic backgrounds, including business, engineering, economics, science, and the humanities. BCG seeks people with strong drive, relentless curiosity, the desire to create their own path, and the passion and leadership to make an impact. At the core of BCG's business is close collaboration – among employees at all levels and with our clients.

Learn how to navigate complexity, draw unique insights, facilitate change, and become a leader responsible for real and lasting impact. Coached by a personal mentor and supported by teams, employees at BCG join a diverse group of highly driven individuals from different backgrounds who respect and trust each other.

A career at BCG offers opportunities to work in many different fields and industries, learning how to navigate complexity, draw unique insights, facilitate change and become a leader responsible for real and lasting impact. Exposure to both breadth and depth of experiences enables employees to pursue any number of career paths.

With on-the-job experience combined with extensive training and mentorship programmes, employees develop analytical, conceptual, and leadership skills, increasing their value at BCG and beyond. The opportunities for educational support, international mobility, social impact work, and connections to our vast alumni network help graduates find deep personal meaning as they develop a platform for future success. Become a part of BCG's heritage of game-changing ideas, business model innovation, and reshaping landscapes.

GRADUATE VACANCIES IN 2016
CONSULTING

NUMBER OF VACANCIES
No fixed quota

LOCATIONS OF VACANCIES

STARTING SALARY FOR 2016
£Competitive
Plus a sign-on bonus.

UNIVERSITY VISITS IN 2015-16
CAMBRIDGE, IMPERIAL COLLEGE LONDON, LONDON SCHOOL OF ECONOMICS, OXFORD, TRINITY COLLEGE DUBLIN, UNIVERSITY COLLEGE DUBLIN
Please check with your university careers service for full details of local events.

MINIMUM ENTRY REQUIREMENTS
2.1 Degree

APPLICATION DEADLINE
31st October 2015

FURTHER INFORMATION
www.Top100GraduateEmployers.com
Register now for the latest news, events information and graduate recruitment details for Britain's leading employers.

ONE DAY
AT BCG

*A BCG Story by Thomasin,
Associate, London office*

← 9AM   ← 9PM

- Researching recent economic trends in a developing nation
- Hashing out the detail of a client presentation with a teammate ● Coffee break
- Delivering answers to our clients on what matters most to them
- Having dinner with my friends at my favorite restaurant

bp

Heat. Light. Power. With great energy comes great responsibility. For BP, it's a responsibility that's shared by every employee. They're the ones finding, developing and producing new supplies of energy every day – energy that's behind the products people around the planet depend on.

People at BP are part of a team. A team of diverse people with different perspectives who work together to make change happen. Scientific breakthroughs, engineering firsts, process improvements – everything they achieve is down to the drive, ambition and collaboration of their people.

Geoscientists sending sound waves through the earth to find new oil and gas reserves. Engineers designing platforms in the ocean for production. Traders anticipating and reacting to changes in the markets. BP takes on graduates and interns at every stage of the energy lifecycle. So whether graduates want to be a future business leader, a world-class scientist or ground-breaking engineer, they have a programme to suit.

The programmes will give graduates the skills and experience they need to be a success – whatever field they're in. For penultimate-year students, the paid internships last for a full 12 months or for 11 weeks over the summer months – giving them a chance to gain valuable insights into how BP works as a business.

With such a breadth of opportunity in engineering, science and business, BP will consider graduates with a good degree in a variety of disciplines. But just as important as their academic achievements are the individual attributes and personal qualities they bring. That's because the BP approach is built on teamwork and respect, inclusion and ambition, and having the support needed to do the right thing. It's this approach that allows BP to deliver energy safely. And it's these values that graduates will share.

"People don't just hear what I have to say, they really listen."

Catherine's perspective on support

Graduate opportunities

Whether you're making innovative suggestions, process improvements or purified terephthalic acid, as a BP graduate, you'll make a real difference from day one. So whatever it is you're doing, you can be sure your voice will be heard.

Search BP careers to find out more.

Procurement Operational Research

Think you know us?

Engineering Analysts

World Cargo Leaders for Business

As part of International Airlines Group, BA is one of the world's leading global premium airlines and the largest international carrier in the UK. The carrier has its home base at London Heathrow, the world's busiest international airport and flies to more than 70 different countries.

This is a business worth getting to know. With almost 40 million customers a year and a 280-strong fleet, it's a major player in global air travel. But the future for BA looks more exciting still. This is an organisation on a journey. One that its people live, feel and shape each day. Individuals drawn together from a surprisingly diverse range of disciplines. Everything from Procurement to Engineering, World Cargo to Data Analysis, and Operational Research to Leaders for Business.

BA is a complex and diverse organisation. But at its heart are its people. Graduates will be a key part of fulfilling a profound purpose - the promise BA makes to each of its customers every day: To Fly. To Serve.

Any graduate joining the business can expect real jobs with real responsibilities. This takes ambition, resilience, and the drive to go above and beyond. They can expect to work across different business areas, to be involved in key business decisions and have opportunities to travel and to work in different locations. With attractive colleague travel benefits, BA's graduates all have the chance to see the world and share unique experiences.

All of the programmes on offer start with a comprehensive induction. Then each one has its own structured development plan to make sure graduates have all the support and opportunities they need to develop, excel and lead.

Think you know us?

Adventure Dispensers

Graduate Opportunities

At British Airways, we bring together a wide variety of brilliant people in a range of fascinating roles. From people managers and business leaders, to researchers, consultants and engineers, this is a place where all kinds of careers take off. Join us and you'll immerse yourself in eye-opening and uniquely complex challenges, to help us achieve one unwavering goal – a premium, seamless customer experience from start to finish. You'll be surprised by where and how far your adventure with us could take you. So if you thought you knew everything we do, maybe you'd like to get to know us a little better?

Every day BT's people touch the lives of millions, providing services that help customers get the most out of their working and personal lives. That's a privilege and a responsibility. At BT, they use the power of communications to make a better world. Helping people, businesses and communities create possibilities.

BT is a truly global business – one of the world's leading companies. They provide an innovative range of communication services to businesses and consumers across more than 170 countries. The organisation is celebrating half a century of communications ingenuity; the BT Tower has been a working icon of innovation for 50 years!

Across the globe BT makes amazing things happen. They have a proven track record in inventions that change the world. But, ground-breaking innovations don't just happen – it takes drive, passion and a thirst for knowledge and solutions in every area of BT and some of the most amazing graduates.

Diversity is at the very heart of the company. In order to provide the very best products and services to a varied customer base they need a diverse workforce to imagine, create and deliver the solutions required both now and into the future. This means creating and maintaining a working environment that includes and values diversity.

BT's graduates are dedicated, bold, ingenious and down to earth. BT looks for all of these qualities. And more. They look for people who don't wait to be told what to do, and who can't wait to get involved. BT's amazing graduate programme focusses on developing the future leaders. They will make sure successful applicants get all the training and development they need to become whatever they want to be. So join BT's ongoing quest to 'make amazing things happen', bring new ideas to life, and make a difference.

GRADUATE VACANCIES IN 2016
GENERAL MANAGEMENT
HUMAN RESOURCES
IT
LAW
MARKETING
RESEARCH & DEVELOPMENT
SALES

NUMBER OF VACANCIES
250 graduate jobs

LOCATIONS OF VACANCIES

STARTING SALARY FOR 2016
£27,500-£31,500

UNIVERSITY VISITS IN 2015-16
BELFAST, BIRMINGHAM, CAMBRIDGE, DURHAM, MANCHESTER, NOTTINGHAM, OXFORD, SHEFFIELD, SOUTHAMPTON, UNIVERSITY COLLEGE LONDON, YORK
Please check with your university careers service for full details of local events.

MINIMUM ENTRY REQUIREMENTS
2.1 Degree
280-320 UCAS points

APPLICATION DEADLINE
Varies by function

FURTHER INFORMATION
www.Top100GraduateEmployers.com
Register now for the latest news, events information and graduate recruitment details for Britain's leading employers.

Make amazing things happen

Change the world

Life today is built on connectivity. As a global innovations company, we use the power of communications to make a better world.

From broadband and TV to mobile, we're driven by the exhilaration of building an ever-growing range of services that help our customers get more out of life. But there's so much more to BT than that. Our research and development teams help vehicle manufacturers make smarter cars, let consultants treat patients remotely, and provide secure fingerprint technology for festival goers.

Our history is all about shaping the future with ground breaking ideas. Today, we're proud to be the UK's number one tech sector investor in R&D, with 14,000 scientists and technologists leading innovation in BT. And if you share our drive and passion for putting customers at the heart of what we do, we'll invest in your future too.

So join our restless quest for innovation. Whichever role you're in, you'll help to change how people live, by bringing new ideas to life.

Make amazing things happen.

For full details on graduate and internship opportunities, please visit:

www.btgraduates.com

graduates.cancerresearchuk.org

graduate@cancer.org.uk ✉

IT'LL TAKE SMART, SHARP
MINDED PEOPLE TO HELP US
BEAT CANCER SOONER.

PEOPLE
LIKE YOU.

Cancer. Be afraid. Cancer Research UK is a world-leading organisation and a prestigious funder of science. Its vision is to bring forward the day when all cancers are cured. In the 1970s, less than a quarter of people with cancer survived. But over the last 40 years, survival has doubled. Its ambition is to see three-quarters of people surviving the disease within the next 20 years.

Every step the charity makes towards beating cancer sooner relies on every person, every team and every effort. Now they are looking for smart, sharp minded individuals to continue to achieve their goals. Its graduates are passionate in their work, determined, unafraid to challenge, stand-out communicators and effective relationship-builders. Not to mention, ready to make a real contribution to bring Cancer Research UK closer to its ambition.

What does a graduate scheme at an organisation like this offer? All graduates are put through their paces from the very beginning. Whether joining Cancer Research UK's Fundraising and Marketing; Scientific Strategy and Funding; Technology, or Policy Information and Communications streams, they will have the exciting opportunity to rotate across four business areas over the course of the two years.

Graduates receive support and challenge from senior mentors, peers and placement managers along their journey. They also benefit from a combination of on-the-job learning and formal training whilst transitioning between placements. Graduates are expected to gain a permanent job at the end of the scheme, subject to performance and business need.

As well as graduate opportunities, Cancer Research UK offers a vast array of volunteering opportunities including award-winning twelve-week internships.

Join Cancer Research UK and help beat cancer sooner.

GRADUATE VACANCIES IN 2016

IT
MARKETING
MEDIA
RESEARCH & DEVELOPMENT

NUMBER OF VACANCIES
7 graduate jobs

LOCATIONS OF VACANCIES

STARTING SALARY FOR 2016
£24,000
*Plus an excellent benefits package
and an annual salary review.*

UNIVERSITY VISITS IN 2015-16
BATH, BELFAST, BIRMINGHAM, BRISTOL,
CAMBRIDGE, CITY, DURHAM, EDINBURGH,
EXETER, IMPERIAL COLLEGE LONDON,
KING'S COLLEGE LONDON, LANCASTER,
LEEDS, LEICESTER, LIVERPOOL,
LONDON SCHOOL OF ECONOMICS,
LOUGHBOROUGH, MANCHESTER,
NEWCASTLE, NOTTINGHAM, OXFORD,
QUEEN MARY LONDON, SHEFFIELD,
SOUTHAMPTON, ST ANDREWS, UNIVERSITY
COLLEGE LONDON, WARWICK, YORK
*Please check with your university careers
service for full details of local events.*

MINIMUM ENTRY REQUIREMENTS
2.1 Degree
280 UCAS points
Relevant degree required for some roles.

APPLICATION DEADLINE
November/December 2015

FURTHER INFORMATION
www.Top100GraduateEmployers.com
*Register now for the latest news, events
information and graduate recruitment
details for Britain's leading employers.*

AMBITIOUS
SMART FAST-PACED
INSPIRING
DRIVING SHARP
CHANGE
UNITED
PIONEERING
VERSATILE CHALLENGING
LIFE-SAVING PERCEPTIONS

THIS IS HOW IT FEELS HELPING TO BEAT CANCER.
For your chance to experience it, go to cruk.org/graduates

CANCER
RESEARCH
UK

centrica

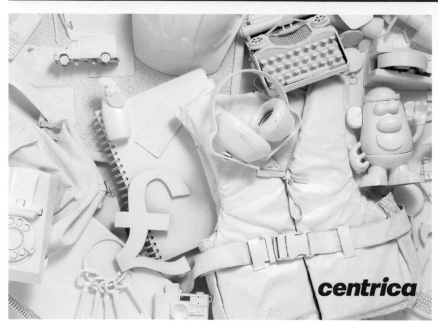

Centrica is an international energy company that sources, generates, processes, stores, trades, supplies, services and helps its customers save energy. Securing energy to power the future is an important priority for Centrica, and the company is making vital investments across the entire energy spectrum.

As a top 30 FTSE 100 company with over 30 million customer accounts, a £29.4 billion turnover and more than 37,000 employees, Centrica is the parent company for a range of global brands. British Gas, Bord Gáis and Direct Energy supply power and related services in the UK, Republic of Ireland and North America respectively; Centrica Energy in the UK manage power generation, gas and oil production and trading operations to ensure day-to-day demand is met and Centrica Storage is the largest gas storage facility in the UK.

Graduates could be getting involved in any area of the energy lifecycle – from exploration and production with Centrica Energy, to front-line customer service management at British Gas – although the exact role will depend on which of the schemes they join. The graduate programme has been designed to offer a broad grounding in the business; those who are ambitious and commercially savvy have an outstanding opportunity to be a future business leader in this diverse organisation.

Developing graduates is important to Centrica; graduate talent boards ensure they have the opportunity to fulfil their potential and are equipped with the right skills and behaviours to help grow the business and implement Centrica's strategy. It all adds up to an award-winning programme that offers graduates who are up for big challenges the opportunity to get involved in a variety of areas – as well as receiving support and reward along the way.

GRADUATE VACANCIES IN 2016

ENGINEERING
FINANCE
GENERAL MANAGEMENT
HUMAN RESOURCES
IT
LOGISTICS
MARKETING

NUMBER OF VACANCIES
50+ graduate jobs

LOCATIONS OF VACANCIES

STARTING SALARY FOR 2016
£27,000+
Plus a £3,000 joining bonus.

UNIVERSITY VISITS IN 2015-16
BATH, BIRMINGHAM, BRISTOL, BRUNEL, CAMBRIDGE, CARDIFF, CITY, DURHAM, EDINBURGH, EXETER, GLASGOW, HERIOT-WATT, IMPERIAL COLLEGE LONDON, KING'S COLLEGE LONDON, LANCASTER, LEEDS, LEICESTER, LIVERPOOL, LONDON SCHOOL OF ECONOMICS, LOUGHBOROUGH, MANCHESTER, NEWCASTLE, NOTTINGHAM, OXFORD, PLYMOUTH, READING, ROYAL HOLLOWAY, SHEFFIELD, SOUTHAMPTON, STRATHCLYDE, UNIVERSITY COLLEGE LONDON, WARWICK
Please check with your university careers service for full details of local events.

MINIMUM ENTRY REQUIREMENTS
2.1 Degree

APPLICATION DEADLINE
4th January 2016

FURTHER INFORMATION
www.Top100GraduateEmployers.com
Register now for the latest news, events information and graduate recruitment details for Britain's leading employers.

Be part **of it all.**

Graduate and Summer Placement Opportunities

centrica

If you've the talent and ambition, then we've the tools and development programmes to help you achieve your potential. From roles involving hard hats to those more suited to laptops, you'll find that each of our graduate programmes comes loaded with everything you need to build a successful and rewarding career.

As the UK's leading energy supplier, we can offer you more than most when it comes to choosing a graduate programme. With opportunities in **Customer Operations, Marketing, Human Resources, Information Systems, Finance, Procurement, Engineering, Health, Safety, Environment & Security or as an Analyst,** there's an excellent chance you'll find something to suit you – whatever it is you're currently studying. We even run a 10-week Summer placement programme, too – perfect if you're looking to gain experience with a company at the top of its game.

Find out how you can be part of it all by visiting our website.

www.centrica.com/Graduates 　f 　🐦 　in 　📷

Since Citi opened its first office in New York in 1812, it has answered the needs of economies, businesses and communities in hundreds of cities, in over 160 countries, thriving in the most challenging times over a 200 year history. Citi's global presence isn't just a question of size, it's a way of thinking.

Citi's success is driven by its exceptional people – their passion, dedication and entrepreneurship – and it will be people with these qualities who will shape its future. At Citi, learning doesn't stop at graduation and they provide one of the best learning and development programmes in banking. Whatever the degree there is a chance to excel at Citi and become of part global firm that provides the most forward-thinking financial products and solutions to the most enterprising corporations, institutions, governments and individuals around the world.

Citi offers full-time, placement and internship opportunities across a number of its business areas, including Investment Banking, Corporate Banking, Capital Markets Origination, Markets and Securities Services, Treasury and Trade Solutions (TTS), Private Bank, Risk Management, Human Resources and Technology.

Citi also offers insight programmes enabling students in their first year (or in their second year of a four year course) to experience first-hand the Citi culture and environment. The most successful candidates on these programmes will also secure an assessment centre for a place on the following year's internship.

Graduates interested in this industry with drive, commitment and a passion for learning are encouraged to apply. This is the opportunity to be part of an exciting period in the development of the global financial services industry, working with the brightest minds to drive responsible, positive change within Citi and beyond.

GRADUATE VACANCIES IN 2016
HUMAN RESOURCES
INVESTMENT BANKING
IT

NUMBER OF VACANCIES
180-220 graduate jobs

LOCATIONS OF VACANCIES

Vacancies also available in Europe and elsewhere in the world.

STARTING SALARY FOR 2016
£Competitive

UNIVERSITY VISITS IN 2015-16
BATH, BRISTOL, CAMBRIDGE, CITY, DURHAM, EDINBURGH, EXETER, IMPERIAL COLLEGE LONDON, KING'S COLLEGE LONDON, LEEDS, LONDON SCHOOL OF ECONOMICS, LOUGHBOROUGH, MANCHESTER, NOTTINGHAM, OXFORD, QUEEN MARY LONDON, ST ANDREWS, TRINITY COLLEGE DUBLIN, UNIVERSITY COLLEGE DUBLIN, UNIVERSITY COLLEGE LONDON, WARWICK
Please check with your university careers service for full details of local events.

MINIMUM ENTRY REQUIREMENTS
2.1 Degree
320 UCAS points

APPLICATION DEADLINE
Year-round recruitment
Early application advised.

FURTHER INFORMATION
www.Top100GraduateEmployers.com
Register now for the latest news, events information and graduate recruitment details for Britain's leading employers.

WE'VE GIVEN GLOBAL TRADE A MAJOR SHORTCUT.

In 1904, Citi financed construction of the Panama Canal, which transformed shipping and economies all over the world. Ready to do more extraordinary things?

Citi provides one of the most highly regarded graduate training programmes in the industry. It's where the best come to get better, so you can excel here – whatever your background. Whether you're in your first or final year, we have a programme for you.

f ⚫ /citigradsEMEA

oncampus.citi.com

PROGRESS STARTS HERE

The World's Citi℠

Civil Service
Fast Stream

www.gov.uk/faststream

faststream@parity.net

twitter.com/faststreamuk 🐦 facebook.com/faststream f

youtube.com/theFaststreamuk ▶️ linkedin.com/company/civil-service-fast-stream in

"Working to create
life changing services
is immensely rewarding."

Sijuwade Salami, Fast Streamer

The Fast Stream is an unrivalled opportunity to lead changes that count and build a career that matters. At the heart of government, Fast Streamers work on some of the most vital and challenging issues facing Britain now and in the future. With a diversity of roles offering incredible professional development.

The Fast Stream is an accelerated learning and development programme for graduates with the motivation and the potential to become the future leaders of the Civil Service. Fast Streamers are given considerable responsibility from the outset: they are stretched and challenged on a daily basis, and they move regularly between posts to gain a wide range of contrasting experiences and build up an impressive portfolio of skills and knowledge.

Work ranges across professional areas including digital, communications, policy development, corporate services, people management, commercial awareness, financial management and project management, giving Fast Streamers a wide understanding of how government delivers public services.

Comprehensive training and development combined with on-the-job learning and support is provided. Successful applicants will receive an excellent package of benefits.

There's no such thing as a typical Fast Streamer, and graduates from widely diverse backgrounds are excited by the idea of making a positive and highly visible impact on the most important and exciting issues facing the country. Society is best served by a Civil Service which is as diverse as itself.

There are opportunities available across the UK in all areas of government, offering graduates a unique perspective of work at the heart of current affairs and key government agendas. There's no limit to where they could lead on the Civil Service Fast Stream. All degree disciplines are welcome.

GRADUATE VACANCIES IN 2016

FINANCE

GENERAL MANAGEMENT

HUMAN RESOURCES

IT

MARKETING

PURCHASING

RESEARCH & DEVELOPMENT

NUMBER OF VACANCIES
900+ graduate jobs

LOCATIONS OF VACANCIES

Vacancies also available in Europe.

STARTING SALARY FOR 2016
£25,000-£27,000

UNIVERSITY VISITS IN 2015-16
Please check with your university careers service for full details of local events.

MINIMUM ENTRY REQUIREMENTS
2.2 Degree

APPLICATION DEADLINE
Early November 2015
The deadline for the Finance and Analytical programmes is the end of September 2015.

FURTHER INFORMATION
www.Top100GraduateEmployers.com
Register now for the latest news, events information and graduate recruitment details for Britain's leading employers.

'Where will you lead?

Education. Health. Justice. Commercial. Human Resources. Defence. Transport. Climate change. International development. Foreign affairs. If the government has a policy on something, it is guaranteed that Fast Streamers are working at the heart of it, putting their brains and their skills at the disposal of the whole of society.

The Civil Service Fast Stream offers the kind of variety of roles and leadership training you simply can't have anywhere else. Choose from an exciting range of generalist and specialist streams with a programme that's ranked among the top five of The Times Top 100 Graduate Employers.

Learn more: www.gov.uk/faststream

Civil Service
Fast Stream

the
future
at work

Credit Suisse is a global financial services company providing a broad range of advisory services, comprehensive solutions and excellent products through two global divisions, Private Banking & Wealth Management and Investment Banking. It serves companies, institutions and private clients around the world.

As a stable company with a long banking tradition, Credit Suisse is one of the most respected banks in the world, recognised by industry publications for its continued excellence and leading position in many key markets around the world.

Credit Suisse is active in more than 50 countries and employs over 46,000 people. Since its founding in 1856, the organisation has continuously set new standards in service and advice, and created intelligent solutions in response to changing client needs. It is renowned for its expertise and valued for its advice, innovation and execution.

Credit Suisse offers entry-level programmes in a variety of business areas. The organisation's programs give graduates the chance to make a difference from day one, and provide world-class training and support to help them to develop into future business leaders. Whichever programme successful candidates choose, they'll contribute to projects that have a significant impact on the business, while building their own expertise. And throughout their career with the company, graduates will benefit from cross-business and international mobility opportunities.

Credit Suisse looks for people with a wide range of experiences, interests and degrees who will add fresh perspectives to the business. The organisation's vision is to become the world's most admired bank. A graduate career with Credit Suisse can help shape the future of the organisation.

GRADUATE VACANCIES IN 2016

FINANCE

INVESTMENT BANKING

IT

SALES

NUMBER OF VACANCIES
150+ graduate jobs

LOCATIONS OF VACANCIES

Vacancies also available in Europe.

STARTING SALARY FOR 2016
£Competitive

UNIVERSITY VISITS IN 2015-16
CAMBRIDGE, IMPERIAL COLLEGE
LONDON, KING'S COLLEGE LONDON,
LONDON SCHOOL OF ECONOMICS,
MANCHESTER, OXFORD, UNIVERSITY
COLLEGE LONDON, WARWICK
*Please check with your university careers
service for full details of local events.*

MINIMUM ENTRY REQUIREMENTS
2.1 Degree

APPLICATION DEADLINE
22nd November 2015

FURTHER INFORMATION
www.Top100GraduateEmployers.com
*Register now for the latest news, events
information and graduate recruitment
details for Britain's leading employers.*

CREDIT SUISSE

Calling all...
Industry Shapers
Idea Igniters
Agile Entrepreneurs

We look for future
leaders with a wide
range of interests,
backgrounds, and
degrees.

To learn more about careers
in financial services and how
to apply visit:

credit-suisse.com/careers

the future at work

DANONE

AT **DANONE** YOU GET TO WORK WITH SOME OF THE WORLD'S **MOST RECOGNISED BRANDS**

BRANDS THAT MAKE A **DIFFERENCE** TO PEOPLE'S LIVES.

GRADUATE VACANCIES IN 2016

- FINANCE
- HUMAN RESOURCES
- IT
- LOGISTICS
- MARKETING
- RESEARCH & DEVELOPMENT
- SALES

NUMBER OF VACANCIES
25+ graduate jobs

LOCATIONS OF VACANCIES

STARTING SALARY FOR 2016
£28,500
Plus a 5-10% bonus and flexible benefits.

UNIVERSITY VISITS IN 2015-16
ASTON, BATH, BIRMINGHAM, BRISTOL, DURHAM, EXETER, LANCASTER, MANCHESTER, NOTTINGHAM
Please check with your university careers service for full details of local events.

MINIMUM ENTRY REQUIREMENTS
2.1 Degree
300-320 UCAS points

APPLICATION DEADLINE
Year-round recruitment
Early application advised.

FURTHER INFORMATION
www.Top100GraduateEmployers.com
Register now for the latest news, events information and graduate recruitment details for Britain's leading employers.

For over 100 years, a unique purpose to 'bring health through food and beverages to as many people as possible', has inspired world leading brands such as evian, Activia, Cow&Gate and Nutricia. Today, this purpose unites 100,000 Danone employees behind products that reach nine million consumers worldwide.

The UK Danone graduate scheme is designed for motivated individuals who are passionate about Danone's mission and values. In return, Danone provides them with the essential skills and behaviours needed to grow into committed and inspirational leaders.

Although a global business, Danone has a non-hierarchical structure that ensures every employee is equally valued, respected and empowered to make a difference. For graduates, that means they are placed in influential roles, with independence and autonomy, gaining extensive experience to support their personal progression. Graduates will be at the cutting edge of the business, playing a key role from the start.

Individual growth and development are an integral part of the company's DNA. A graduate's learning journey is completely personalised, based on their career aspirations and developmental targets. Along the way, they are fully supported by an internal coach and a network of key individuals who are committed to helping them achieve their goals.

Danone was built on the pioneering spirit of its founders. It's their spirit that underpins the core values of the entire organisation and their legacy is the development of a business that began and remains at the forefront of innovation. In its graduates, Danone is looking for new and exciting visionaries to continue this legacy and to contribute to a healthier world.

CAN WE INSPIRE THE **leader** IN YOU?

No. 1 worldwide in Fresh **DAIRY PRODUCTS**

No. 1 in Western Europe in **MEDICAL NUTRITION**

No. 2 worldwide in **WATERS** (packaged & by volume)

No. 2 worldwide in **EARLY LIFE NUTRITION**

SALES & MARKETING /// BUSINESS PARTNERING /// NUTRITION

FIND OUT MORE ONLINE
DANONE.CO.UK/GRADUATES

DANONE

Making an impact that matters. Five small words that sum up everything Deloitte stands for. By drawing on their diverse talents and wide-ranging industry expertise, the firm influence the big decisions organisations make, helping them grow their reputation and build on their success.

Making an impact that matters is about more than just helping clients build on their success. It's about enabling Deloitte people to realise their potential too. It's about contributing to the communities in which the organisation operates, influencing the wider world of business and making a positive difference to society as whole.

In a fast-changing world, that's an ongoing challenge. One that involves harnessing the power of new technologies, challenging conventional business thinking and adopting a more consultative approach in everything the firm does.

In purely economic terms, the impact Deloitte makes is clear to see. Last year alone, working with clients in virtually all industry sectors, the firm contributed £1 in every £1000 to the UK GDP. At the same time, the standards of governance and transparency its people promote brought confidence to the policy decisions of government too.

A £27 million firm-wide investment in learning and development in 2015 underlines Deloitte's commitment to developing well-rounded business skills that can take students and graduates virtually anywhere.

With roles in Audit, Risk Advisory, Tax Consulting, Financial Advisory, Consulting or Technology, students and graduates are always exposed to a range of inspiring and innovative projects. And with 21 offices across the UK, opportunities are available at a range of different locations too.

GRADUATE VACANCIES IN 2016

ACCOUNTANCY

CONSULTING

FINANCE

IT

PROPERTY

NUMBER OF VACANCIES
1,200 graduate jobs

LOCATIONS OF VACANCIES

STARTING SALARY FOR 2016
£Competitive
Plus 25 days holiday, pension, life assurance, accident insurance and a mobile phone.

UNIVERSITY VISITS IN 2015-16
ABERDEEN, ASTON, BATH, BELFAST, BIRMINGHAM, BRISTOL, CAMBRIDGE, CARDIFF, CITY, DUNDEE, DURHAM, EAST ANGLIA, EDINBURGH, EXETER, GLASGOW, HERIOT-WATT, HULL, IMPERIAL COLLEGE LONDON, KING'S COLLEGE LONDON, KENT, LANCASTER, LEEDS, LEICESTER, LIVERPOOL, LONDON SCHOOL OF ECONOMICS, LOUGHBOROUGH, MANCHESTER, NEWCASTLE, NORTHUMBRIA, NOTTINGHAM, NOTTINGHAM TRENT, OXFORD, OXFORD BROOKES, QUEEN MARY LONDON, READING, ROYAL HOLLOWAY, SHEFFIELD, SOUTHAMPTON, ST ANDREWS, STRATHCLYDE, SURREY, SUSSEX, ULSTER, UNIVERSITY COLLEGE LONDON, WARWICK, YORK
Please check with your university careers service for full details of local events.

MINIMUM ENTRY REQUIREMENTS
2.1 Degree
280-360 UCAS points

APPLICATION DEADLINE
Year-round recruitment
Early application advised.

FURTHER INFORMATION
www.Top100GraduateEmployers.com
Register now for the latest news, events information and graduate recruitment details for Britain's leading employers.

£27 million
says you'll
never stop
learning

That's the sum we invested last year in our people's training and development. A big chunk of which was allocated to graduates just like you. Couple that commitment with the ever-more consultative nature of our work, and you'll realise what makes this such an inspiring place to launch your career. You'll also understand how Deloitte can help you become the kind of rounded business professional who makes a positive impact out there in the real world. Start by visiting our website.

www.deloitte.co.uk/students

Audit and Risk Advisory • Tax Consulting • Financial Advisory • Consulting • Technology

Deloitte.

DIAGEO

GRADUATE VACANCIES IN 2016
ENGINEERING
FINANCE
HUMAN RESOURCES
MARKETING
SALES

NUMBER OF VACANCIES
50+ graduate jobs

LOCATIONS OF VACANCIES

Vacancies also available in Europe.

STARTING SALARY FOR 2016
£Competitive

UNIVERSITY VISITS IN 2015-16
BATH, BELFAST, BRISTOL, CAMBRIDGE,
DUNDEE, EDINBURGH, HERIOT-WATT,
LOUGHBOROUGH, MANCHESTER,
NOTTINGHAM, SHEFFIELD, STRATHCLYDE,
TRINITY COLLEGE DUBLIN, ULSTER,
UNIVERSITY COLLEGE DUBLIN
*Please check with your university careers
service for full details of local events.*

MINIMUM ENTRY REQUIREMENTS
2.1 Degree

APPLICATION DEADLINE
November 2015

FURTHER INFORMATION
www.Top100GraduateEmployers.com
*Register now for the latest news, events
information and graduate recruitment
details for Britain's leading employers.*

Diageo is the world's leading premium drinks company, with iconic brands such as Guinness®, Smirnoff®, Johnnie Walker® and Tanqueray®, and a company purpose to celebrate life everyday, everywhere. At the core of the company are its values; passionate about customers and consumers, freedom to succeed, proud of what they do, be the best and valuing each other.

A young company born from an incredible entrepreneurial legacy, Diageo employs over 33,000 talented people globally and considers its people its biggest asset. Walking in the footsteps of industry giants such as Arthur Guinness, Alexander Walker who cared deeply about the people and businesses they fostered, Diageo continues to stand on their shoulders and act with the same entrepreneurial spirit and determination in creating an environment where graduates are set up to succeed. Successful applicants to the three-year programme will receive exceptional development and lead in real roles within a global, vibrant and diverse company.

Diageo is looking for graduates who have the capability to succeed in the organisation today but also have the potential to be the leaders for tomorrow. Being fully committed to their role from the beginning, showing energy and enthusiasm in everything they do – following their instincts and standing up for what they feel is right both for them and for Diageo.

Diageo's culture is rooted in a deep sense of its purpose and values, fostering an environment that provides opportunities for all while celebrating cultural and individual diversity. Encouraging a flexible approach to working and emphasising the importance of treating individuals fairly and inclusively. With competitive salaries, great benefits and opportunities to work on local or global community initiatives, Diageo gives graduates the perfect springboard to start their career.

DLA PIPER

DLA Piper is a global law firm with lawyers located in more than 30 countries throughout the Americas, Asia Pacific, Europe and the Middle East, positioning the firm to help companies with their legal needs anywhere in the world. In the UK, it provides legal advice from London and the other major centres.

Unlike many law firms, DLA Piper is organised to provide clients with a range of essential business advice, not just on large scale mergers and acquisitions and banking deals but also on people and employment, commercial dealings, litigation, insurance, real estate, IT, intellectual property, plans for restructuring and tax. It has a comprehensive, award winning client relationship management programme and the brand is built upon local legal excellence and global capability.

DLA Piper looks for opportunities to use its strength as a leading business law firm to make a positive contribution in their local and global communities. The firm's Corporate Responsibility initiatives demonstrate how their values are embedded in the way the firm engages with its people, its clients and its communities.

Within its trainee cohort the firm needs a diverse group of highly talented individuals who have a consistently strong academic performance, formidable commercial acumen, who are articulate, ambitious and driven with sharp minds, enthusiasm and intellectual curiosity. In return, DLA Piper offers a dynamic and diverse environment in which people can build a long and fruitful career and have their success rewarded.

Trainees complete four six-month seats and are given an opportunity to express what areas of law they would like to experience during their training contracts. They have the opportunity to do a seat abroad, or a client secondment.

GRADUATE VACANCIES IN 2016

LAW

NUMBER OF VACANCIES
85 graduate jobs
For training contracts starting in 2018.

LOCATIONS OF VACANCIES

STARTING SALARY FOR 2016
£24,000-£40,000

UNIVERSITY VISITS IN 2015-16
ABERDEEN, BIRMINGHAM, BRISTOL, CAMBRIDGE, CITY, DUNDEE, DURHAM, EDINBURGH, EXETER, GLASGOW, KING'S COLLEGE LONDON, LANCASTER, LEEDS, LONDON SCHOOL OF ECONOMICS, MANCHESTER, NEWCASTLE, NOTTINGHAM, OXFORD, QUEEN MARY LONDON, SHEFFIELD, ST ANDREWS, STRATHCLYDE, UNIVERSITY COLLEGE LONDON, WARWICK, YORK
Please check with your university careers service for full details of local events.

MINIMUM ENTRY REQUIREMENTS
2.1 Degree

APPLICATION DEADLINE
Law: 31st July 2016
Non-law: 31st July 2016

FURTHER INFORMATION
www.Top100GraduateEmployers.com
Register now for the latest news, events information and graduate recruitment details for Britain's leading employers.

BIGGER

OPPORTUNITIES

DLA Piper offers big opportunities to ambitious graduates – big firm, big clients, big careers.

Don't just take our word for it. Find out more at www.dlapipergraduates.co.uk

dyson

The world's first bagless vacuum. A hand dryer that doesn't use heat. A fan with no blades. For over 20 years, Dyson has been looking beyond the existing solutions to invent new technology. It's a philosophy this global, cutting-edge engineering firm calls 'wrong thinking'. And it's in the blood of every Dyson person.

It took 15 years, rejection after rejection and over 5,000 failed prototypes before James Dyson's cyclonic vacuum cleaner found success. But since going it alone to take on the big boys in 1993, Dyson vacuums now lead the market in the UK, Europe, Japan and the USA. Most recently, they've moved into robotic vacuums, as well as the LED lighting industry. New ideas are always springing up at Dyson. And to realise their ambitious future, they're looking for grads with ideas of their own. There's no traditional graduate scheme at Dyson – just graduate jobs. Live global projects from the off. No fluff. No shadowing. No watching from the sidelines. And with the support to help them develop in a direction that suits their ambition, where they go – and how far – is up to them.

Dyson graduates will be joining over 3,000 engineers, scientists, marketing creatives, business development executives, web developers, financial analysts and more on the eve of the largest expansion in Dyson's history – with a £250m investment to double the size of their research and design HQ in Wiltshire, and a 25-year pipeline of exciting future technologies to develop. Dyson doesn't look for a particular type of degree or experience.

And they don't just recruit engineers – there's a lot going on outside the labs too. They want intelligent, articulate minds with the right attitude. People with a passion for technology. People who go beyond the job description. People who demonstrate the same qualities that drove James Dyson on through all those prototypes and rejections – perseverance, perfectionism and wrong thinking.

Inventive engineering requires more than inventive engineers.

It doesn't just take engineers to make a Dyson machine work. We need problem solvers in all sorts of areas – including Finance, Marketing and IT. It is a broad combination of different skill sets that makes Dyson a successful technology company. So if you see problems as opportunities, whether

twitter.com/EU-Careers   facebook.com/EU.Careers.EPSO

youtube.com/EUCareers   linkedin.com/company/3040469

Looking for a challenging career in a dynamic environment? Based in the heart of Europe, the EU Institutions offer a truly international career to ambitious and capable graduates. Serving 500 million citizens, a range of options are available, all with the chance to make a real and lasting difference.

For final-year students and graduates, entry-level positions are available in various fields, from law to economics or languages, as well as more general policy or project management roles. New recruits could be drafting legislation, helping to implement EU law, developing communication strategies, or managing projects and resources.

Most positions are based either in Brussels or Luxembourg, with around 20% of staff based in offices throughout the world. Applying for an EU Career could in practice mean working for the European Commission, Council of the EU, European Parliament, European External Action Service, European Court of Justice, European Court of Auditors, as well as other EU bodies and agencies or any of the other main EU Institutions or Agencies.

Interested applicants will need to prove their strong analytical, organisational and communication skills, a drive to deliver the best possible results, the ability to work effectively as part of a multi-cultural team, and a potential for leadership and personal development.

Candidates are selected through a process of open competition, which generally consists of a first round of computer-based tests in centres throughout the EU, followed by an assessment centre in Brussels or Luxembourg for the best performers. The main graduate recruitment cycle normally opens in the spring, but all of the EU Institutions offer paid graduate traineeships throughout the year – a great way to gain a first taste of a future EU career.

GRADUATE VACANCIES IN 2016

FINANCE

GENERAL MANAGEMENT

HUMAN RESOURCES

IT

LAW

MARKETING

MEDIA

RESEARCH & DEVELOPMENT

NUMBER OF VACANCIES

No fixed quota

LOCATIONS OF VACANCIES

Vacancies available in Europe.

STARTING SALARY FOR 2016

£41,500+

UNIVERSITY VISITS IN 2015-16

ABERDEEN, BELFAST, BRISTOL, CAMBRIDGE, CARDIFF, DURHAM, EDINBURGH, EXETER, KING'S COLLEGE, KENT, LEEDS, LEICESTER, LIVERPOOL, NEWCASTLE, OXFORD, SHEFFIELD, ST ANDREWS, STRATHCLYDE, SURREY

Please check with your university careers service for full details of local events.

APPLICATION DEADLINE

Varies by function

FURTHER INFORMATION

www.Top100GraduateEmployers.com

Register now for the latest news, events information and graduate recruitment details for Britain's leading employers.

FACE A BIGGER CHALLENGE

"What I really love about my job is that I'm working right at the heart of international politics and at the top of the news agenda. One day I might be live tweeting from a European Council summit or the G7, and the next working on the Council's long-term social media strategy or advising upcoming Council presidencies on their social media activities.

"I get to travel a lot, speak different languages, and meet new people from all over the world. But what I really appreciate is how the EU institutions invest in their staff, and the opportunities to build my career through new skills and experiences."

Alexandra coordinates social media for the Council of the European Union. She studied History.

eu careers

eu-careers.eu

ExxonMobil

Global fundamentals

Consider how modern energy enriches your life. Now consider the 7 billion other people on earth who also use energy each day to make their own lives richer, more productive, safer and healthier. Then you will recognize what is perhaps the biggest driver of energy demand: the human desire to sustain and improve the well-being of ourselves, our families and our communities. Through 2040, population and economic growth will drive demand higher, but the world will use energy more efficiently and shift toward lower-carbon fuels.

25%

The world's population will rise by more than 25 percent from 2010 to 2040, reaching nearly 9 billion people. Population and economic growth are key factors behind increasing demand for energy.

Imagine working for the world's largest publicly traded oil and gas company, on tasks that affect nearly everyone in the world today and for future generations to come. ExxonMobil in the UK is better known for its Esso and Mobil brands due to the success of its service stations and high performance lubricants.

ExxonMobil offers challenging long-term careers to high performing graduates, as well as summer and year placements with real responsibility!

There's no such thing as an average day at ExxonMobil and there are many different career paths available from a technical career to a leadership position to a commercial role. For graduates who are looking for a long-term career that will be challenging, rewarding and certainly varied, then a career with ExxonMobil might just be for them.

What are ExxonMobil looking for? For the technical schemes, applications are welcomed from Chemical, Electrical and Mechanical Engineers with a 2:1 minimum. For the commercial schemes, applications from a number of disciplines including Science/Engineering/IT/Business degrees with a 2:1 minimum are accepted.

In addition to the competitive base salary and relocation allowance, employees are also offered a matched 2-for-1 share scheme, final salary pension plan, private health care scheme, 33 days holiday per annum (including public holidays), interest-free loan, tailored graduate training and continuous development, support towards studying for professional qualifications such as CIMA and IChemE, free sports facilities and subsidised dining facilities at most locations, voluntary community activities, international opportunities and regular job rotations (typically every one to three years) with opportunities to develop and hone skills.

GRADUATE VACANCIES IN 2016
ENGINEERING
FINANCE
HUMAN RESOURCES
IT
MARKETING
SALES

NUMBER OF VACANCIES
No fixed quota

LOCATIONS OF VACANCIES

STARTING SALARY FOR 2016
£37,500+
Plus a relocation allowance.

UNIVERSITY VISITS IN 2015-16
BATH, BIRMINGHAM, CAMBRIDGE, EDINBURGH, IMPERIAL COLLEGE LONDON, LOUGHBOROUGH, MANCHESTER, NEWCASTLE, NORTHUMBRIA, NOTTINGHAM, SOUTHAMPTON, STRATHCLYDE, SURREY, UNIVERSITY COLLEGE LONDON
Please check with your university careers service for full details of local events.

MINIMUM ENTRY REQUIREMENTS
2.1 Degree
Relevant degree required for some roles.

APPLICATION DEADLINE
Varies by function

FURTHER INFORMATION
www.Top100GraduateEmployers.com
Register now for the latest news, events information and graduate recruitment details for Britain's leading employers.

exxonmobil.com/UKrecruitment

EY
Building a better working world

GRADUATE VACANCIES IN 2016

ACCOUNTANCY

CONSULTING

FINANCE

IT

NUMBER OF VACANCIES
1,400 graduate jobs

LOCATIONS OF VACANCIES

EY is a global professional services organisation. Its work impacts at the highest level of business as it advises many of the world's most important companies on the issues that are shaping tomorrow. It's the perfect environment for graduates who want to make an impact on business and their own careers.

EY offers graduates the world-class training, contacts and experiences to drive lasting change and make a big impact on business. They have ambitious plans for growth, aiming to double turnover by 2020. And with 210,000 people working out of 700 offices in 150 countries across their four Service Lines: Assurance, Consulting, Tax and Transactions all contributing to this growth, the size and scale of opportunity for graduates is huge.

EY people ask the better questions that lead to better answers, and work with their clients on better solutions. With a deep understanding of how businesses work, they create and implement the innovations that enable clients to do better business, seize better opportunities and make better decisions on the issues that matter most.

EY engages early on with students and plays an active role in undergraduate life, hosting on-campus workshops, talks and debates, and publishing content designed to increase employability, sharpen skills and improve understanding of the business world.

By recruiting graduates based on their natural strengths and future potential, EY invests in training and development to have these strengths for use in a truly global inclusive business environment. Bright, curious ambitious graduates will join EY to drive lasting change, create an impact on business and their own careers, and make their own contribution to EY's purpose of building a better working world.

STARTING SALARY FOR 2016
£Competitive

UNIVERSITY VISITS IN 2015-16
ABERDEEN, ASTON, BATH, BELFAST, BIRMINGHAM, BRISTOL, CAMBRIDGE, CARDIFF, CITY, DURHAM, EDINBURGH, EXETER, GLASGOW, HERIOT-WATT, HULL, IMPERIAL COLLEGE LONDON, KING'S COLLEGE LONDON, LANCASTER, LEEDS, LEICESTER, LIVERPOOL, LONDON SCHOOL OF ECONOMICS, LOUGHBOROUGH, MANCHESTER, NEWCASTLE, NOTTINGHAM, OXFORD, READING, SHEFFIELD, SOUTHAMPTON, ST ANDREWS, STRATHCLYDE, ULSTER, UNIVERSITY COLLEGE DUBLIN, UNIVERSITY COLLEGE LONDON, WARWICK, YORK
Please check with your university careers service for full details of local events.

APPLICATION DEADLINE
Year-round recruitment

FURTHER INFORMATION
www.Top100GraduateEmployers.com
Register now for the latest news, events information and graduate recruitment details for Britain's leading employers.

Start today.
Change tomorrow.

Our work impacts at the highest level of global business. We advise some of the world's most important organisations on the issues that are shaping tomorrow.

It's the perfect environment for graduates who want to make an impact on business and their own careers.

Start thinking today about the impact you want to make tomorrow.

Find out more and apply **ey.com/uk/students**

EY
Building a better working world

First Derivatives plc

FD

DATA TRADING RISK

First Derivatives (FD) is a leading provider of products and consulting services to the capital markets industry. Focused on financial institutions that work cross-asset, the company scopes, designs, develops, implements and supports a broad range of mission critical data and trading systems.

Now is a fantastic time to be joining First Derivatives plc. Despite challenging market conditions FD have continued to build its business and assert its position as one of the leading capital markets consultancy and software providers. FD's expansion plans are ongoing with exciting plans for the years ahead.

The Graduate Options Programme is a fast track consulting programme which combines intense theoretical financial and technical training with on the job experience working as a consultant on client sites globally!

FD are seeking high calibre graduates from a range of backgrounds including Finance, Computer Science, Maths, Business, Physics and Engineering to join the team as Financial and Software Engineers, Technology Traders and Data Scientists.

FD can promise positions with travel, working in the hustle and bustle of tier one banks in top financial cities – with accommodation and expenses costs covered.

FD don't hire any average graduate; they seek students with a difference. FD want students that are ambitious, intelligent and motivated individuals, passionate about Finance/IT and keen to kick-start an exciting career into the Capital Markets industry. Within weeks of joining, FD's junior consultants are exposed to exciting projects worldwide, building on their financial and technical expertise with leading global institutions. There is no better time to join the success story at First Derivatives plc!

GRADUATE VACANCIES IN 2016

ACCOUNTANCY
CONSULTING
ENGINEERING
FINANCE
INVESTMENT BANKING
IT
LAW

NUMBER OF VACANCIES
200 graduate jobs

LOCATIONS OF VACANCIES

Vacancies also available in Europe, Asia, the USA and elsewhere in the world.

STARTING SALARY FOR 2016
£Competitive
Plus expenses and accommodation. Graduate package exceeds the value of £50,000 from year one.

UNIVERSITY VISITS IN 2015-16
BELFAST, BIRMINGHAM, BRISTOL, CAMBRIDGE, CARDIFF, CITY, DUNDEE, DURHAM, EAST ANGLIA, EDINBURGH, ESSEX, EXETER, GLASGOW, HERIOT-WATT, IMPERIAL COLLEGE LONDON, KEELE, KING'S COLLEGE LONDON, KENT, LIVERPOOL, LONDON SCHOOL OF ECONOMICS, MANCHESTER, OXFORD, QUEEN MARY LONDON, ROYAL HOLLOWAY, ST ANDREWS, STIRLING, STRATHCLYDE, TRINITY COLLEGE DUBLIN, ULSTER, UNIVERSITY COLLEGE DUBLIN, UNIVERSITY COLLEGE LONDON, WARWICK
Please check with your university careers service for full details of local events.

MINIMUM ENTRY REQUIREMENTS
2.1 Degree

APPLICATION DEADLINE
Year-round recruitment

FURTHER INFORMATION
www.Top100GraduateEmployers.com
Register now for the latest news, events information and graduate recruitment details for Britain's leading employers.

Careers at FD

Take the plunge and enter a world where the emphasis is on problem solving using a combination of analytics, imagination and business understanding. Join our Graduate Options Programme. We are calling all alumni and recent graduates, FD are recruiting!

We have lots of exciting opportunities currently available with a guarantee that our junior consultants will be placed on client projects within the first three months of joining our organisation.

Do you fancy a new role working in the hustle and bustle of a Tier 1 Bank in top financial cities? FD can promise these positions with travel, accommodation and expenses costs covered.

FD don't hire any average graduate; we seek students with a difference. Are you an ambitious, intelligent and motivated individual, passionate about Finance/IT and keen to kick-start an exciting career into the Capital Markets industry? First Derivatives Plc is the place for you.

If excellent remuneration (including accommodation, flights and expenses), rapid career progression and an impressive benefits programme sounds like the package you want, don't waste time. Apply now!

First Derivatives plc

FD

DATA | TRADING | RISK

www.firstderivatives.com/careers

facebook.com/FreshfieldsGraduates **f**   ukgraduates@freshfields.com ✉

linkedin.com/company/freshfields **in**   twitter.com/freshfieldsgrad 🐦

As an international law firm, Freshfields Bruckhaus Deringer advises some of the world's biggest companies on how to grow, strengthen and defend their businesses. Graduates who are keen to pursue a career in commercial law will find the firm offers some of the best and most interesting work around.

Because Freshfields supports clients wherever in the world they operate, trainees will be involved in delivering a consistent, high-quality service across the globe.

Trainees are likely to work in a team – usually with an associate and a partner. It's the team's job to work out how to help clients achieve what they want to do. Is it possible? What's the best way to structure the deal or tackle the problem? What are the risks?

The team will need to come up with solutions that work in the real, commercial world – not just ones that reflect what's right or wrong in law. By working in teams, trainees find out how.

Freshfields lawyers focus on at least one industry sector and work in one of seven practice groups: antitrust, competition and trade; corporate; dispute resolution; employment, pensions and benefits; finance; real estate; and tax.

Flexibility is key in the firm's training contract. Trainees can try up to eight areas of law. That's twice as many as most law firms.

There's also the chance to spend time on secondment to a client or to one of Freshfields' offices in the US, Asia or Europe.

The firm looks for graduates from any background, university or degree course. To do well, trainees need to have intellectual talent, and excellent written and spoken English. They also need to work well with other people.

The work at Freshfields is nearly always complicated, so the trainees who do best are those who enjoy being challenged.

GRADUATE VACANCIES IN 2016

LAW

NUMBER OF VACANCIES
80 graduate jobs
For training contracts starting in 2018.

LOCATIONS OF VACANCIES

STARTING SALARY FOR 2016
£41,000
Plus maintenance grants for GDL and LPC students.

UNIVERSITY VISITS IN 2015-16
ABERDEEN, BATH, BELFAST, BIRMINGHAM, BRISTOL, CAMBRIDGE, CARDIFF, CITY, DURHAM, EDINBURGH, EXETER, GLASGOW, KING'S COLLEGE LONDON, KENT, LANCASTER, LEEDS, LEICESTER, LIVERPOOL, LONDON SCHOOL OF ECONOMICS, MANCHESTER, NEWCASTLE, NOTTINGHAM, OXFORD, QUEEN MARY LONDON, READING, SCHOOL OF AFRICAN STUDIES, SHEFFIELD, SOUTHAMPTON, ST ANDREWS, TRINITY COLLEGE DUBLIN, UNIVERSITY COLLEGE DUBLIN, UNIVERSITY COLLEGE LONDON, WARWICK, YORK
Please check with your university careers service for full details of local events.

APPLICATION DEADLINE
Law: 31st July 2016
Non-law: 6th January 2016

FURTHER INFORMATION
www.Top100GraduateEmployers.com
Register now for the latest news, events information and graduate recruitment details for Britain's leading employers.

MAKE NO MISTAKE, THIS IS A CLIMB. BUT THE VIEW WILL BE SENSATIONAL.

A career in law is demanding, so choose somewhere that makes it all worthwhile.

Choose a firm where your curiosity, ideas and hard work will be rewarded. Where you can experience everything that a career in commercial law has to offer, through a distinctively flexible training contract and beyond. A firm whose international outlook and world-class reputation open up a multitude of opportunities.

See the whole story at **freshfields.com/ukgraduates**

Freshfields Bruckhaus Deringer LLP

FRONTLINE

CHANGING LIVES

www.thefrontline.org.uk

recruitment@thefrontline.org.uk

twitter.com/FrontlineSW
facebook.com/FrontlineChangingLives

youtube.com/FrontlineSW
linkedin.com/company/frontline-org

GRADUATE VACANCIES IN 2016
GENERAL MANAGEMENT
HUMAN RESOURCES
LAW
RESEARCH & DEVELOPMENT

NUMBER OF VACANCIES
180 graduate jobs

LOCATIONS OF VACANCIES

STARTING SALARY FOR 2016
£Competitive

UNIVERSITY VISITS IN 2015-16
ASTON, BIRMINGHAM, BRISTOL,
CAMBRIDGE, CARDIFF, DURHAM,
EDINBURGH, ESSEX, EXETER, GLASGOW,
KENT, KING'S COLLEGE LONDON,
LANCASTER, LEEDS, LEICESTER, LIVERPOOL,
LONDON SCHOOL OF ECONOMICS,
LOUGHBOROUGH, MANCHESTER,
NEWCASTLE, NOTTINGHAM, OXFORD,
QUEEN MARY LONDON, READING,
ST ANDREWS, SUSSEX, UNIVERSITY
COLLEGE LONDON, WARWICK, YORK
*Please check with your university careers
service for full details of local events.*

MINIMUM ENTRY REQUIREMENTS
2.1 Degree
*Most applicants have 300 UCAS points –
please see website for full details.*

APPLICATION DEADLINE
November 2015
Early application advised.

FURTHER INFORMATION
www.Top100GraduateEmployers.com
*Register now for the latest news, events
information and graduate recruitment
details for Britain's leading employers.*

There are lots of graduate programmes out there. Most involve nice, comfortable office jobs. Frontline is different. Participants work with families, schools, courts and the police to change lives. 99% would run in the opposite direction. But Frontline is seeking the 1% who really want to make a difference.

Frontline's two-year graduate programme is a new opportunity for exceptional individuals to join one of Britain's toughest and most rewarding professions. An innovative approach to social work training, this demanding programme places graduates and career changers in child protection teams in Greater Manchester, Greater London, North East, East and South East of England.

The programme begins with a five-week summer residential where a team of world-leading academics and individuals with care experience provide participants with master classes in social work practice. In September, participants join a local authority and start the first year, learning 'on-the-job' in teams of four. They receive full-time supervision from an experienced social worker and ongoing academic input. Upon qualification, the second year consists of 12 months guaranteed employment as a children's social worker and the opportunity to study towards a Masters qualification.

An integral part of Frontline's approach is its focus on leadership as a tool to transform lives. The best social workers have the leadership skills to bring together a wide range of agencies, establish a vision with a family and influence people to act accordingly. Frontline is committed to instilling these skills in participants so they can drive positive change both in social work and in broader society. Its leadership development programme will give participants the confidence to drive change whatever their future career path.

Frontline welcomes applicants with a range of experiences from any discipline.

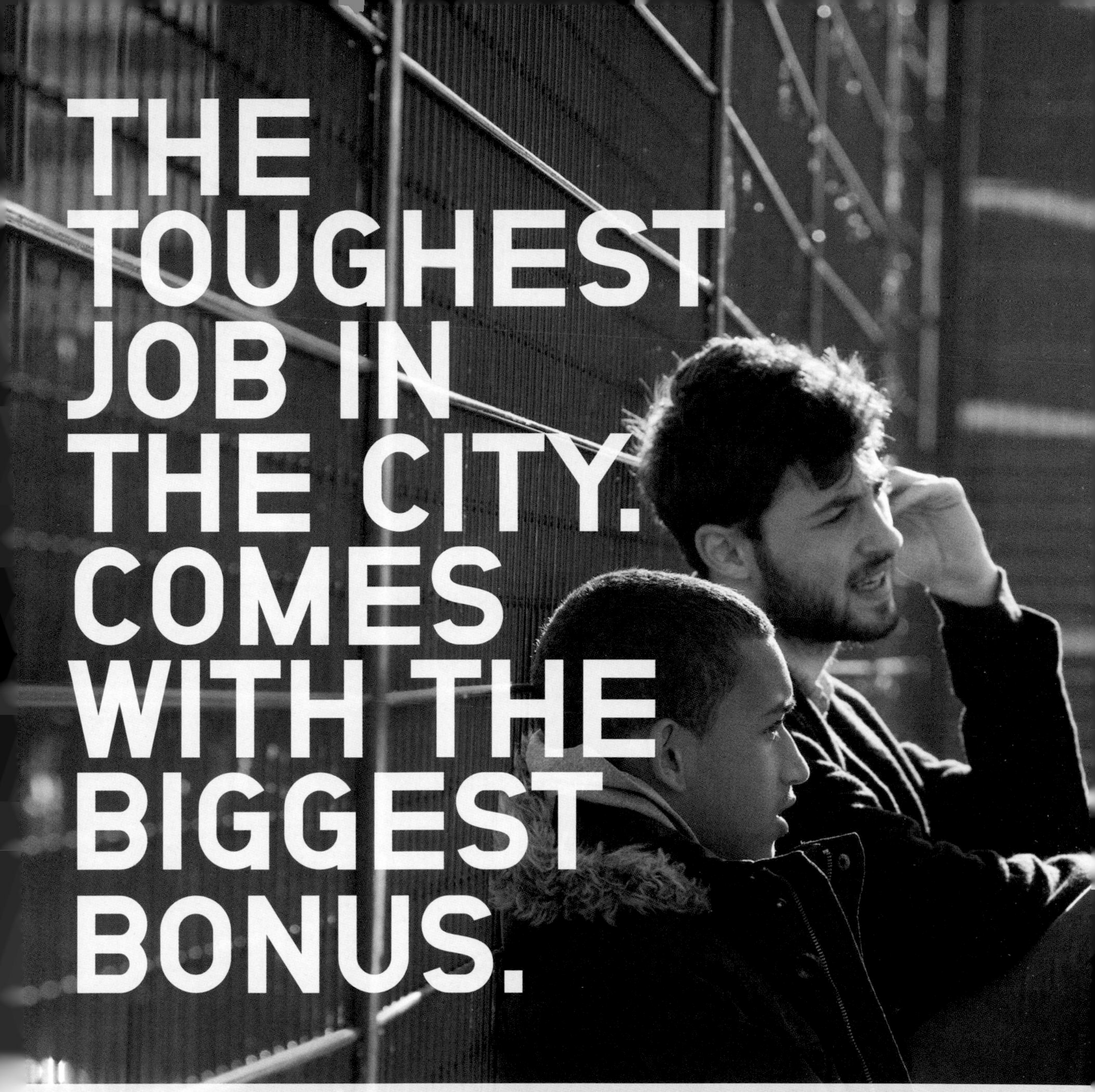

THE
TOUGHEST
JOB IN
THE CITY.
COMES
WITH THE
BIGGEST
BONUS.

FRONTLINE

CHANGING LIVES

Frontline is a new initiative designed to recruit outstanding graduates to be leaders in social work and in broader society. Successful applicants will take part in an intensive and innovative two year leadership programme, and gain a masters degree. But most importantly, they'll be working to transform the lives of vulnerable children and young people.

Because there's no bigger bonus than changing a life for the better.
www.thefrontline.org.uk

do more
feel better
live longer

GRADUATE VACANCIES IN 2016

ENGINEERING

FINANCE

HUMAN RESOURCES

IT

MARKETING

RESEARCH & DEVELOPMENT

SALES

NUMBER OF VACANCIES
50+ graduate jobs

LOCATIONS OF VACANCIES

One of the world's leading healthcare companies, GSK gives its people the chance to answer some of the planet's biggest questions. Questions about future healthcare needs and about building an innovative, global business to meet them, as well as questions about their personal and professional growth.

Dedicated to helping millions of people around the world to do more, feel better and live longer, GSK is revolutionising its business to meet changing healthcare needs from London to Lima, Lusaka, Luzhou and Lahore. GSK invested £3.1 billion in R&D in 2014 and topped the Access to Medicine Index, underlining its commitment to tackle some of the world's deadliest diseases by embracing new, open and innovative ways of working.

GSK discover, develop, manufacture and distribute vaccines, prescription medicines and consumer health products. Based in the UK, with operations in over 100 countries, GSK produce a huge range of healthcare products from lifesaving prescription medicines and vaccines to popular consumer products like Maximuscle, Sensodyne, Aquafresh and Panadol. In fact, every year GSK screen about 65 million compounds, make over four billion packs of medicines and healthcare products, and supply one quarter of the world's vaccines.

GSK is deeply committed to developing people through a range of ongoing development opportunities that includes tailored, 2-3 year rotational graduate programmes and industrial or summer placements. So it offers graduates the trust and respect to be themselves, and develop their careers across an incredibly diverse collection of businesses and geographies, in an environment where personal growth can play a vital part in the changing face of the business.

Most of all, GSK graduates enjoy the sense of purpose that comes from leading change in an industry that touches millions every day.

STARTING SALARY FOR 2016
£Competitive

UNIVERSITY VISITS IN 2015-16
ASTON, CAMBRIDGE, BIRMINGHAM, BRISTOL, IMPERIAL COLLEGE LONDON, LEEDS, LOUGHBOROUGH, MANCHESTER, NOTTINGHAM, OXFORD, SHEFFIELD, SOUTHAMPTON, UNIVERSITY COLLEGE LONDON
Please check with your university careers service for full details of local events.

MINIMUM ENTRY REQUIREMENTS
2.1 Degree

APPLICATION DEADLINE
Year-round recruitment
Early application advised.

FURTHER INFORMATION
www.Top100GraduateEmployers.com
Register now for the latest news, events information and graduate recruitment details for Britain's leading employers.

www.goldmansachs.com/careers

campusrecruiting@gs.com

plus.google.com/+GoldmanSachs/posts &+ twitter.com/gscareers

youtube.com/GoldmanSachs linkedin.com/company/goldman-sachs/careers in

The Goldman Sachs Group, Inc. is a leading global investment banking, securities and investment management firm that provides a wide range of financial services to a substantial and diversified client base that includes corporations, financial institutions, governments and high-net-worth individuals.

At Goldman Sachs, graduates will have many opportunities to make an impact. The unique perspectives that its people bring to the firm and their shared passion for working on projects of great global, economic and social significance, help drive progress and create results.

Goldman Sachs is structured in a series of divisions: Executive Office, Finance, Global Compliance, Global Investment Research, Human Capital Management, Internal Audit, Investment Banking, Investment Management, Legal, Merchant Banking, Operations, Securities, Services and Technology.

From the first day, successful applicants will be immersed in a collaborative environment with people of all levels who share the firm's values. Nearly everyone – from the junior analysts to the most senior leaders – is actively involved in recruiting talented people from a variety of backgrounds, because Goldman Sachs recognises that a diverse workforce enables them to serve their clients most effectively and in the most innovative ways.

The diversity of talents and educational backgrounds in Goldman Sachs's people is crucial to its performance and business success. To that end, the organisation is committed to an environment that values diversity, promotes inclusion and encourages teamwork.

Whatever the background or area of academic study, Goldman Sachs values the intellect, personality and integrity of an individual. While an interest in and appreciation for finance is important, one's personal qualities are key.

GRADUATE VACANCIES IN 2016

ACCOUNTANCY
FINANCE
HUMAN RESOURCES
INVESTMENT BANKING
IT
LAW

NUMBER OF VACANCIES
Around 400 graduate jobs

LOCATIONS OF VACANCIES

Vacancies also available in Europe.

STARTING SALARY FOR 2016
£Competitive

UNIVERSITY VISITS IN 2015-16
BATH, BIRMINGHAM, BRISTOL, CAMBRIDGE, CITY, DURHAM, EDINBURGH, GLASGOW, IMPERIAL COLLEGE LONDON, KING'S COLLEGE LONDON, LONDON SCHOOL OF ECONOMICS, LOUGHBOROUGH, MANCHESTER, NOTTINGHAM, OXFORD, QUEEN MARY LONDON, READING, SOUTHAMPTON, STRATHCLYDE, SURREY, TRINITY COLLEGE DUBLIN, UNIVERSITY COLLEGE DUBLIN, UNIVERSITY COLLEGE LONDON, WARWICK, YORK
Please check with your university careers service for full details of local events.

APPLICATION DEADLINE
1st November 2015

FURTHER INFORMATION
www.Top100GraduateEmployers.com
Register now for the latest news, events information and graduate recruitment details for Britain's leading employers.

Goldman Sachs

HOW WILL YOU
MAKE AN IMPACT

CONTRIBUTE, COLLABORATE AND SUCCEED WITH A CAREER AT GOLDMAN SACHS

If you're the kind of person who can't wait to make a difference, consider a career at Goldman Sachs. We believe that good ideas and innovations can come from anyone, at any level. We offer meaningful opportunities, best-in-class training and a wide variety of career paths for talented people from all academic backgrounds. Plus, with access to important clients and projects, you'll have the chance to make an impact with global significance.

APPLICATION DEADLINES

NEW ANALYST: 1 November 2015
SUMMER PROGRAMME: 6 December 2015
SPRING PROGRAMME: 3 January 2016
WORK PLACEMENT PROGRAMME: 3 January 2016

Please note we encourage early applications and may interview ahead of deadlines.

Goldman Sachs Careers

DOWNLOAD OUR APP
to learn more about how you can make an impact.

goldmansachs.com/careers
   @GSCareers

plus.google.com/+GoogleStudents   g+

twitter.com/googlestudents   🐦   facebook.com/GoogleStudents   f

youtube.com/GoogleStudents   ▶   linkedin.com/company/google/careers   in

Google™

GRADUATE VACANCIES IN 2016

CONSULTING
ENGINEERING
HUMAN RESOURCES
IT
MARKETING
MEDIA
SALES

NUMBER OF VACANCIES
No fixed quota

LOCATIONS OF VACANCIES

Vacancies also available in Europe, Asia and the USA.

STARTING SALARY FOR 2016
£Competitive
Plus world-renowned perks and benefits.

UNIVERSITY VISITS IN 2015-16
Please check with your university careers service for full details of local events.

MINIMUM ENTRY REQUIREMENTS
2.1 Degree

APPLICATION DEADLINE
Year-round recruitment

FURTHER INFORMATION
www.Top100GraduateEmployers.com
Register now for the latest news, events information and graduate recruitment details for Britain's leading employers.

Founders Larry Page and Sergey Brin met at Stanford University in 1995. By 1996, they had built a search engine that used links to determine the importance of individual web pages. Today, Google is a tech company that helps businesses of all kinds succeed on and off the web.

It's really the people that make Google the kind of company it is. Google hire people who are smart and determined, and favour ability over experience.

New grads joining Google will enter either the Small-to-Medium Business (SMB) Sales or Global Customer Experience Teams. As small business experts, Googlers in SMB help to get local entrepreneurs on the map, and deliver a beautifully simple, intuitive experience that enables customers to grow their businesses. By spotting and analysing customer needs and trends, Google's innovative teams of strategists, account developers and customer support specialists work together on scalable solutions for each business, no matter its age or size.

Google hires graduates from all disciplines, from humanities and business related courses to engineering and computer science. The ideal candidate is someone who can demonstrate a passion for the online industry and someone who has made the most of their time at university through involvement in clubs, societies or relevant internships. Google hires graduates who have a variety of strengths and passions, not just isolated skill sets. For technical roles within engineering teams, specific skills will be required.

The Google Business Associate Programme is a two-year developmental programme that supplements a Googler's core role in SMB. It offers world-class training, equipping new joiners with the business, analytical and leadership skills needed to be successful at Google.

THE IDEA FOR GMAIL
BEGAN WITH 1 GOOGLER.

TODAY, IT HAS MORE THAN 425 MILLION USERS AND COUNTING.

DO COOL THINGS THAT MATTER

How to sum up a complex and exciting business like Grant Thornton? Simply put, they're part of a global organisation providing business and financial advice to dynamic organisations right at the heart of growth. In the UK alone, they deliver solutions to 40,000 clients in over 100 countries.

Grant Thornton are a shared enterprise – meaning their people share ideas, share responsibility and share reward. It's never been a more exciting time to be a part of a firm that are passionate about their higher purpose – unlocking growth for clients and driving a vibrant economy. Business and the way we do it is changing, Grant Thornton are at the start of an exciting journey and they recognise the need for agility and collaboration in today's environment. They're starting from within – all 4,500 people thinking and behaving according to their shared mindset for growth.

Over 400 ambitious graduates, interns and placement students join Grant Thornton each year. They enjoy variety and responsibility from the start on exciting client assignments, from multinationals to fast-growth companies such as start-ups. The structured training, varied on-the-ground client experience and supportive working environment gives trainees the chance to develop and grow as trusted advisers with a deep understanding of business, as well as achieving a respected professional qualification and a competitive salary.

So what makes a business adviser at the go-to firm for growth? People with a passion for business, who combine technical thinking with their shared insight to give the kind of advice that makes a real difference to the organisations they work with and the wider economy. They listen critically and have the confidence to challenge assumptions right from day one. They seek out opportunities, collaborate and add real value to clients by unlocking their potential for growth.

GRADUATE VACANCIES IN 2016
ACCOUNTANCY

NUMBER OF VACANCIES
300+ graduate jobs

LOCATIONS OF VACANCIES

STARTING SALARY FOR 2016
£Competitive

UNIVERSITY VISITS IN 2015-16
ASTON, BATH, BIRMINGHAM, BRISTOL, BRUNEL, CARDIFF, CITY, DURHAM, EAST ANGLIA, EDINBURGH, EXETER, GLASGOW, IMPERIAL COLLEGE LONDON, KING'S COLLEGE LONDON, KENT, LANCASTER, LEEDS, LEICESTER, LIVERPOOL, LONDON SCHOOL OF ECONOMICS, LOUGHBOROUGH, MANCHESTER, NEWCASTLE, NOTTINGHAM, NOTTINGHAM TRENT, PLYMOUTH, READING, SHEFFIELD, SOUTHAMPTON, STRATHCLYDE, SURREY, SUSSEX, UNIVERSITY COLLEGE LONDON, WARWICK, YORK
Please check with your university careers service for full details of local events.

MINIMUM ENTRY REQUIREMENTS
Flexible academic entry requirements.

APPLICATION DEADLINE
Year-round recruitment
Early application advised.

FURTHER INFORMATION
www.Top100GraduateEmployers.com
Register now for the latest news, events information and graduate recruitment details for Britain's leading employers.

DON'T EAT YELLOW SNOW

What will your advice be?

HERBERT
SMITH
FREEHILLS

www.herbertsmithfreehills.com
facebook.com/HSFgraduatesUK graduatesuk@hsf.com
linkedin.com/company/herbert-smith twitter.com/HSFgraduatesUK

GRADUATE VACANCIES IN 2016
LAW

NUMBER OF VACANCIES
70 graduate jobs
For training contracts starting in 2018.

LOCATIONS OF VACANCIES

Vacancies also available in Europe, Asia, the USA and elsewhere in the world.

STARTING SALARY FOR 2016
£42,000

UNIVERSITY VISITS IN 2015-16
BIRMINGHAM, BRISTOL, CAMBRIDGE, CARDIFF, DURHAM, EDINBURGH, EXETER, GLASGOW, KING'S COLLEGE LONDON, LEEDS, LEICESTER, LONDON SCHOOL OF ECONOMICS, MANCHESTER, NEWCASTLE, NOTTINGHAM, OXFORD, READING, SOUTHAMPTON, ST ANDREWS, UNIVERSITY COLLEGE LONDON, WARWICK, YORK
Please check with your university careers service for full details of local events.

MINIMUM ENTRY REQUIREMENTS
2.1 Degree

APPLICATION DEADLINE
16th January 2016

FURTHER INFORMATION
www.Top100GraduateEmployers.com
Register now for the latest news, events information and graduate recruitment details for Britain's leading employers.

Corporate and litigation. Arbitration and advocacy. Herbert Smith Freehills has it all. And as one of the world's leading law firms, Herbert Smith Freehills works with some of the biggest and most ambitious organisations across the globe on some of their biggest and most ambitious projects.

The firm is a global force with more than 2,800 lawyers across Asia, Australia, Europe, the Middle East and the USA. The quality of Herbert Smith Freehills' international network means it can provide integrated cross-border services to its high-profile clients.

Herbert Smith Freehills' dispute resolution practice is number one in the UK, Asia and Australia, and includes both the firm's leading international arbitration practice and award-winning in-house advocacy unit. The firm has a market-leading corporate practice plus other quality practices like finance, competition and regulation and trade. Herbert Smith Freehills prides itself on being a full-service firm that's able to do more for its clients.

And Herbert Smith Freehills trainees can be a part of it all. The training contract balances contentious and non-contentious work with pro bono opportunities and real responsibility. Trainees rotate around four six-month seats with the opportunity to go on secondment either to a client, or to one of the firm's international offices.

Herbert Smith Freehills looks for people with the drive to become brilliant lawyers. As well as a great academic record, applicants should be commercially minded and willing to build relationships with clients and colleagues alike. For people who are assured, perceptive, empathetic and ambitious, Herbert Smith Freehills offers more than the chance to experience everything. It offers the chance to be a part of it.

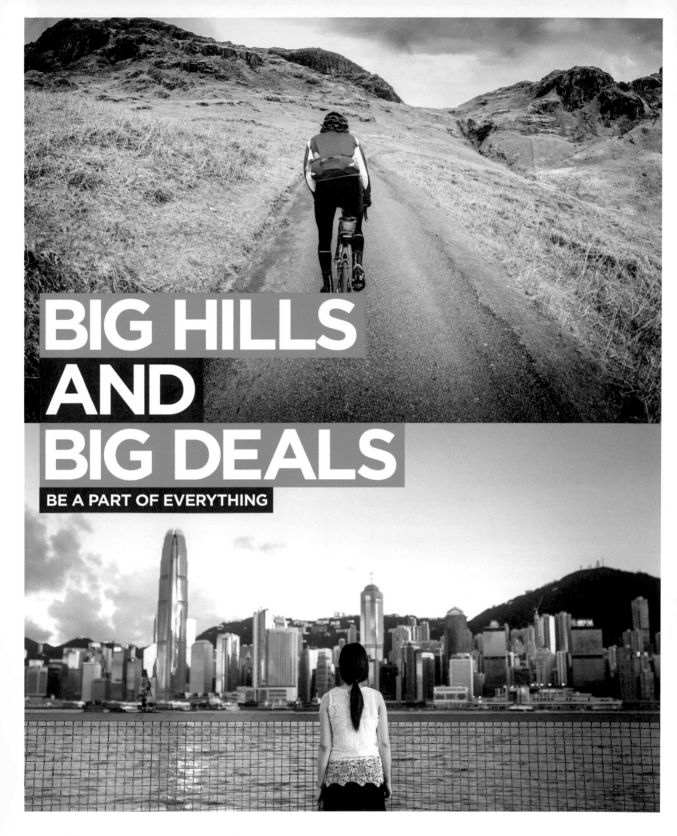

BIG HILLS AND BIG DEALS

BE A PART OF EVERYTHING

HERBERT SMITH FREEHILLS

INTERNATIONAL GRADUATE CAREERS IN LAW

Setting off with clients on a charity cycle event. Settling in to finish a £1.4bn merger agreement. We'll give you the chance to make a real impact. And to enjoy the rewards that come with working hard.

Don't just experience everything, be a part of it.

SEARCH HSF GRADUATE FOR MORE f t in

Hogan Lovells is a top global law firm that tackles the toughest legal issues in major industries and commercial centres around the world. The firm is recognised for its balance of ambition and approachability, straight-talking advice and thinking around corners, and supportive culture that ensures trainees' success.

Known for their global diversity, Hogan Lovells is home to more than 2,500 lawyers operating out of over 45 offices across Africa, Asia, Australia, Europe, Latin America, the Middle East and North America. The firm has a strong reputation for corporate, finance, dispute resolution, government regulatory and intellectual property. It is also recognised for its commitment to high quality training and development.

Each year they take on 60 trainee solicitors, composed of law and non-law graduates. The two-year training contract is split into four six-month periods of work experience known as 'seats'. Trainee solicitors move around four different practice areas during their two years, gaining a range of experiences and spending time in either corporate or finance, as well as litigation. During the second year of the contract, they also offer options for secondment at their international offices and in-house with clients.

Hogan Lovells also offers up to 90 vacation scheme places, split between their highly-regarded spring, summer and winter vacation schemes. Lasting up to three weeks, students will have the chance to work alongside partners, associates and trainees – gaining insight into key practice areas such as corporate, finance and litigation. Vacation scheme students are exposed to real projects on a daily basis. They learn to draft documents, carry out legal research and co-ordinate meetings. There is even the opportunity to attend court. This hands-on learning is complemented by tailored workshops, discussions and social events.

GRADUATE VACANCIES IN 2016

LAW

NUMBER OF VACANCIES
60 graduate jobs
For training contracts starting in 2018.

LOCATIONS OF VACANCIES

STARTING SALARY FOR 2016
£41,000

UNIVERSITY VISITS IN 2015-16
BELFAST, BIRMINGHAM, BRISTOL, CAMBRIDGE, CARDIFF, DURHAM, EAST ANGLIA, EDINBURGH, EXETER, HULL, IMPERIAL COLLEGE LONDON, KING'S COLLEGE LONDON, LANCASTER, LEEDS, LEICESTER, LONDON SCHOOL OF ECONOMICS, MANCHESTER, NEWCASTLE, NOTTINGHAM, OXFORD, QUEEN MARY LONDON, SHEFFIELD, SOUTHAMPTON, ST ANDREWS, TRINITY COLLEGE DUBLIN, UNIVERSITY COLLEGE DUBLIN, UNIVERSITY COLLEGE LONDON, WARWICK, YORK
Please check with your university careers service for full details of local events.

MINIMUM ENTRY REQUIREMENTS
2.1 Degree

APPLICATION DEADLINE
Law: 31st July 2016
Non-law: 31st March 2016

FURTHER INFORMATION
www.Top100GraduateEmployers.com
Register now for the latest news, events information and graduate recruitment details for Britain's leading employers.

HSBC ◆

HSBC is one of the world's leading international banks and it is looking for progressive minds to join its Global Graduate and Intern Programmes. With over 6,100 offices serving around 51 million customers, its ambition is to be where the growth is, connecting customers to opportunities and enabling businesses to thrive and economies to prosper.

This leading international bank offers a wide choice of programmes in many areas of its organisation and in many parts of the world. It values diversity with an inclusive environment that supports flexible working and treats everyone with respect. Being open to different ideas and cultures is just one of its values which is at the heart of everything it does. These values define HSBC and makes it distinctive.

HSBC is looking for students and graduates who share its values. People who are forward-thinking, driven and perceptive. Who want to create foundations for businesses to grow, enjoy being part of a team and are excited by the challenge of new ideas. Dependable people who are open to different cultures and different ideas. As well as having the support of a line manager, mentor and buddy, successful applicants will be learning from great colleagues. Connecting with customers and clients, communities and colleagues, they will be making a tangible contribution to their own success.

For those who join one of HSBC's Global Graduate Programmes, the journey will begin with the Global Induction in either Commercial Banking, Global Banking and Markets, Global Private Banking or Retail Banking and Wealth Management which includes Asset Management. Their Summer Internship is up to 10 weeks long. Their selection process includes two on-line tests, a telephone interview and an assessment centre.

GRADUATE VACANCIES IN 2016

FINANCE

INVESTMENT BANKING

RETAILING

SALES

NUMBER OF VACANCIES
500+ graduate jobs

LOCATIONS OF VACANCIES

Vacancies also available in Europe, Asia, the USA and elsewhere in the world.

STARTING SALARY FOR 2016
£Competitive

UNIVERSITY VISITS IN 2015-16
ASTON, BATH, BIRMINGHAM, BRISTOL, CAMBRIDGE, CARDIFF, CITY, DURHAM, EDINBURGH, EXETER, GLASGOW, IMPERIAL COLLEGE LONDON, KING'S COLLEGE LONDON, LANCASTER, LEEDS, LEICESTER, LIVERPOOL, LONDON SCHOOL OF ECONOMICS, LOUGHBOROUGH, MANCHESTER, NEWCASTLE, NOTTINGHAM, OXFORD, QUEEN MARY LONDON, READING, ROYAL HOLLOWAY, SHEFFIELD, SOUTHAMPTON, SWANSEA, UNIVERSITY COLLEGE LONDON, WARWICK, YORK
Please check with your university careers service for full details of local events.

MINIMUM ENTRY REQUIREMENTS
2.1 Degree
300 UCAS points

APPLICATION DEADLINE
Varies by function

FURTHER INFORMATION
www.Top100GraduateEmployers.com
Register now for the latest news, events information and graduate recruitment details for Britain's leading employers.

DRIVERS WANTED

To take us in new directions. To steer our future. To help drive new ideas forward.

At HSBC, we're looking for forward-thinking, perceptive and motivated people to join our Global Graduate Programmes, to help fulfil our customers' hopes, dreams and ambitions. Along the road, we'll help guide and encourage you to explore new paths and support you on your own journey.

Are you ready to take the wheel?

PROGRESSIVE MINDS APPLY

hsbc.com/careers

HSBC ►◄

Issued by HSBC Holdings plc. Approved for issue in the UK by HSBC Bank plc. **AC32935**

The world is changing, and it's innovative companies like IBM who are driving this transformation. At IBM, graduates will have limitless opportunities to do meaningful work using data and technology to make the world better and more efficient in an organisation full of passionate and dedicated individuals.

IBM work with some of the greatest and best known names on the planet, providing IT services and consultancy across all industries including retail, sport, business, finance, health, media and entertainment.

IBM look for the best and brightest graduates, from all universities, degree backgrounds and abilities. They want creative and passionate people who will share their dedication to tackling the world's toughest problems. Whether graduates want to pursue a career in consulting, technology, business, design or sales they'll have the chance to collaborate with extraordinary people in a creative environment to make the world work better.

IBM are dedicated to giving graduates every opportunity to enhance their career development. They'll work in an environment that cultivates creativity and individual differences, rewarding their best work.

IBM's award winning, bespoke training is designed to give graduates the personal, business and technical skills to take their career wherever they want to go. Graduates will continuously learn and develop new skills and have the opportunity to contribute to the enhancement of their field.

IBM will encourage graduates to extend their expertise through customised professional development and leadership training, allocating every graduate a professional development manager and a mentor to ensure graduates get the most out of the programme.

Be part of a global transformation and join IBM.

GRADUATE VACANCIES IN 2016
CONSULTING
IT
SALES

NUMBER OF VACANCIES
300+ graduate jobs

LOCATIONS OF VACANCIES

STARTING SALARY FOR 2016
£30,000+

UNIVERSITY VISITS IN 2015-16
ASTON, BATH, BIRMINGHAM, BRISTOL, CAMBRIDGE, CARDIFF, DURHAM, EDINBURGH, EXETER, GLASGOW, IMPERIAL COLLEGE LONDON, KING'S COLLEGE LONDON, LANCASTER, LEEDS, LIVERPOOL, LONDON SCHOOL OF ECONOMICS, LOUGHBOROUGH, MANCHESTER, NEWCASTLE, NOTTINGHAM, OXFORD, SHEFFIELD, SOUTHAMPTON, UNIVERSITY COLLEGE LONDON, WARWICK, YORK
Please check with your university careers service for full details of local events.

MINIMUM ENTRY REQUIREMENTS
2.1 Degree

APPLICATION DEADLINE
Year-round recruitment

FURTHER INFORMATION
www.Top100GraduateEmployers.com
Register now for the latest news, events information and graduate recruitment details for Britain's leading employers.

your future
made with
IBM

What will you make with IBM?

ibm.com/jobs/uk

BEHIND THE EXCELLENCE

Home to some of the most iconic nameplates ever to take to the road, Jaguar Land Rover has a proud and enviable heritage. One that has seen them continually redefine the global benchmark for quality, performance and innovation and set the standards that others want to follow.

With such momentum behind them, the organisation's future is set to be even more exciting. Increasing demand and significant investment in new products, facilities and markets, means finding the next-generation of innovators who will shape Jaguar Land Rover's future has never been more important.

Reflecting the scale of their ambition is Jaguar Land Rover's extensive and expanding graduate offering. Opportunities lie right across the business in everything from Engineering and Manufacturing disciplines to their Commercial and Business areas.

Whichever role graduates make their own, they'll discover a dedication to excellence runs throughout the business. They'll find a requirement for innovative and creative thinking that pushes the boundaries of their potential, and ensures they develop a rigorous and commercially-focused approach to their work. With ongoing support to gain further professional qualifications and accreditation, in-house training and a thorough induction programme, the graduate scheme has been designed to be as inspiring as the pioneering vehicles they'll help produce.

As would be expected from two of the world's most revered brands, an outstanding range of rewards and benefits await those who have the initiative, vision and drive to contribute to the organisation's global success – including a competitive salary, joining bonus, pension scheme and discounted car purchase scheme. All this and more makes Jaguar Land Rover an enviable place to start the journey and put their excellence in motion.

BEHIND THE NEXT GENERATION

GRADUATE & UNDERGRADUATE OPPORTUNITIES
ENGINEERING & COMMERCIAL BUSINESS AREAS

Our heritage is enviable. Our future will be breathtaking. As home to two of the world's most iconic brands, there has never been a more exciting time to join our journey. The scale of our ambition is reflected by the ever-expanding breadth of our graduate programmes and undergraduate placements. From our Manufacturing and Engineering disciplines to our Commercial and Business functions, this is a place where you'll use your creativity to redefine the benchmark for excellence. Where you'll continually push the boundaries of your own potential. Where you'll develop specialist and commercial skills working alongside an industry-revered team.

To put your excellence in motion, visit:
jaguarlandrovercareers.com

The John Lewis Partnership is a multi-award winning retail business and incorporates two of the high street's most renowned brands – John Lewis and Waitrose. Combining the best of traditional and modern, it has responded to customers' needs to become a truly omni-channel business.

This commitment to innovation and outstanding customer service is part of what makes the John Lewis Partnership so different and successful. But perhaps the most unique aspect is that everyone that joins the organisation becomes a Partner. This means they own a share in the business and get to have a say in how it's run.

And key to its ongoing success are graduates. The organisation is keen to give graduates early responsibility as well as challenges that give them every opportunity to make a difference. The Partnership runs a number of schemes that are all geared up to create future leaders of the business. These fast-paced and stimulating programmes offer real experiences, superb training and support, the chance to work with different individuals and to create a strong graduate community. Exposure to the most successful leaders in retail today, support from a buddy or mentor and a comprehensive induction are also core aspects of development.

A lot is expected in return. A sense of pride in ownership and the ability to make things happen. To deliver excellent service, work together, bring commitment to personal and professional development and openness and adaptability to change are all things that the John Lewis Partnership look for (along with specific generalist or specialist skills of course). Graduates that bring these qualities can expect to start a unique journey with the organisation consistently voted as the nation's most loved retailer.

GRADUATE VACANCIES IN 2016

FINANCE
GENERAL MANAGEMENT
IT
PURCHASING
RETAILING

NUMBER OF VACANCIES
40+ graduate jobs

LOCATIONS OF VACANCIES

STARTING SALARY FOR 2016
Dependent on scheme
Please see website for full details.

UNIVERSITY VISITS IN 2015-16
Please check with your university careers service for full details of local events.

MINIMUM ENTRY REQUIREMENTS
Dependent on scheme
Please see website for full details.

APPLICATION DEADLINE
22nd November 2015

FURTHER INFORMATION
www.Top100GraduateEmployers.com
Register now for the latest news, events information and graduate recruitment details for Britain's leading employers.

J.P.Morgan

GRADUATE VACANCIES IN 2016

FINANCE
HUMAN RESOURCES
INVESTMENT BANKING
IT

NUMBER OF VACANCIES
No fixed quota

LOCATIONS OF VACANCIES

Vacancies also available in Europe, the USA and Asia.

STARTING SALARY FOR 2016
£Competitive

UNIVERSITY VISITS IN 2015-16
BATH, CAMBRIDGE, DURHAM, EDINBURGH, EXETER, GLASGOW, IMPERIAL COLLEGE LONDON, LONDON SCHOOL OF ECONOMICS, OXFORD, SOUTHAMPTON, ST ANDREWS, STRATHCLYDE, UNIVERSITY COLLEGE LONDON, WARWICK
Please check with your university careers service for full details of local events.

MINIMUM ENTRY REQUIREMENTS
2.1 Degree

APPLICATION DEADLINE
Please see website for full details.

FURTHER INFORMATION
www.Top100GraduateEmployers.com
Register now for the latest news, events information and graduate recruitment details for Britain's leading employers.

Banking is a vital part of the world's economy and everyday life. Over the last 200 years, J.P. Morgan has evolved as a business to meet the needs of some of the world's largest companies as well as many of the smaller businesses that are a cornerstone of local communities. Their team of employees work tirelessly to do the right thing for their clients, shareholders and the firm every day.

J.P. Morgan's strength lies not only in the quality of its products, but also within the invaluable power of its employees. Harnessing the diversity of its people, J.P. Morgan values those with different talents, ranging from Investment Banking to Technology, Operations and Human Resources.

Career opportunities are available across the firm, so it pays to learn as much as possible about the industry, business areas and the roles available. Be sure to take advantage of pre-internship programmes, such as Insight Days and Spring Week, which give students a chance to get noticed early – many interns are hired directly from the firm's Spring Week programme.

J.P. Morgan offers internship and graduate opportunities in the following areas: Finance, Global Investment Management, Global Wealth Management, Human Resources, Investment Banking, Investor Services, Operations, Quantitative Research, Risk, Sales, Trading & Research, Technology and Treasury Services.

J.P. Morgan is looking for collaborative future leaders who have passion, creativity and exceptional interpersonal skills. Impeccable academic credentials are important, but so are achievements outside the classroom.

Working with a team committed to doing their best, earning the trust of their clients and encouraging employees to fulfil their potential. That's what it means to be part of J.P. Morgan.

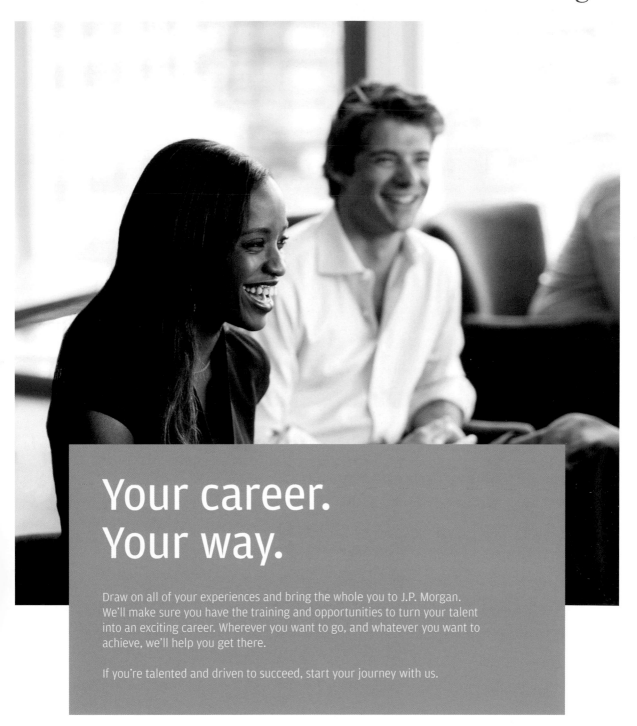

J.P.Morgan

Your career.
Your way.

Draw on all of your experiences and bring the whole you to J.P. Morgan. We'll make sure you have the training and opportunities to turn your talent into an exciting career. Wherever you want to go, and whatever you want to achieve, we'll help you get there.

If you're talented and driven to succeed, start your journey with us.

Start your journey.
jpmorgan.com/careers

cutting through complexity

KPMG in the UK has 22 offices and is part of a global network of member firms offering Audit, Tax and Advisory to some of the world's biggest businesses. KPMG's vision is simple – to turn knowledge into value for the benefit of its clients, people and stakeholders. Striving to be better is the KPMG difference.

At the heart of KPMG's continued success is its people. Being part of KPMG is being part of a community of talented and innovative people who work together to make a wide-reaching and positive impact on government, business and society as a whole.

There's no one type of person that succeeds at KPMG. KPMG welcomes all kinds of personalities, characters, skill sets and degree disciplines. Talented and ambitious graduates can expect responsibility from day one. The range of clients and project work can be fascinating and challenging, and graduates will use their own individual unique set of skills, experiences and competencies to achieve their business, and personal goals.

To help graduates achieve their full potential, KPMG gives all the support and guidance they need to succeed through The Academy. This provides access to diverse KPMG communities, support and learning opportunities to build skills and knowledge. The full-time Professional Qualification Training team is dedicated to helping graduates pass professional exams first time.

The work is definitely challenging and in return, KPMG launched 'Our Deal', to reward colleagues for giving their best. From introducing secondment programmes, preferential banking, cash towards student loan payments and birthdays off, KPMG is making sure that its people have a rewarding and supportive experience to help them be their best. Just a few reasons why KPMG is an award-winning employer and a place for graduates to learn and grow.

GRADUATE VACANCIES IN 2016

ACCOUNTANCY
CONSULTING
FINANCE
HUMAN RESOURCES
IT
MARKETING

NUMBER OF VACANCIES
1,000 graduate jobs

LOCATIONS OF VACANCIES

STARTING SALARY FOR 2016
£Competitive
Plus benefits.

UNIVERSITY VISITS IN 2015-16
ABERDEEN, BATH, BIRMINGHAM, BRISTOL, CARDIFF, DURHAM, EDINBURGH, EXETER, IMPERIAL COLLEGE LONDON, KING'S COLLEGE LONDON, LEEDS, LONDON SCHOOL OF ECONOMICS, LOUGHBOROUGH, MANCHESTER, NEWCASTLE, NOTTINGHAM, SHEFFIELD, SOUTHAMPTON, ST ANDREWS, STRATHCLYDE, UNIVERSITY COLLEGE LONDON, WARWICK, YORK
Please check with your university careers service for full details of local events.

MINIMUM ENTRY REQUIREMENTS
2.1 Degree
300 UCAS points
However, it's not just academic performance KPMG is interested in. Please see website for specific programme requirements.

APPLICATION DEADLINE
Year-round recruitment
Early application advised.

FURTHER INFORMATION
www.Top100GraduateEmployers.com
Register now for the latest news, events information and graduate recruitment details for Britain's leading employers.

L'ORÉAL

Think 32 iconic international brands, selling in 130 countries. Think Ralph Lauren. Think Diesel. Think Garnier. Think The Body Shop. And now, think about the adventure graduates can have, when they work for the world's number one cosmetics group. It's time to start a L'Oréal adventure.

At the forefront of a booming £10 billion industry in the UK, L'Oréal continues to invent and revolutionise. In 2014, the group registered a stunning 501 patents for newly invented products and formulae. That constant creativity, and determined exploration of every possibility, is what makes L'Oréal a global success symbol.

So, when it comes to their Management Trainee Programme, L'Oréal need more than just graduates. They need inventors, explorers, leaders, and entrepreneurs. Graduates who know that when it comes to success, inspirational talent and hard work go hand in hand. Graduates who know that they should never stop exploring new ideas.

On the Management Trainee Programme, graduates work in functions across the business, gaining a sharp sense of life at L'Oréal. With three different rotations in marketing, operations, commercial and finance, they're free to develop their talent and discover new possibilities. More than that, the graduates also move through different brands – from Kiehl's to La Roche-Posay; from Armani Beauty to Maybelline – each with their own unique culture and identity to explore.

With on-the-job training and their own personal HR sponsor, graduates will progress into operational roles within as little as a year. They'll take on real responsibility, and make a palpable contribution to an international success story. From the start, they'll shape their own career and choose their own direction; their own adventure with L'Oréal's outstanding brands.

GRADUATE VACANCIES IN 2016

FINANCE
LOGISTICS
MARKETING
SALES

NUMBER OF VACANCIES
40 graduate jobs

LOCATIONS OF VACANCIES

STARTING SALARY FOR 2016
£29,000

UNIVERSITY VISITS IN 2015-16
BATH, BIRMINGHAM, CAMBRIDGE, CARDIFF, DURHAM, EDINBURGH, EXETER, LANCASTER, LEEDS, LONDON SCHOOL OF ECONOMICS, LOUGHBOROUGH, MANCHESTER, NEWCASTLE, NORTHUMBRIA, NOTTINGHAM, NOTTINGHAM TRENT, OXFORD, READING, ST ANDREWS, SUSSEX, WARWICK, YORK
Please check with your university careers service for full details of local events.

MINIMUM ENTRY REQUIREMENTS
2.1 Degree
320 UCAS points

APPLICATION DEADLINE
31st January 2016

FURTHER INFORMATION
www.Top100GraduateEmployers.com
Register now for the latest news, events information and graduate recruitment details for Britain's leading employers.

L'ORÉAL

STEVE. FINANCE GRADUATE

ON HIS WAY TO PRESENT
THE BUDGET.
THIS IS ONE SMALL STEP
FOR L'ORÉAL;
ONE GIANT LEAP
FOR STEVE.

Start your L'Oréal adventure
For graduate careers in finance, marketing, commercial
and logistics, visit **careers.loréal.com/UKgrads**

Quality products. Quality people.

GRADUATE VACANCIES IN 2016
GENERAL MANAGEMENT
LOGISTICS
PROPERTY
PURCHASING
RETAILING
SALES

NUMBER OF VACANCIES
100 graduate jobs

LOCATIONS OF VACANCIES

As one of the UK's retail success stories, Lidl's simple retail philosophy and efficient working practices allow them to focus on what they do best – providing top quality products at the lowest possible prices. Their principles ensure clear structures, simple processes, flat hierarchies and short decision paths.

Lidl is an established international food retailer with more than 10,000 stores trading across Europe. With 620 stores in the UK alone, they have an impressive schedule of new store openings planned for the next few years and are increasing their portfolio with further warehouses to support their new in-store bakeries.

Uncompromising on quality, they look for the same in their graduates. They are looking for talented, motivated and ambitious people who are excellent communicators and possess good commercial awareness. They offer graduate opportunities in positions across the UK, based in their stores, Regional Distribution Centres and Head Office. A structured and hands-on approach to training allows Lidl graduates to take on early responsibility with support being provided throughout the training by experienced colleagues.

At Lidl, initiative is encouraged with achievements being recognised; this is supported by their promise that internal candidates come first in all career opportunities. In fact, nearly all of their senior professionals started their careers in store operations and have successfully progressed in career paths through sales, property, construction, logistics and a wide range of head office positions.

With opportunities to travel internationally and an excellent rewards package, this could be one of the most exciting opportunities on the market. For graduates who have what it takes to be part of one of the fastest paced industries on the graduate market then Lidl could offer the perfect career opportunity.

STARTING SALARY FOR 2016
£38,000

UNIVERSITY VISITS IN 2015-16
ASTON, BIRMINGHAM, DURHAM, EDINBURGH, EXETER, LEEDS, MANCHESTER, NEWCASTLE, NOTTINGHAM, NOTTINGHAM TRENT, READING, ST ANDREWS, STRATHCLYDE, WARWICK
Please check with your university careers service for full details of local events.

MINIMUM ENTRY REQUIREMENTS
2.1 Degree

APPLICATION DEADLINE
Varies by function

FURTHER INFORMATION
www.Top100GraduateEmployers.com
Register now for the latest news, events information and graduate recruitment details for Britain's leading employers.

Quality products. Quality people.

Step into the limelight.

Are you ready to take the limelight? If you're a natural leader, with the ability to inspire excellence in a team, take the next step towards the best decision you've ever made.

For more information or to download our graduate brochure, please visit:

www.lidlgraduatecareers.co.uk

#LidlSurprises

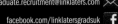

As one of the world's most prestigious law firms, Linklaters is the place where graduates can make the most of their talents. Amongst a team of exceptional lawyers, a network of international offices and through unparalleled training and development opportunities, people can live their ambition.

With the ambition to be the leading global law firm, if graduates want to make the most of their potential in commercial law, Linklaters is the place to be.

Linklaters attracts and recruits people from a range of subject disciplines and backgrounds. What they all have in common is a desire to achieve their full potential through a career in commercial law.

Linklaters helps its trainees achieve their ambitions by providing an environment in which to succeed. For non-law graduates, it starts with the Graduate Diploma in Law, giving them all the legal knowledge required to start their professional training. All graduates then come together to complete the bespoke Legal Practice Course.

Once the initial training is complete, it's time to begin working on real client matters through four six-month seats in Linklaters' global practice groups. Each seat not only builds skills and expertise in a particular area, but with ongoing training, feedback and support, it develops the professional and commercial skills that every successful lawyer needs.

As Linklaters believes in continuous learning, the unique Linklaters Law and Business School delivers the tools, knowledge and confidence for lawyers throughout their careers.

With complex and high-profile deals across a global network of 29 offices and beyond, international secondment opportunities and great rewards, Linklaters offers its trainees broad and rich experiences to springboard their careers.

GRADUATE VACANCIES IN 2016
LAW

NUMBER OF VACANCIES
110 graduate jobs
For training contracts starting in 2018.

LOCATIONS OF VACANCIES

STARTING SALARY FOR 2016
£42,000
Plus eligibility for a bonus.

UNIVERSITY VISITS IN 2015-16
BELFAST, BIRMINGHAM, BRISTOL, CAMBRIDGE, CARDIFF, DURHAM, EDINBURGH, EXETER, GLASGOW, KING'S COLLEGE LONDON, LANCASTER, LEEDS, LONDON SCHOOL OF ECONOMICS, MANCHESTER, NEWCASTLE, NOTTINGHAM, OXFORD, QUEEN MARY LONDON, SCHOOL OF AFRICAN STUDIES, SHEFFIELD, SOUTHAMPTON, ST ANDREWS, TRINITY COLLEGE DUBLIN, UNIVERSITY COLLEGE DUBLIN, UNIVERSITY COLLEGE LONDON, WARWICK, YORK
Please check with your university careers service for full details of local events.

MINIMUM ENTRY REQUIREMENTS
2.1 Degree

APPLICATION DEADLINE
Varies by function
Please see website for full details.

FURTHER INFORMATION
www.Top100GraduateEmployers.com
Register now for the latest news, events information and graduate recruitment details for Britain's leading employers.

Linklaters

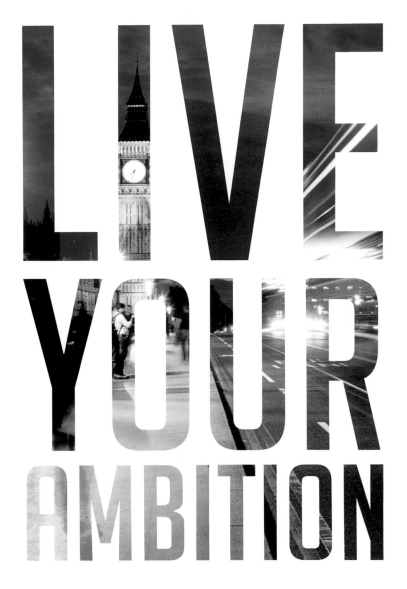

LIVE YOUR AMBITION

What do you want from your career in commercial law? To work on the most exciting and high-profile deals in a world-leading law firm? To receive top-class training from the brightest talent in the legal sector? To be generously rewarded throughout your career, including through global opportunities?

These are the kind of goals we love. So we'll do everything to make sure you succeed – giving you the tailored, supportive and long-term training that helps you craft the career you want.

Live your ambition with Linklaters.

www.linklaters.com/ukgrads

LLOYD'S

www.lloyds.com/graduates

facebook.com/Lloyds **f**   graduate.enquiries@lloyds.com ✉

lloyds.com/linkedin **in**   twitter.com/LloydsofLondon 🐦

Lloyd's is the world's specialist insurance market, insuring some of the world's most complex risks, from hurricanes to terrorism, sporting events to space travel, cybercrime to fine art. Based in the City of London, in the iconic Lloyd's building, it has increasing business and presence in more than 200 countries and territories around the world.

As well as working in the centre of the City, at the heart of the insurance industry, graduates at Lloyd's are provided with a holistic view of the market covering claims, underwriting, broking and the Corporation on the generalist programme. Lloyd's also offers an inspiring eight week summer internship for undergraduates looking for insight before choosing their career path.

Graduates explore the many roles that Lloyd's has to offer by rotation, experiencing anything from managing relationships with international regulators, to examining the potential impact of a catastrophe, to helping develop insight into emerging risks. There is a chance to shape the future as Lloyd's needs sharp, commercial thinkers to develop new approaches and products to meet the needs of an ever changing global outlook.

Placements offer a six month opportunity to undertake a live project with real responsibility. Lloyd's makes sure everyone is confident and up to speed with everything before they start with a thorough induction and continuous training and support.

Lloyd's is looking for graduates from any discipline with sharp analytic and problem solving skills, numerical ability, openness to change and strong relationship building capability. With their impressive benefits package, intellectual challenge and real career building opportunities in the heart of the City, Lloyd's is a superb choice.

GRADUATE VACANCIES IN 2016

FINANCE

NUMBER OF VACANCIES
15-20 graduate jobs

LOCATIONS OF VACANCIES

STARTING SALARY FOR 2016
£26,000
Plus £1,000 every six months for 18 months.

UNIVERSITY VISITS IN 2015-16
KENT, LEICESTER, LONDON SCHOOL OF ECONOMICS, NOTTINGHAM, WARWICK
Please check with your university careers service for full details of local events.

MINIMUM ENTRY REQUIREMENTS
2.2 Degree

APPLICATION DEADLINE
8th January 2016

FURTHER INFORMATION
www.Top100GraduateEmployers.com
Register now for the latest news, events information and graduate recruitment details for Britain's leading employers.

LLOYD'S

A new generation of risks requires a new generation of insurers.

That's why Lloyd's, the world's only specialist re/insurance market, is looking for dynamic and creative graduates to join its Graduate Programme.

Help shape the future.
Join the Lloyd's Graduate Programme today.

Contact graduate.enquiries@lloyds.com or visit www.lloyds.com/graduates for more information

 Follow us on Twitter: @Lloydsoflondon

 lloyds.com/linkedin

Lloyds Banking Group is a major UK financial institution. A third of the population has a relationship with the organisation through brands such as Lloyds, Halifax and Bank of Scotland. The Group has a huge business management and technology workforce, and the career opportunities to match.

This is an organisation where talented individuals can explore their potential and find a more meaningful career path. The development journey is powerful, balanced and diverse – where deep on-the-job learning complements formal training and the funding to earn renowned professional qualifications. Mentoring, alumni networks, agile working and support systems are in place – all underpinning influential post-programme opportunities.

Graduates emerge from their chosen programme with robust customer experience, consulting, managerial, commercial and innovation skills – everything they need for a far-reaching and substantial business career.

Culture plays a big part in the graduate experience too. The emphasis is always on ownership, collaboration, ethics and the strongest customer advocate mindset.

The individuals who thrive in this environment are those who appreciate diversity and come together to create a positive impact for their colleagues, customers and society. The Group has an inherent spirit of inclusion that embraces all talented, energetic and open-minded people. People who want to do work that truly matters and create a lasting impression. Maybe even leave a legacy.

This is vitally important because Lloyds Banking Group looks to its graduates to shape the direction of the organisation, its culture and the way that Britain banks in the future.

GRADUATE VACANCIES IN 2016
ACCOUNTANCY
CONSULTING
FINANCE
GENERAL MANAGEMENT
HUMAN RESOURCES
INVESTMENT BANKING
IT
MARKETING
RETAILING

NUMBER OF VACANCIES
Around 450 graduate jobs

LOCATIONS OF VACANCIES

STARTING SALARY FOR 2016
£Competitive

UNIVERSITY VISITS IN 2015-16
BIRMINGHAM, BRISTOL, CAMBRIDGE, DURHAM, EDINBURGH, EXETER, IMPERIAL COLLEGE LONDON, KING'S COLLEGE LONDON, LANCASTER, LEEDS, LEICESTER, LIVERPOOL, LONDON SCHOOL OF ECONOMICS, LOUGHBOROUGH, MANCHESTER, NEWCASTLE, NOTTINGHAM, OXFORD BROOKES, SHEFFIELD, SOUTHAMPTON, STRATHCLYDE, SWANSEA, UNIVERSITY COLLEGE LONDON, WARWICK, YORK
Please check with your university careers service for full details of local events.

MINIMUM ENTRY REQUIREMENTS
Please see website for full details.

APPLICATION DEADLINE
31st December 2015

FURTHER INFORMATION
www.Top100GraduateEmployers.com
Register now for the latest news, events information and graduate recruitment details for Britain's leading employers.

M&S

EST. 1884

GRADUATE VACANCIES IN 2016
GENERAL MANAGEMENT
HUMAN RESOURCES
IT
LOGISTICS
MARKETING
PURCHASING
RESEARCH & DEVELOPMENT
RETAILING

NUMBER OF VACANCIES
200 graduate jobs

LOCATIONS OF VACANCIES

M&S always strives for perfection. This passion to improve and meticulous attention to detail has led them to create products that millions of people love. Not to mention the on and offline experiences that push the boundaries for the entire retail industry and perfect careers for the talented people who work for them.

For ambitious graduates, there's no better place to begin their working life. Covering everything from Software Engineering and IT to Logistics, Retail Management, Marketing and beyond, each M&S graduate programme comes packed with unique opportunities for bright people to achieve the best for themselves and the business.

As an example, for those starting in Retail Management, the path to Commercial Manager level is clearly set out and, for many, achievable in as little as 9 months. But whichever part of the business a graduate joins, the day they start is the first step on a long and rewarding career with M&S – one where they'll be in an excellent position to achieve their potential as they help one of Britain's best-loved brands do the same.

It's truly an exciting time to be at M&S. With retail moving faster than ever before, anyone joining the company now will be building the business of the future. Whether it's spotting today's trends and turning them into tomorrow's reality, refining retail channels and enhancing shopping experiences or developing products and services on offer, it's all for the taking at M&S.

For graduates with high standards, a hard work ethic and an unwavering commitment to doing the right thing, a career at the forefront of retail awaits – along with a competitive salary and a host of other great benefits.

STARTING SALARY FOR 2016
£23,500-£28,000

UNIVERSITY VISITS IN 2015-16
ASTON, BIRMINGHAM, EAST ANGLIA,
IMPERIAL COLLEGE LONDON, KENT,
LEEDS, LOUGHBOROUGH, OXFORD,
READING, ROYAL HOLLOWAY, SHEFFIELD,
SURREY, YORK
*Please check with your university careers
service for full details of local events.*

MINIMUM ENTRY REQUIREMENTS
Dependent on scheme
Please see website for more details.

APPLICATION DEADLINE
Mid December 2015

FURTHER INFORMATION
www.Top100GraduateEmployers.com
*Register now for the latest news, events
information and graduate recruitment
details for Britain's leading employers.*

MARS

Start your own story.

Think 'work, rest and play'. Think M&M's®, Uncle Ben's®, Pedigree®, Whiskas® and Wrigley®, iconic billion-dollar brands. Think the world's third-largest food company with international operations in 370 locations. Know what makes Mars special? Think again.

Sure, Mars is one of the world's leading food companies, but it's more like a community than a corporate. Because it's still privately owned. And that means it's a place without any of the trappings of typical big business. It has a sense of humanity and a lack of vanity around leadership. It's somewhere that encourages open communication and collaboration, where people can get to grips with challenging work and take on high levels of responsibility early on.

The flat, open structure is a big plus for graduates when it comes to grabbing the opportunity to shape Mars' future. It makes for a truly creative and dynamic environment, whichever programme graduates join on. But it takes more than just freedom and responsibility to create the Mars leaders of the future. What graduates at Mars get is high levels of responsibility, a variety of possibilities and the opportunity to improve things for everyone else along the way.

Mars provides a fantastic support structure, financial sponsorship to pursue professional qualifications, extensive learning and development opportunities and personal mentoring from some of the brightest and best people in the industry. All Mars employees are called associates, and are treated as individuals, not numbers, driving their own performance and development.

In return, Mars gives its associates the autonomy to grab each and every opportunity that presents itself, and commit to improving how Mars treats its customers, communities and the planet. So that ultimately, they can make Mars mean more.

GRADUATE VACANCIES IN 2016

ENGINEERING
FINANCE
GENERAL MANAGEMENT
IT
LOGISTICS
MARKETING
PURCHASING
RESEARCH & DEVELOPMENT
SALES

NUMBER OF VACANCIES
50 graduate jobs

LOCATIONS OF VACANCIES

Vacancies also available in Europe.

STARTING SALARY FOR 2016
Up to £32,000
Plus a £2,000 joining bonus.

UNIVERSITY VISITS IN 2015-16
BATH, BIRMINGHAM, BRISTOL, CAMBRIDGE, EXETER, LEEDS, MANCHESTER, NOTTINGHAM, OXFORD, SHEFFIELD
Please check with your university careers service for full details of local events.

MINIMUM ENTRY REQUIREMENTS
2.1 Degree
280-300 UCAS points
Relevant degree required for some roles.

APPLICATION DEADLINE
20th November 2015

FURTHER INFORMATION
www.Top100GraduateEmployers.com
Register now for the latest news, events information and graduate recruitment details for Britain's leading employers.

When the heat was on, Órla had a cool idea.

We love it when demand for our products soars. But in the Middle East and Africa, demand for MALTESERS® was growing so fast that we simply couldn't keep up. Enter Órla, from our Management Development Programme. When we asked her to create a global demand plan she didn't break a sweat. Instead, she considered all the facts and successfully presented her case – for building a brand new production line on the other side of the world. It was a bold idea, but the potential returns were huge. Which left just one problem: how could we meet global demand for MALTESERS® in the meantime? Órla had an idea for that too – introducing a new superfast wrapping machine in the UK. It can wrap more than double the number of bags per minute than before, meaning we can keep our fans happy the world over. It just goes to show. Give people freedom and responsibility, and they'll go further than you ever imagined. **mars.co.uk/graduates**

GRADUATE VACANCIES IN 2016
GENERAL MANAGEMENT
RETAILING

NUMBER OF VACANCIES
250-350 graduate jobs

LOCATIONS OF VACANCIES

Training and developing people has been at the heart of McDonald's business throughout the 40 years in the UK. Each year, the company invests £43 million in developing its people and providing opportunities to the 100,000 employees to progress, whilst achieving nationally recognised qualifications.

McDonald's arrived in the UK in 1974 and currently operates 1,300 restaurants, employing 100,000 people. The company has a proven track record of career progression; with the entire UK Operations executive team starting their careers on the graduate Trainee Manager programme. Prospective managers can create a long-term career with one of the world's most recognised and successful brands.

A graduate job at McDonald's is focused on restaurant management – it involves overseeing the performance and development of an average 90 employees, and identifying ways in which to improve customer service, build sales and profitability. Following the training period, which can last up to six months, Trainee Managers are promoted to Assistant Managers and become part of the core restaurant management team. Successful Trainee Managers can, in future, progress to managing all aspects of a £multi-million business – opportunities can then arise to progress to area management roles or secondments in support departments. Trainee Managers need to be logical thinkers, have a great attitude and be committed to delivering a great customer experience.

Working for a progressive company has its perks – including a host of benefits such as a quarterly bonus scheme, six weeks holiday, meal allowance, private healthcare and access to discounts at over 1,600 retailers.

STARTING SALARY FOR 2016
£21,000-£24,000

UNIVERSITY VISITS IN 2015-16
NOTTINGHAM TRENT
Please check with your university careers service for full details of local events.

APPLICATION DEADLINE
Year-round recruitment

FURTHER INFORMATION
www.Top100GraduateEmployers.com
Register now for the latest news, events information and graduate recruitment details for Britain's leading employers.

The McDonald's Trainee Manager Programme is the first step to managing a £multi-million restaurant employing 80 staff.

After six months training and learning all the basics, our Trainee Managers are promoted to Assistant Managers - but if you've got the drive and ambition, there's no limit to how far you can go.

To find out more about working and learning with us visit

mcdonalds.co.uk/people

Sammy Jo
Stockport

TRAINEE
MANAGER

McKinsey&Company

McKinsey & Company helps world-leading clients in the public, private and third sectors to meet their biggest strategic, operational and organisational challenges. Their goal is to provide distinctive and long-lasting performance improvements – in short, it is about having an impact. Making a difference.

As a consultant in this truly global firm, graduates will have the opportunity to work with colleagues and clients from all around the world. They will come into contact with CEOs, government leaders and the foremost charitable organisations, and work together with them on their most exciting and challenging issues.

Working as part of a small team, and dedicated to one project at a time, graduates will be fully involved from the very start of their first project. No two weeks will be the same: from gathering and analysing data, to interviewing stakeholders or presenting findings to clients, the range of industries and business issues to which successful applicants have exposure will mean that they are constantly acquiring new skills and experience. Bright, motivated newcomers can expect their ideas and opinions to be encouraged and valued, right from day one.

Graduates will also enjoy world-class personal and professional development. Formal training programmes, coupled with a culture of mentoring and coaching, will provide the best possible support.

Working in consulting is challenging, but McKinsey encourages a healthy work-life balance. Successful applicants will find like-minded individuals, and a thriving range of groups, initiatives and events that bring people together.

McKinsey & Company is welcoming applications for both full time and summer internship applications.

GRADUATE VACANCIES IN 2016

CONSULTING

NUMBER OF VACANCIES
No fixed quota

LOCATIONS OF VACANCIES

STARTING SALARY FOR 2016
£Competitive

UNIVERSITY VISITS IN 2015-16
BELFAST, BRISTOL, CAMBRIDGE,
EDINBURGH, IMPERIAL COLLEGE LONDON,
LONDON SCHOOL OF ECONOMICS,
OXFORD, TRINITY COLLEGE DUBLIN,
UNIVERSITY COLLEGE DUBLIN, WARWICK
*Please check with your university careers
service for full details of local events.*

MINIMUM ENTRY REQUIREMENTS
2.1 Degree

APPLICATION DEADLINE
29th October 2015

FURTHER INFORMATION
www.Top100GraduateEmployers.com
*Register now for the latest news, events
information and graduate recruitment
details for Britain's leading employers.*

METROPOLITAN POLICE

TOTAL POLICING

www.metpolicecareers.co.uk

The Metropolitan Police Service (MPS) is respected throughout the world as a leading authority on policing. It is their job to make London a safe place for the millions of people who live there – plus the millions more who work in and visit the capital each year.

Reducing crime, and the fear of crime, in a vibrant multicultural city requires an equally diverse workforce. The MPS must continue to recruit the brightest and the best people from every background. They need the kind of individuals who can forge close relationships, build trust and understand the complex issues that affect different communities. With the full spectrum of skills, knowledge and experience they can make London safer for everybody.

With thousands of people, the MPS is one of the capital's largest employers. Many of these individuals work as frontline police officers with the people of London. Dealing with the day-to-day challenges of policing one of the world's largest cities is one of the most important, rewarding and absorbing roles around. In order for them to fulfil their roles, however, they rely on the support of a host of people working behind the scenes.

From Human Resources, IT to Accountancy, Forensics and Marketing and Communications, the MPS encompasses every department found in a large corporate organisation (and a few that are not). So there is a wide range of roles for graduates to choose from – all of which come with the in-depth training and support necessary to progress their careers.

Working for the Metropolitan Police Service can open doors to many different areas, such as voluntary work as a special constable (volunteer police officer).

But whatever role they play, graduates can be sure of joining an organisation with unique challenges.

GRADUATE VACANCIES IN 2016

POLICING

NUMBER OF VACANCIES
To be confirmed

LOCATIONS OF VACANCIES

STARTING SALARY FOR 2016
Dependent on scheme
New Police Constables will be paid circa £28,000.

UNIVERSITY VISITS IN 2015-16
LONDON
Please check with your university careers service for full details of local events.

APPLICATION DEADLINE
Please see website for full details.

FURTHER INFORMATION
www.Top100GraduateEmployers.com
Register now for the latest news, events information and graduate recruitment details for Britain's leading employers.

SOME CAREERS IMPROVE COMPANIES. YOU'LL TRANSFORM COMMUNITIES.

BE THERE FOR LONDON

CAREERS IN THE METROPOLITAN POLICE SERVICE

You've spent the last few years learning, growing, honing your skills and laying the groundwork for a career that's worthy of your degree. To find out more about the range of career paths and graduate opportunities, visit **www.metpolicecareers.co.uk**

METROPOLITAN POLICE **TOTAL POLICING**

MI5 helps safeguard the UK against threats to national security including terrorism and espionage. It investigates suspect individuals and organisations to gather intelligence relating to security threats. MI5 also advises the critical national infrastructure on protective security measures, to help them reduce their vulnerability.

Graduates from a range of backgrounds join MI5 for stimulating and rewarding careers. Some join to use languages such as Russian or Mandarin, or many graduates join the Intelligence Officer Development Programme, which is a structured 3-5 year programme designed to teach new joiners about MI5 investigations and give them the skills to run them. After completing one post of two years or two posts of one year, and subject to successful completion of performance reviews and assessments, those on the programme will then be eligible to undertake Foundation Investigative Training (FIT). After successfully completing FIT, they will then take up an investigative posting, after which they will be a fully trained Intelligence Officer and can then choose to remain in investigative work, or move into an operational, assessment or policy role.

MI5 deals with vast amounts of data and interpreting that data is vital to its intelligence work. The Intelligence and Data Analyst Development Programme is a structured two-year programme which prepares graduates to be part of this specialist careers stream within MI5. It will take new joiners from the basics through to the most advanced data analytical techniques. As they progress they will have the opportunity to work in different teams across the range of MI5's investigations using their analytical expertise. Some analysts progress into management roles, taking responsibility for delivering analysis across wide areas of the business whilst others stay focused on data analysis, becoming subject experts.

GRADUATE VACANCIES IN 2016
GENERAL MANAGEMENT
IT

NUMBER OF VACANCIES
80+ graduate jobs

LOCATIONS OF VACANCIES

STARTING SALARY FOR 2016
£28,500-£30,000

UNIVERSITY VISITS IN 2015-16
Please check with your university careers service for full details of local events.

MINIMUM ENTRY REQUIREMENTS
Relevant degree required for some roles.

APPLICATION DEADLINE
Varies by function

FURTHER INFORMATION
www.Top100GraduateEmployers.com
Register now for the latest news, events information and graduate recruitment details for Britain's leading employers.

"I NEVER THOUGHT MY SKILLS COULD HELP PROTECT A NATION"

The future is in your hands.

With a range of skills, backgrounds and cultures, our people bring fresh perspectives to our work. Join MI5 and you'll discover an environment that nurtures and develops your talents and offers the flexibility to fit work around your personal and family commitments wherever possible. Most importantly, you'll be working with people who share your commitment to protecting the UK from serious threats. Find out how you'll fit in at www.mi5.gov.uk/careers

To apply to MI5 you must be a born or naturalised British citizen, over 18 years old and normally have lived in the UK for nine of the last ten years. You should not discuss your application, other than with your partner or a close family member, providing that they are British. They should also be made aware of the importance of discretion.

 **Microsoft**

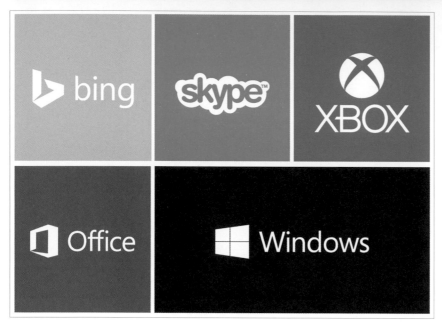

When smart, creative, passionate people get together, the result can be astounding and the opportunities limitless. Microsoft are empowering their customers to do more and achieve more. They are obsessing about individuals and organisations across the globe by creating products and services for them which will enable them to thrive in todays digital world.

The opportunity to stretch existing skills and build new ones is there for the taking. Curiosity, questions and ideas are encouraged, valued and respected. Graduates will benefit from being part of an organisation that's re-inventing and enabling productivity through groundbreaking products and services.

Graduate opportunities provide individuals with a real job role alongside the perfect training platform to launch their career. With opportunities in Sales, IT, Business Consulting or Project Management, graduates will work on major projects from day one. As well as learning from senior colleagues and mentors from across the business, they'll have the chance to meet peers from around the world on a number of international networking and training events.

Highlights of the 18-month training include: a four day induction which provides a spring-board into the business; mentoring and a self-learning curriculum, plus international formal training camps aimed at developing cross-profession skills and specialist expertise.

Microsoft also run an award-winning one year internship scheme. With a comprehensive induction followed by in-depth on-the-job learning and skills training, it's an insightful introduction to Microsoft. Intern roles are hugely varied and stretch across a number of exciting business areas including Marketing, Bing, Xbox, Studios and more.

GRADUATE VACANCIES IN 2016
CONSULTING
IT
SALES

NUMBER OF VACANCIES
36 graduate jobs

LOCATIONS OF VACANCIES

STARTING SALARY FOR 2016
£34,700
Plus a sign-on bonus.

UNIVERSITY VISITS IN 2015-16
ASTON, BATH, BIRMINGHAM, CARDIFF, EXETER, IMPERIAL COLLEGE LONDON, LOUGHBOROUGH, MANCHESTER, NOTTINGHAM TRENT, READING, SURREY, UNIVERSITY COLLEGE LONDON, WARWICK
Please check with your university careers service for full details of local events.

MINIMUM ENTRY REQUIREMENTS
2.1 Degree

APPLICATION DEADLINE
Mid November
Early application advised.

FURTHER INFORMATION
www.Top100GraduateEmployers.com
Register now for the latest news, events information and graduate recruitment details for Britain's leading employers.

MAKE IT. BREAK IT. MAKE IT BETTER.

When smart, creative, passionate people get together, the result can be astounding and the opportunities limitless. Microsoft are looking ahead and empowering their customers to do more and achieve more. They are obsessing about building products to solve hard challenges. They are reinventing productivity. As a graduate you will help build the future in a cloud-first, mobile-first world.

www.microsoft.co.uk/students

GRADUATE VACANCIES IN 2016

ENGINEERING
FINANCE
HUMAN RESOURCES
LOGISTICS
MARKETING
RESEARCH & DEVELOPMENT
SALES

NUMBER OF VACANCIES
Around 40 graduate jobs

LOCATIONS OF VACANCIES

Vacancies also available in Europe.

STARTING SALARY FOR 2016
£27,000-£29,000
Plus a joining bonus and an annual performance bonus.

UNIVERSITY VISITS IN 2015-16
BATH, BIRMINGHAM, CARDIFF,
DURHAM, LANCASTER, LEEDS,
LOUGHBOROUGH, MANCHESTER,
NEWCASTLE, NOTTINGHAM, SHEFFIELD
Please check with your university careers service for full details of local events.

MINIMUM ENTRY REQUIREMENTS
2.1 Degree

APPLICATION DEADLINE
15th November 2015

FURTHER INFORMATION
www.Top100GraduateEmployers.com
Register now for the latest news, events information and graduate recruitment details for Britain's leading employers.

Mondelēz International is the world's pre-eminent maker of snacks. Not only are they the name behind much-loved brands like Cadbury, Milka, Belvita and Trident, but they're ranked 1st globally in Chocolate, Biscuits and Candy, and 2nd in Gum. What's more, they market their products in 165 countries, enjoy annual net revenues of $34 billion and employ 100,000 people worldwide.

What makes working at Mondelēz International special? The iconic brands and global nature of the business. The fast-paced, constantly changing environment. The on-the-job training and mentoring by senior leaders. The chance every day, to create delicious moments of joy for people all around the world.

Mondelēz International offers exciting graduate opportunities in Sales & Marketing, Engineering, Supply Chain, Finance, HR and Research and Development. Each opportunity includes real roles on live projects, continuous challenge, collaboration with industry experts and exposure to every corner of the business.

They also give graduates the chance to work with a variety of people both inside and outside the company, from a range of business areas and markets. Whether graduates are gaining new skills or networking with senior leaders, they'll put themselves in the perfect position to lead Mondelēz International forward.

Who are Mondelēz International looking for? They want people who are hungry to grow and succeed, and who never shy away from a challenge. They're after team players who could become future leaders, and for self-starters who can adapt to the changing needs of a global business. Solid academic results are a must, as are bold ideas and the motivation to put those ideas into action.

In return, Mondelēz International gives graduates a highly competitive salary, a generous holiday entitlement, an impressive array of benefits – and endless opportunities to progress.

Mondelēz
International
the power of big. and small.

big enough to make the world's most delicious brands.
small enough to look after the people behind them.

We're Mondelēz International, the world's leading maker of Chocolate, Biscuits, Candy and Gum. Even if you haven't heard of us, you've almost certainly heard of our brands. Brands like Cadbury, Oreo, Trident and Toblerone. Names known and loved all around the world. Join one of our commercial, engineering or science-based graduate programmes, and you'll enjoy live projects, exposure to industry experts and continuous development opportunities. Everything you need to drive our brands forward – and become a future leader of the business.

Interested? To learn more about who we are and the opportunities available for graduates, interns, apprentices and school-leavers, visit **careers.mondelezinternational.com/Europe**

You can also follow us on: 🅵 MondelezInternational 🐦 @MDLZ

Morgan Stanley

morganstanley.com/campus

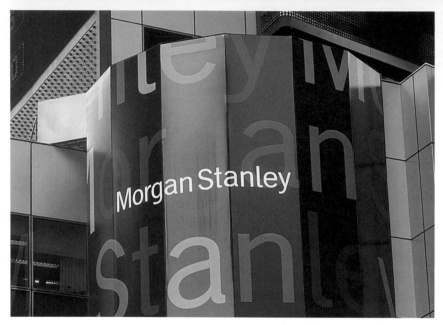

Morgan Stanley has a distinguished history of serving clients for over 75 years. Since its founding in 1935, the firm has been known for the important clients it serves, its innovative approach to solving complex problems, and its agility in embracing change.

Morgan Stanley is a firm that inspires people to be their best – and always finds new opportunities to offer them. Its mission is to build a community of talent that can deliver the finest financial thinking and products in the world.

There is no typical person at Morgan Stanley. People come from a wide variety of backgrounds and interests – all are high achievers who share integrity, intellectual curiosity and the desire to work in a collegial environment. Individuality is prized and people are encouraged to be themselves.

Morgan Stanley offers a variety of Graduate Programmes and internship opportunities for students who demonstrate the entrepreneurial drive, team working and communication skills to take the business forward. All Graduate Programmes are designed to provide graduates with the knowledge and toolkit they require to quickly become effective and successful professionals in their chosen area. Training is not limited to the first weeks or months on the job but continues throughout the graduate's career.

The summer and industrial placement programmes are considered first class and designed to attract, develop and continually assess those students who are most likely to succeed in the long-term. Through classroom-based and on-the-job training, seminars, regular mentoring, social events and the experience of working with top people in the industry throughout a period of either 10 or 48 weeks, students gain a unique insight into the industry and Morgan Stanley's culture – all necessary foundations for a truly exceptional and rewarding career.

GRADUATE VACANCIES IN 2016
FINANCE
HUMAN RESOURCES
INVESTMENT BANKING
IT

NUMBER OF VACANCIES
No fixed quota

LOCATIONS OF VACANCIES

Vacancies also available in Europe.

STARTING SALARY FOR 2016
£Competitive
Plus benefits and a discretionary bonus.

UNIVERSITY VISITS IN 2015-16
BATH, BELFAST, BRISTOL, CAMBRIDGE, CITY, DURHAM, EDINBURGH, EXETER, GLASGOW, HERIOT-WATT, IMPERIAL COLLEGE LONDON, KING'S COLLEGE LONDON, LONDON SCHOOL OF ECONOMICS, LOUGHBOROUGH, MANCHESTER, NOTTINGHAM, OXFORD, ST ANDREWS, STIRLING, STRATHCLYDE, TRINITY COLLEGE DUBLIN, ULSTER, UNIVERSITY COLLEGE DUBLIN, UNIVERSITY COLLEGE LONDON, WARWICK, YORK
Please check with your university careers service for full details of local events.

MINIMUM ENTRY REQUIREMENTS
2.1 Degree

APPLICATION DEADLINE
Varies by function
Early application advised.

FURTHER INFORMATION
www.Top100GraduateEmployers.com
Register now for the latest news, events information and graduate recruitment details for Britain's leading employers.

Morgan Stanley

Who starts the start ups?

A start up needs a great idea to get off the ground, sure. But it also needs people who believe in that idea and foster its growth — as well as the research that attracts that support. We want to crunch the data and make the calls that illustrate what the future will bring. Let's decide together what tomorrow looks like. Join us.

What Will You Create?

morganstanley.com/campus

Neel
Research Analyst

facebook.com/mottmacdonaldgroup **f**   graduate.recruitment@mottmac.com ✉
linkedin.com/company/mott-macdonald **in**   twitter.com/MottMacGraduate **y**
youtube.com/mottmacdonaldgroup ▶   plus.google.com/+mottmacdonald **g+**

Mott MacDonald is a global management, engineering and development consultancy adding value for public and private clients on agenda-setting, next-generation projects worldwide. They use their ingenuity to save customers money and time, reduce risks, increase efficiency, maximise sustainable outcomes and advance best practice.

Employees are united by the vision to be the consultant of choice, recognised for the quality of their people. They deliver technical expertise across 12 core sectors: buildings; communications; education; environment; health; industry; international development; oil and gas; power; transport; urban development and water.

Mott MacDonald's ambition is that their people are able to enjoy a long and rewarding career. To support this they encourage and enable people to achieve their full potential. Their award-winning graduate programme will support graduates in gaining experience across all core business areas through providing opportunities to work on some the most exciting projects across the world. Graduates are supported with a tailored programme allowing progression within one of the leading engineering consultancies and so support their development.

Professional excellence is important at Mott MacDonald and graduates' ambitions and needs are also valued. Working within a multidisciplinary team and involved in an array of leading industry projects, they will gain vital on-the-job experience and skills that can be utilised throughout their careers.

Mott MacDonald's professional development schemes are accredited and enable graduates to gain chartered status with their chosen institution. At the start of their careers they will enrol onto the Mott MacDonald Academy, a four-year development programme for entry-level professionals. The programme introduces key business and commercial competencies that will drive their careers.

GRADUATE VACANCIES IN 2016
CONSULTING
ENGINEERING
PROPERTY

NUMBER OF VACANCIES
300 graduate jobs

LOCATIONS OF VACANCIES

STARTING SALARY FOR 2016
£24,000-£28,000

UNIVERSITY VISITS IN 2015-16
BATH, BIRMINGHAM, BRISTOL, CAMBRIDGE, CARDIFF, EDINBURGH, GLASGOW, HERIOT-WATT, IMPERIAL COLLEGE LONDON, LEEDS, LIVERPOOL, LOUGHBOROUGH, MANCHESTER, NEWCASTLE, NORTHUMBRIA, NOTTINGHAM, READING, SHEFFIELD, SOUTHAMPTON, STRATHCLYDE, SURREY, UNIVERSITY COLLEGE LONDON, WARWICK
Please check with your university careers service for full details of local events.

MINIMUM ENTRY REQUIREMENTS
2.1 Degree

APPLICATION DEADLINE
15th November 2015

FURTHER INFORMATION
www.Top100GraduateEmployers.com
Register now for the latest news, events information and graduate recruitment details for Britain's leading employers.

WE WANT TO HIRE YOU

OK, that's not quite accurate. Let's rephrase it. If you're hard working, talented, brave, smart, innovative, humble, confident, nice and most important, you LOVE working in engineering, then we want to hire you.

Check out our amazing projects and find your next challenge at mottmac.com/careers/graduate

Make the World you Love

www.nestlecareers.co.uk/academy

facebook.com/Nestle.Academy.Careers **f**

linkedin.com/company/nestle-s-a- **in**   twitter.com/nestleacademy **y**

As the world's leading nutrition, health and wellness company, people will definitely have come across Nestlé before. Nescafé®, Kit Kat® and Shredded Wheat are just some of their household names. Not to mention Buxton® mineral water, Felix®, Rowntree's Fruit Pastilles® and After Eight®.

But behind all the world-famous brands, there are lots of other things that Nestlé does that people might not be so familiar with.

For example, Nestlé's research is pushing back the boundaries of health and nutrition. They also have offices, factories and plants not just across the UK but throughout Europe and around the world. In fact, across 86 countries they employ over 330,000 people.

Joining Nestlé gives graduates the opportunity not only to work on their successful brands, but also to explore this hugely diverse and complex organisation by moving through different roles, different teams, different business areas and, potentially, different countries as well.

Despite being the world's leading nutrition, health and wellness company, a graduate career with Nestlé will have a local emphasis as well as a potential global reach.

And thanks to the world-class learning and development offered by the Nestlé Academy, successful applicants will, at the same time, be able to build on their existing strengths to become a highly skilled and experienced expert in their field.

The Academy provides a variety of career development routes through the organisation including on the job training, providing graduates the opportunities for continuous improvement at every stage of their career.

To find out more about what it takes to join Nestlé, visit their website.

GRADUATE VACANCIES IN 2016

ENGINEERING
FINANCE
HUMAN RESOURCES
MARKETING
SALES

NUMBER OF VACANCIES
30-35 graduate jobs

LOCATIONS OF VACANCIES

STARTING SALARY FOR 2016
£27,000
Plus a £2,000 joining bonus.

UNIVERSITY VISITS IN 2015-16
ASTON, BIRMINGHAM, DURHAM,
EDINBURGH, GLASGOW, KING'S COLLEGE
LONDON, LANCASTER, LONDON SCHOOL
OF ECONOMICS, LOUGHBOROUGH,
NEWCASTLE, NORTHUMBRIA, STRATHCLYDE,
UNIVERSITY COLLEGE LONDON, YORK
*Please check with your university careers
service for full details of local events.*

MINIMUM ENTRY REQUIREMENTS
2.1 Degree

APPLICATION DEADLINE
Varies by function

FURTHER INFORMATION
www.Top100GraduateEmployers.com
*Register now for the latest news, events
information and graduate recruitment
details for Britain's leading employers.*

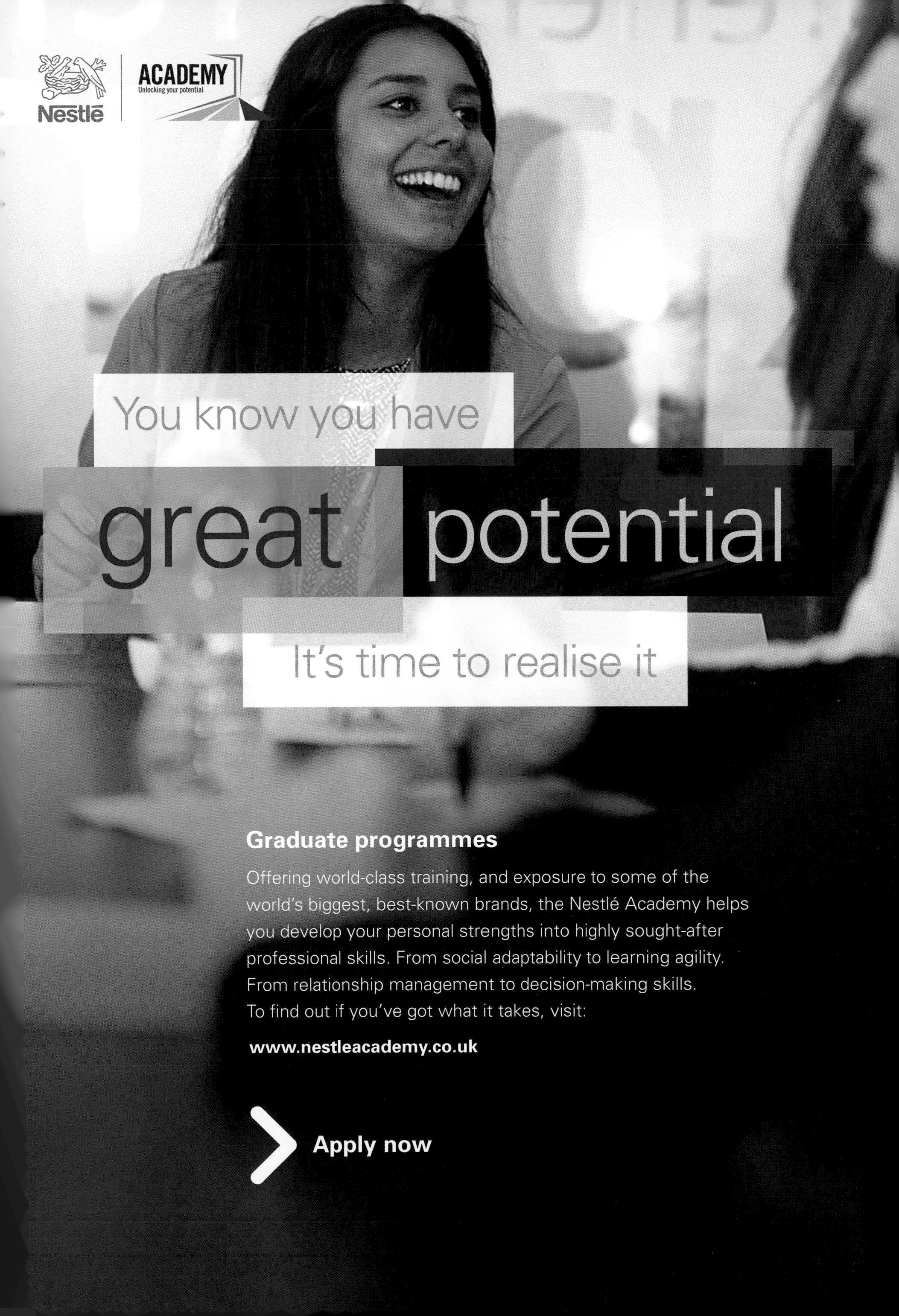

You know you have

great potential

It's time to realise it

Graduate programmes

Offering world-class training, and exposure to some of the
world's biggest, best-known brands, the Nestlé Academy helps
you develop your personal strengths into highly sought-after
professional skills. From social adaptability to learning agility.
From relationship management to decision-making skills.
To find out if you've got what it takes, visit:

www.nestleacademy.co.uk

 **Apply now**

GRADUATE VACANCIES IN 2016

ENGINEERING

FINANCE

GENERAL MANAGEMENT

HUMAN RESOURCES

IT

LOGISTICS

PROPERTY

NUMBER OF VACANCIES
Around 200 graduate jobs

LOCATIONS OF VACANCIES

STARTING SALARY FOR 2016
£26,500
Plus a £2,000 welcome bonus.

UNIVERSITY VISITS IN 2015-16
ASTON, BATH, BIRMINGHAM, BRISTOL,
CARDIFF, EXETER, IMPERIAL COLLEGE
LONDON, KING'S COLLEGE LONDON, KENT,
LANCASTER, LEEDS, LEICESTER, LIVERPOOL,
LOUGHBOROUGH, MANCHESTER,
NOTTINGHAM, NOTTINGHAM TRENT,
OXFORD, PLYMOUTH, READING, SHEFFIELD,
SOUTHAMPTON, STRATHCLYDE, UNIVERSITY
COLLEGE LONDON, WARWICK, YORK
*Please check with your university careers
service for full details of local events.*

MINIMUM ENTRY REQUIREMENTS
2.2 Degree

APPLICATION DEADLINE
December 2015

FURTHER INFORMATION
www.Top100GraduateEmployers.com
*Register now for the latest news, events
information and graduate recruitment
details for Britain's leading employers.*

Network Rail run, maintain and develop Britain's rail tracks, signalling, bridges, tunnels, level crossings and many key stations. With £38 billion earmarked to invest in an incredibly diverse range of landmark projects and initiatives over the next five years, there's never been a better time to join as a graduate.

Network Rail look for dedicated, enthusiastic individuals with a passion for shaping a positive future and seeking ways to make things better rather than accepting how they are. As one of their future leaders, there will be the opportunity to gain people management experience early on.

There are two overarching routes for graduates; Engineering and Business Management programmes. Within engineering, there are three specific schemes: Civil Engineering, Electrical & Electronic Engineering, and Mechanical Engineering. In Business Management, they have a number of different schemes: Finance, General Management, Property, Strategic Planning, Project Management, Supply Chain, HR and Business Technology.

From route modernisation through to the redevelopment of London Bridge station, Network Rail are tackling some ambitious, hugely complex engineering challenges. They own 7,400 commercial properties, giving them one of the largest property portfolios in the UK which includes 600,000sq ft of retail space (sales at stations have even been outperforming the high street). They are also behind some of the biggest, most innovative projects in the country – from the world's largest solar bridge at Blackfriars through to electrification and HS2.

When graduates join, they're put on a special path which begins at Network Rail's leadership centre, Westwood. The development offered is second to none and Network Rail will support graduates to achieve professional qualifications where appropriate.

www.newtoneurope.com/careers

facebook.com/NewtonEurope **f**   recruitment@newtoneurope.com ✉

linkedin.com/company/newton-europe-limited/careers **in**   twitter.com/NewtonCareers 🐦

Newton implements transformational, award-winning change across a wide range of sectors and projects, from construction of the nation's warships, to increasing beer production, improving transport operations, and making significant savings across NHS trusts while transforming patient care.

Newton brings together the world's most talented individuals, including more engineers and scientists than any other operational consultancy. With a unique approach, they work hands-on to generate sustainable results and real financial and operational improvement for some of the world's most successful, innovative organisations. They're great communicators from diverse backgrounds spanning engineering, science, mathematics, business, economics, languages, law, social sciences and beyond. Their talents include strong numeracy and analytical skills, problem solving and the ability to engage with people at all levels.

Unlike management consultants and improvement specialists who simply assess companies and deliver reports, the Newton team immerse themselves in businesses and actively implement change through working alongside their clients' people to achieve sustainable results. They are invested and passionately involved each step of the way, not only because the work is meaningful and rewarding, but also because Newton confidently guarantees fees only on the reality of achieving results.

Newton provides opportunities to graduates who want to achieve real, sustainable, positive change across diverse sectors including defence, healthcare, local government, business services, transport, and manufacturing, and potential applicants should head to their careers site to find out more and apply.

GRADUATE VACANCIES IN 2016
CONSULTING

NUMBER OF VACANCIES
60 graduate jobs

LOCATIONS OF VACANCIES

Vacancies also available in Europe and the USA.

STARTING SALARY FOR 2016
£39,000
Plus a sign-on bonus of £3,000.

UNIVERSITY VISITS IN 2015-16
BATH, BIRMINGHAM, BRISTOL, CAMBRIDGE, DURHAM, EXETER, IMPERIAL COLLEGE LONDON, LEEDS, LONDON SCHOOL OF ECONOMICS, NOTTINGHAM, OXFORD, STRATHCLYDE, UNIVERSITY COLLEGE LONDON, WARWICK, YORK
Please check with your university careers service for full details of local events.

MINIMUM ENTRY REQUIREMENTS
2.2 Degree

APPLICATION DEADLINE
Year-round recruitment
Early application advised.

FURTHER INFORMATION
www.Top100GraduateEmployers.com
Register now for the latest news, events information and graduate recruitment details for Britain's leading employers.

LEADING
the way

We're searching for outstanding operational improvement specialists to join our team.

Newton works hands-on with some of the best organisations in the world to implement transformational, award-winning change.

Our operational improvement specialists make a difference to the lives of a wide range of people, from top executives to factory workers, engineers, hospital patients, and children in social care.

Our people drive our business. They're great communicators from diverse backgrounds spanning engineering, science, mathematics, business, economics, languages, law, social sciences and beyond. Their talents include strong numeracy and analytical skills, problem solving and the ability to engage with people at all levels.

Newton's track record of delivering significant results, and our entrepreneurial, inspiring work culture means headcount and turnover continues to grow at a rate of 25% annually.

If you like the sound of achieving real, sustainable, positive change across diverse sectors including defence, healthcare, local government, business services, transport, and manufacturing, please head to our careers site to find out more and apply.

T: +44 (0) 1865 601 300
E: recruitment@newtoneurope.com
W: www.newtoneurope.com/careers

Newton
The science of performance

NATIONAL GRADUATE
DEVELOPMENT PROGRAMME

ngdp

FOR LOCAL GOVERNMENT

www.ngdp.org.uk

twitter.com/ngdp_LGA 🐦 ngdp@local.gov.uk ✉

GRADUATE VACANCIES IN 2016
GENERAL MANAGEMENT

NUMBER OF VACANCIES
120 graduate jobs

LOCATIONS OF VACANCIES

STARTING SALARY FOR 2016
£23,698+

UNIVERSITY VISITS IN 2015-16
ASTON, BIRMINGHAM, BRISTOL,
CAMBRIDGE, CARDIFF, CITY, DURHAM,
EAST ANGLIA, KING'S COLLEGE LONDON,
LANCASTER, LEEDS, LEICESTER, LIVERPOOL,
LONDON SCHOOL OF ECONOMICS,
LOUGHBOROUGH, MANCHESTER,
NEWCASTLE, NORTHUMBRIA, NOTTINGHAM,
NOTTINGHAM TRENT, OXFORD, QUEEN
MARY LONDON, SHEFFIELD, UNIVERSITY
COLLEGE LONDON, WARWICK, YORK
*Please check with your university careers
service for full details of local events.*

MINIMUM ENTRY REQUIREMENTS
2.1 Degree

APPLICATION DEADLINE
11th January 2016

FURTHER INFORMATION
www.Top100GraduateEmployers.com
*Register now for the latest news, events
information and graduate recruitment
details for Britain's leading employers.*

The ngdp is a two-year graduate development programme
which gives committed graduates the opportunity and training
to make a positive difference in local communities. Run by the
Local Government Association, the ngdp is looking to equip the
sector's next generation of high-calibre managers.

Local government is the largest and most diverse employer in the UK, with
around 1.2 million staff based in nearly 400 local authorities and in excess of
500 different occupational areas. Almost 900 graduates have completed the
ngdp since 2002 and gained access to rewarding careers in and beyond the
sector, with many currently holding influential managerial and policy roles.

In the midst of huge changes taking place within the public sector,
ngdp graduates are positioned to make a real contribution to shaping and
implementing new ideas and initiatives from day one. Graduate trainees are
employed by a participating council (or group of councils) for a minimum of
two years, during which time they rotate between a series of placements in key
areas of the council. Trainees can experience a range of roles in strategy, frontline service and support to expand their perspective of local government's many
different capacities and gain a flexible, transferable skill set.

ngdp graduates also benefit from being part of a national cohort of like-minded
peers. Together they will participate in a national induction event, join an
established knowledge-sharing network and gain a post-graduate qualification
in Leadership and Management. The learning and development programme
gives graduates the chance to learn from established professionals and each other.

The ngdp has enabled graduates to build varied and rewarding careers
for almost twenty years. Join now to start working in an exciting period of
opportunity and change for the benefit of local communities.

www.nhsgraduates.co.uk

facebook.com/NHSGraduateScheme

youtube.com/NHSGraduates twitter.com/NHSGradScheme

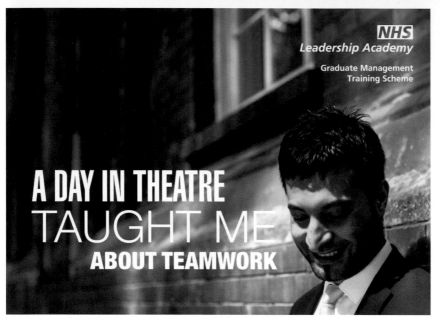

NHS
Leadership Academy

Graduate Management
Training Scheme

A DAY IN THEATRE
TAUGHT ME
ABOUT TEAMWORK

GRADUATE VACANCIES IN 2016

FINANCE

GENERAL MANAGEMENT

HUMAN RESOURCES

IT

NUMBER OF VACANCIES
100+ graduate jobs

LOCATIONS OF VACANCIES

As Europe's largest employer with an annual budget of over £100 billion, there is no other organisation on Earth quite like the NHS. And with the ability to have a positive impact on over 53 million people, the NHS Graduate Management Training Scheme really is nothing less than a life defining experience.

It's unquestionably hard work, but this multi-award-winning, fast-track development scheme, enables graduates to become the healthcare leaders of the future.

Graduates specialise in one of four areas: Finance, Health Informatics, Human Resources and General Management. As they grow personally and professionally they'll gain specialist skills while receiving full support from a dedicated mentor at Executive level.

Graduate induction includes 20 days in which they can set the agenda, experiencing NHS life on the frontline, with the option of arranging a 'flexi-placement' and the chance to acquire new perspectives.

Success is granted only to those who are prepared to give their heart and souls to their profession. The responsibility of the NHS demands that their future leaders have the tenacity, the focus, and the determination to deliver nothing but the best.

Because the scheme offers a fast-track route to a senior-level role, graduates will soon find themselves facing complex problems head on and tackling high-profile situations. Working for the NHS means standing up to high levels of public scrutiny and having decisions closely inspected. Graduates who want to succeed will need to be resilient and able to respond to constant change.

This is a career where the hard work and unfaltering commitment of graduates not only affects the lives of others, but it will ultimately define their own.

STARTING SALARY FOR 2016
£22,269
Plus a location allowance where appropriate.

UNIVERSITY VISITS IN 2015-16
Please check with your university careers service for full details of local events.

MINIMUM ENTRY REQUIREMENTS
2.2 Degree

APPLICATION DEADLINE
December 2015

FURTHER INFORMATION
www.Top100GraduateEmployers.com
Register now for the latest news, events information and graduate recruitment details for Britain's leading employers.

MY WORK IS
HELPING PREVENT
FEMALE GENITAL MUTILATION.
HOW MANY GRADUATE MANAGEMENT SCHEMES OFFER THAT?

The NHS Graduate Management Training Scheme is nothing less than a life defining experience. Whether you join our HR, Finance, Health Informatics or General Management streams, you'll receive everything you need to make a positive impact on the lives of 53 million people across England.

These aren't clinical opportunities, but this is about developing exceptional healthcare leaders. High-calibre management professionals who will lead the NHS through a profound transformation and shape our services around ever-evolving patient needs. Inspirational people who will push up standards, deliver deeper value for money and continue the drive towards a healthier nation.

nhsgraduates.co.uk

Life Defining

NHS
Leadership Academy

Graduate Management Training Scheme

ᶺNORTON ROSE FULBRIGHT

Progress with purpose

Norton Rose Fulbright is a global legal practice. It provides the world's pre-eminent corporations and financial institutions with a full business law service. The practice has more than 3,800 lawyers based in over 50 cities across Europe, the United States, Canada, Latin America, Asia, Australia, Africa, the Middle East and Central Asia.

Recognised for its industry focus, the practice is strong across all the key sectors: financial institutions; energy; infrastructure, mining and commodities; transport; technology and innovation; and life sciences and healthcare.

Norton Rose Fulbright recruits up to 50 trainee solicitors each year. Its training contract is based on a four-seat pattern, allowing trainees to get the widest possible exposure to different practice areas and offices around the world. Trainees have the opportunity to spend one of their seats on an international or client secondment, in addition to seats in Corporate, Banking and Litigation, enabling them to make the best and most informed choice of qualification area.

Each year, Norton Rose Fulbright runs three vacation schemes for law and non-law applicants which are designed to provide an invaluable insight into life and work inside a global legal practice. Successful applicants will have the opportunity to participate in actual work with clients – which could involve anything from legal research to attending meetings or court. Students will also attend training sessions, breakfast briefings about Norton Rose Fulbright's practice areas and social events with current trainees, lawyers, and partners.

Norton Rose Fulbright also runs two open days for penultimate-year undergraduates, finalists and graduates, as well as a First step programme for first-year undergraduates.

GRADUATE VACANCIES IN 2016
LAW

NUMBER OF VACANCIES
Up to 50 graduate jobs
For training contracts starting in 2018.

LOCATIONS OF VACANCIES

Vacancies also available in Europe, Asia, the USA and elsewhere in the world.

STARTING SALARY FOR 2016
£41,000

UNIVERSITY VISITS IN 2015-16
BIRMINGHAM, BRISTOL, CAMBRIDGE, DURHAM, EDINBURGH, ESSEX, EXETER, IMPERIAL COLLEGE LONDON, KING'S COLLEGE LONDON, LEEDS, LEICESTER, LONDON SCHOOL OF ECONOMICS, MANCHESTER, NOTTINGHAM, OXFORD, QUEEN MARY LONDON, SHEFFIELD, SOUTHAMPTON, ST ANDREWS, TRINITY COLLEGE DUBLIN, UNIVERSITY COLLEGE DUBLIN, UNIVERSITY COLLEGE LONDON, WARWICK, YORK
Please check with your university careers service for full details of local events.

MINIMUM ENTRY REQUIREMENTS
2.1 Degree
340 UCAS points

APPLICATION DEADLINE
Please see website for full details.

FURTHER INFORMATION
www.Top100GraduateEmployers.com
Register now for the latest news, events information and graduate recruitment details for Britain's leading employers.

Six reasons our trainees chose Norton Rose Fulbright

. . . .

The impressive work.

"Our industry focus means that there is plenty of high quality work. You can get involved in some huge deals here."

For me, it was the practice's ambitions.

"We're growing and ambitious, and we continue to establish ourselves at the top of the league tables."

I knew I would go places here.

"We don't just offer secondments – we actively encourage all trainees to undertake one."

I could see this was a place I could grow.

"I wanted challenging work and a steep learning curve. I get that here, in an environment where those around me look to help me improve."

The international focus.

"It's more than a list of offices - there is a real emphasis on working with colleagues and clients in different jurisdictions. Pick somewhere in the world, and we've probably got an office there."

The culture felt right.

"It's collegiate, and open to individuality. There's an understanding here that people need to feel free to explore opportunities outside of their immediate role."

. . . .

*We know that choosing the right legal practice is a big decision.
So we thought we would tell you what persuaded our trainees to come here.
If you join us, we'll keep on supporting you to choose wisely throughout your career.*

nortonrosefulbrightgraduates.com

NORTON ROSE FULBRIGHT

Progress with purpose

GRADUATE VACANCIES IN 2016

HUMAN RESOURCES

MARKETING

MEDIA

RESEARCH & DEVELOPMENT

RETAILING

NUMBER OF VACANCIES
50+ voluntary internships

LOCATIONS OF VACANCIES

Few organisations offer such a unique opportunity to contribute towards overcoming poverty and suffering. Oxfam has been fighting it for 70 years and graduates can be part of it. Poverty isn't inevitable, so Oxfam gives people what they need to fight it.

Oxfam is one of the most experienced development agencies in the world, working in more than 70 countries. It has run its Voluntary Internship scheme since 2006 and has helped to provide valuable experience and skills to hundreds of people. Voluntary Internships provide a structured, time-bound opportunity, so that graduates can get the most out of volunteering.

Oxfam's Voluntary Internships are based on projects where its people are able to contribute and add significant value to an area of the organisation. Voluntary Internships are usually between 3 and 7 months, depending on the project. Oxfam pays local travel and lunch expenses so that its volunteers aren't out of pocket whilst volunteering.

The roles could be in Oxfam's Oxford Headquarters, a shop or a regional office. They range from Voluntary Assistant Shop Managers, to Marketing & Communications Assistants working in Oxfam's Community Fundraising team, to HR & Recruitment Advisors, to Research Executives in the Campaigns Division. Regardless of whether graduates want to plan a fundraising event, work on a campaign project, or help to run a shop, they will get to experience how a major international Non Government Organisation works and enjoy a friendly, open and passionate working environment.

Voluntary Internships are a great way to learn new skills, experience how a large NGO operates and help to contribute towards Oxfam's goal of overcoming poverty and suffering around the world.

STARTING SALARY FOR 2016
£Voluntary

UNIVERSITY VISITS IN 2015-16
OXFORD, OXFORD BROOKES
Please check with your university careers service for full details of local events.

APPLICATION DEADLINE
Year-round recruitment

FURTHER INFORMATION
www.Top100GraduateEmployers.com
Register now for the latest news, events information and graduate recruitment details for Britain's leading employers.

WORLD CHANGERS WANTED

VOLUNTARY INTERNSHIP OPPORTUNITIES, UK-WIDE

Ever wanted to change the world? To right wrongs and make a real difference? Take up an internship that takes on poverty, suffering and injustice, and help us change lives worldwide.

Apply now at **www.oxfam.org.uk/getinvolved**

Work every day with lots of

BRANDS YOU KNOW.

P&G

Nearly five billion times a day, P&G brands touch the lives of people around the world. Whether they're shaving with a Gillette Fusion ProGlide or Venus Razor; washing their hair with Pantene or Head & Shoulders; wearing a scent from Hugo Boss; or cleaning the dishes with Fairy Liquid.

As one of the world's largest consumer goods companies, P&G has one of the strongest portfolios of trusted, globally recognised leading brands of any company in the world. The P&G community includes operations in approximately 70 countries worldwide and our employees represent over 140 nationalities.

P&G recruits the finest people in the world, because they develop talent almost exclusively from within. This means graduates won't just get their first job out of university; they are being hired into a career, with the expectation that they will grow into one of P&G's future leaders... maybe even the next CEO. New starters with P&G can expect a job with responsibility from day one and a career with a variety of challenging roles that develop and broaden their skills, together with the support of training and coaching to help them succeed.

P&G look beyond just good academic records from their applicants. They are looking for graduates who are smart, and savvy, leaders who stand out from the crowd, who are able to get things done. They want to hear about achievements at work, in clubs, societies, voluntary and community activities and to see how graduates have stretched and challenged themselves and others.

The commercial functions welcome applicants from any degree discipline. Product Supply (Manufacturing, Engineering, and Supply Network Operations) requires a technical degree. R&D requires an engineering or science degree.

GRADUATE VACANCIES IN 2016

ENGINEERING
FINANCE
HUMAN RESOURCES
IT
LOGISTICS
MARKETING
RESEARCH & DEVELOPMENT
SALES

NUMBER OF VACANCIES
100 graduate jobs

LOCATIONS OF VACANCIES

Vacancies also available in Europe.

STARTING SALARY FOR 2016
£30,000

UNIVERSITY VISITS IN 2015-16
BATH, BRISTOL, CAMBRIDGE, DURHAM, EDINBURGH, EXETER, GLASGOW, LEEDS, LONDON SCHOOL OF ECONOMICS, MANCHESTER, NOTTINGHAM, OXFORD, STRATHCLYDE, UNIVERSITY COLLEGE LONDON, WARWICK
Please check with your university careers service for full details of local events.

APPLICATION DEADLINE
Varies by function

FURTHER INFORMATION
www.Top100GraduateEmployers.com
Register now for the latest news, events information and graduate recruitment details for Britain's leading employers.

We Develop the World's Best... How Long Before It's You?

As a Build-From-Within Company, P&G hires individuals who we believe have the potential to become future leaders of the business.

You bring your passion....

.... P&G gives you challenges that will inspire you!

We invest a lot into training and developing our people, through a variety of different methods, including on the job training, mentoring and coaching from more experienced leaders, and formal training via our P&G Leadership Academy.

You will have a role with real responsibility and ownership from day one, whilst being supported and coached by your manager, mentor and other colleagues.

Learn More:
uki.experiencePG.com

 Venus BRAUN Pampers. GUCCI AUSSIE

 P&G

Penguin
Random House
UK

www.penguinrandomhousecareers.co.uk

facebook.com/PRHCareersUK **f**   PRHCareersUK@penguinrandomhouse.co.uk

linkedin.com/company/penguin-random-house-uk **in**   twitter.com/PRHcareersUK **y**

At Penguin Random House, they believe that what they do really matters. The business is committed to finding the very best stories from the very best minds, and then connecting them to as many people as possible. Publishing used to follow a linear model. Today, things work very differently.

Penguin Random House works with a wide range of talent – from animators and developers, to toy manufacturers and producers – which means that they act more like broadcasters as they find new ways to tell stories and different ways to capture the attention of the world for the stories, ideas and writing that matter.

Penguin Random House launches 2000 start-ups a year – they are called books – and they believe that by connecting these stories to readers they can help to transform people's lives.

The company boasts a show-stopping portfolio of authors and brands across fiction and non-fiction: Jamie Oliver, EL James, Nigella Lawson, James Patterson, Lee Child, Peppa Pig, Zadie Smith, Roald Dahl and Mary Berry.

Penguin Random House works with a wide range of talent internally too, with creative colleagues supported by dynamic teams specialising in Technology, Finance, Data and Sales – to name a few.

Collaboration, creativity and experimentation are at the heart of what they do. As Penguin Random House continues to build its newly-created company, it recognises the opportunity ahead to enable their employees to do the best work of their lives as they make and publish extraordinary books together.

Penguin Random House has three publishing sites in London: The Strand, Vauxhall Bridge Road and Ealing Broadway, distribution centres in Frating, Grantham and Rugby, and number of regional offices, employing over 2,000 people in the UK.

Your Story Starts Here

Finding a great story - editor, publisher, sales director, finance team. Making it look good - designer, copy writer, art director, illustrator. Making the finished book - production controller, product manager, quality controller. Getting it out there - marketing assistant, publicity manager, sales executive, social media manager.

Come and be part of the first of a new kind of publisher that captures the attention of the world through the stories, ideas and writing that matter.

Penguin Random House UK

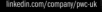

pwc.com/uk/careers

twitter.com/PwC_UK_Careers facebook.com/PwCCareersUK

youtube.com/careerspwc linkedin.com/company/pwc-uk

pwc

The opportunity of a lifetime

Opportunities are at the heart of a career with PwC. Opportunities to grow as an individual, to build lasting relationships and make an impact in a place where people, value and quality mean everything. Their purpose is to build trust in society and solve important problems for their clients.

PwC's continued success, size and scale, not forgetting their extensive client base, creates an environment where undergraduates and graduates get access to the best career and work experience opportunities. They choose the best people to join them, but it might be surprising to learn they're from a wide range of backgrounds and have studied all sorts of degree subjects. Along with strong academics, PwC are looking for graduates keen to develop, with business awareness, intellectual and cultural curiosity and the ability to build strong relationships, while making a positive impact with their clients and each other.

Graduates get access to the best learning and development around; learning by doing, learning from others and more formal approaches to learning. For some business areas this could mean the opportunity to work towards a professional qualification. With PwC graduates are in the driving seat of their development, and have the support of a structured career development programme.

For undergraduates and graduates exploring work experience opportunities, or ways to help them decide where their skills, interests and career goals could best fit, they could attend a PwC career open day, or apply to a summer internships or work placement.

Join PwC. They're focused on helping graduates reach their full potential while providing a competitive salary and personally tailored benefits package. Take the opportunity of a lifetime.

English degree

Our training & development programmes are designed to help you learn the most from an outstanding variety of work

We hire graduates from a huge range of degree subjects

Your degree is just the start

Arts degree

History degree

Last year, almost half the graduates who joined us came from an arts & humanities, science, law or social sciences degree subject

Science degree

Geography degree

pwc

pwc.com/uk/careers

Diverse people make us stronger

 **RBS**

Early Careers at RBS
Your passion. Your potential.

GRADUATE VACANCIES IN 2016

ACCOUNTANCY
FINANCE
GENERAL MANAGEMENT
HUMAN RESOURCES
INVESTMENT BANKING
IT

NUMBER OF VACANCIES
500+ graduate jobs

LOCATIONS OF VACANCIES

STARTING SALARY FOR 2016
£Competitive

UNIVERSITY VISITS IN 2015-16
BRISTOL, CAMBRIDGE, CITY, DURHAM,
EDINBURGH, IMPERIAL COLLEGE
LONDON, LEICESTER, LONDON SCHOOL
OF ECONOMICS, MANCHESTER,
NOTTINGHAM, OXFORD, UNIVERSITY
COLLEGE LONDON, WARWICK
*Please check with your university careers
service for full details of local events.*

MINIMUM ENTRY REQUIREMENTS
2.1 Degree

APPLICATION DEADLINE
Varies by function

FURTHER INFORMATION
www.Top100GraduateEmployers.com
*Register now for the latest news, events
information and graduate recruitment
details for Britain's leading employers.*

**RBS is one of the UK's leading financial services groups.
As the organisation moves forward, graduates have a real
opportunity to apply their passions and turn them into a
rewarding career. Regardless of degree discipline, there are
roles nationwide across the organisation.**

The company believes that the future of banking lies in the enthusiasm,
passion for customer service and talent of its graduates, interns and apprentices,
so they do their very best to make sure they each have access to all the latest
support and training that they need.

As a result, RBS is proud to have been recognised as an employer of choice by
the Investors in Young People accreditation. If students want somewhere they can
grow, whilst reaching their full potential, joining RBS as a graduate or intern will
help them transform their passions into an exciting, varied and dynamic career.

Whatever their degree, RBS has a varied number of core functions that value
students' curiosity, passion and talent. The insights they gain today, will help
them drive the bank's agenda for tomorrow. The bank offers a broad range of
opportunities, from commercial and corporate schemes in banking, technical
programmes in their services functions, to roles in areas such as HR. In return,
graduates and interns can develop a career that both challenges and rewards
them. As well as world-class training and development, they will enjoy exposure
to business disciplines, and early responsibility.

At every stage, there will be support and guidance from a strong network of
managers and mentors. There are also opportunities to build relationships outside
of work, through a variety of educational, social events and CSR initiatives.

RBS believes passion and inspiration leads to potential and success, and
encourage all who join them to help create a safer and stronger bank.

 **RBS**

Everyone likes recognition for hard work.

Want to feel valued and recognised for your work? At RBS, we want you to as well. Our commitment to developing students and graduates means we've been recognised as an employer of choice by the Investors in Young People Accreditation.

Join a graduate and intern programme with a company that continues to recognise talented young people and offer them the best training, experience and opportunities throughout the bank.

For more information visit **www.yourpassionyourpotential.rbs.com**

CREATE | BETTER

For over 100 years, Rolls-Royce has delivered excellence for customers in the aerospace, marine and nuclear markets. In 2014, their order book totalled £73.7 billion and they invested £1.2 billion in research and development. They employ over 50,000 people in more than 50 international offices.

From the Spitfire to the A350, Rolls-Royce engines have always powered impressive aircraft. However, their reputation for engineering excellence extends far beyond aerospace, to nuclear reactors and submarine propulsion as well as rail and off-road vehicle applications.

A single Rolls-Royce engine can contain 17,998 individual parts, around a third of the elements from the periodic table and blades accurate to within one-tenth of the width of a human hair. It's a level of precision that demands excellence, commitment and unwavering customer focus from everyone involved.

Graduates and interns can join in Engineering or one of the company's diverse business functions. The latter includes opportunities in areas as varied as HR, Project Management, Commercial and Customer Management, while the former spans electrical engineering, fluid dynamics, manufacturing engineering and much more. Wherever they join, individuals are expected to be logical, analytical, innovative and enthusiastic.

Graduates can look forward to placements across the business, plus learning and development opportunities that can include gaining professional accreditation and comprehensive, programme-specific training courses. And because every graduate works on live projects, they have every opportunity to make a real contribution. In previous years, graduates have driven improvements worth millions of pounds, implemented cultural change, refined complex engines and supported customers from some of the most famous airlines in the world.

GRADUATE VACANCIES IN 2016

ENGINEERING
GENERAL MANAGEMENT
HUMAN RESOURCES
PURCHASING
SALES

NUMBER OF VACANCIES
350+ graduate jobs

LOCATIONS OF VACANCIES

Vacancies also available in Europe, the USA and Asia.

STARTING SALARY FOR 2016
£28,000
Plus a £2,000 joining bonus.

UNIVERSITY VISITS IN 2015-16
BATH, BRISTOL, CAMBRIDGE, DURHAM, EDINBURGH, EXETER, GLASGOW, IMPERIAL COLLEGE LONDON, LANCASTER, LIVERPOOL, LOUGHBOROUGH, MANCHESTER, NOTTINGHAM, OXFORD, SOUTHAMPTON, STRATHCLYDE, WARWICK
Please check with your university careers service for full details of local events.

MINIMUM ENTRY REQUIREMENTS
2.1 Degree

APPLICATION DEADLINE
Year-round recruitment
Early application advised.

FURTHER INFORMATION
www.Top100GraduateEmployers.com
Register now for the latest news, events information and graduate recruitment details for Britain's leading employers.

Throughout the course of history, a life at sea has always attracted those with a taste for travel and adventure; but there are plenty of other reasons for graduates and final-year students to consider a challenging and wide-ranging career with the Royal Navy.

The Royal Navy is, first and foremost, a fighting force. Serving alongside Britain's allies in conflicts around the world, it also vitally protects UK ports, fishing grounds and merchant ships, helping to combat international smuggling, terrorism and piracy. Increasingly, its 33,000 personnel are involved in humanitarian and relief missions; situations where their skills, discipline and resourcefulness make a real difference to people's lives.

Graduates are able to join the Royal Navy as Officers – the senior leadership and management team in the various branches, which range from Engineering and Warfare to Medical, the Fleet Air Arm and Logistics. Starting salaries of at least £25,472 – rising to £30,617 in the first year – compare well with those in industry.

Those wanting to join the Royal Navy as an Engineer – either Marine, Weapon or Engineer Officer, above or below the water – could work on anything from sensitive electronics to massive gas-turbine engines and nuclear weapons. What's more, the Royal Navy can offer a secure, flexible career and the potential to extend to age 50.

The Royal Navy offers opportunities for early responsibility, career development, sport, recreation and travel which exceed any in civilian life. With its global reach and responsibilities, the Royal Navy still offers plenty of adventure and the chance to see the world, while pursuing one of the most challenging, varied and fulfilling careers available.

GRADUATE VACANCIES IN 2016
ENGINEERING
FINANCE
GENERAL MANAGEMENT
HUMAN RESOURCES
IT
LAW
LOGISTICS
RESEARCH & DEVELOPMENT

NUMBER OF VACANCIES
No fixed quota

LOCATIONS OF VACANCIES

Vacancies also available elsewhere in the world.

STARTING SALARY FOR 2016
£25,472
Plus a one-off joining bonus of £27,000 (subject to specialisation – see website for full details).

UNIVERSITY VISITS IN 2015-16
BATH, BELFAST, CARDIFF, DUNDEE, DURHAM, EDINBURGH, EXETER, HULL, IMPERIAL COLLEGE LONDON, KING'S COLLEGE LONDON, LEEDS, LIVERPOOL, LOUGHBOROUGH, NEWCASTLE, NOTTINGHAM, OXFORD, SHEFFIELD, SOUTHAMPTON, STIRLING, SURREY, ULSTER, UNIVERSITY COLLEGE LONDON, WARWICK, YORK
Please check with your university careers service for full details of local events.

MINIMUM ENTRY REQUIREMENTS
Relevant degree required for some roles.

APPLICATION DEADLINE
Year-round recruitment

FURTHER INFORMATION
www.Top100GraduateEmployers.com
Register now for the latest news, events information and graduate recruitment details for Britain's leading employers.

YOU MAKE A DIFFERENCE NOT MAKE UP THE NUMBERS

ROYAL NAVY OFFICER

Being an officer in the Royal Navy is a career like any other, but the circumstances and places are sometimes extraordinary. With opportunities ranging from Engineer Officer to Medical Officer, it's a responsible, challenging career that will take you further than you've been before. If you want more than just a job, join the Royal Navy and live a life without limits.

LIFE WITHOUT LIMITS
08456 07 55 55
ROYALNAVY.MOD.UK/CAREERS

Shell is a global group of energy and petrochemicals companies. With approximately 90,000 employees in over 70 countries, our aim is to help meet the world's growing demand for energy in economically, environmentally and socially responsible ways.

Shell offers a wide range of career routes. The scale and global reach of the business means they have a huge range of technical, commercial and corporate roles across most types of Engineering, Finance, HR, IT, Contracts & Procurement, Sales & Marketing and Maritime.

The Shell Graduate Programme is open to graduates and early career professionals. Most are from Engineering, Science, Social Science or Humanities courses but, with relevant work experience, other subject areas are welcomed. The structured Graduate Programme gives graduates immediate immersion in their business with real, high levels of responsibility from day one. The Programme is typically 3 years, although this can depend on your area of the business, and graduates usually complete at least 2 assignments within this time. Throughout they receive comprehensive support from mentors, work buddies, the graduate network (Energie) and access to senior business leaders. Students apply to the Graduate Programme by completing an Assessed Internship or by applying to attend a Shell Recruitment Day.

Assessed Internships are open to penultimate year students. They are usually 12 week placements undertaken over the summer. During this time students are supported through delivery of a live project for which they have responsibility. Project topics are determined based on the student's interests and the needs of the business. Shell Internships are very sought after roles that give a fantastic insight into a fascinating business – one that has an impact on us all.

GRADUATE VACANCIES IN 2016

ENGINEERING
FINANCE
HUMAN RESOURCES
IT
LOGISTICS
MARKETING
RESEARCH & DEVELOPMENT

NUMBER OF VACANCIES
80-100 graduate jobs

LOCATIONS OF VACANCIES

STARTING SALARY FOR 2016
£32,500

UNIVERSITY VISITS IN 2015-16
ABERDEEN, BATH, CAMBRIDGE, HERIOT-WATT, IMPERIAL COLLEGE LONDON, LEEDS, LONDON SCHOOL OF ECONOMICS, MANCHESTER, OXFORD, SHEFFIELD, STRATHCLYDE, WARWICK
Please check with your university careers service for full details of local events.

APPLICATION DEADLINE
31st March 2016

FURTHER INFORMATION
www.Top100GraduateEmployers.com
Register now for the latest news, events information and graduate recruitment details for Britain's leading employers.

IN SEARCH OF EXPLORERS

IN SEARCH OF REMARKABLE GRADUATES

To be a true explorer is a remarkable quality. After all, how many people are really prepared to continuously seek out new ideas, opportunities and experiences? At Shell, we're in search of remarkable people. So if you want to explore what you can achieve when you're encouraged to challenge the status quo, join us.

Discover the opportunities at www.shell.com/graduates

SIEMENS

www.siemens.co.uk/grads

graduate.recruitment.cp.gb@siemens.com

linkedin.com/company/siemens **in**   twitter.com/SiemensUKJobs **y**

As the leading global engineering company, Siemens is behind a diverse range of technologies and services, many of which people take for granted in their daily lives. They design and manufacture products and systems from traffic lights and wind turbines, to rail systems and motor drives.

From keeping cities at the cutting edge of technology, to providing greener energy solutions for the way people live, work and travel – Siemens graduates are helping to provide the solutions for a sustainable future.

For those who are looking to develop a career in Engineering or Business, Siemens offer early responsibility, mentoring and continuous professional development. Graduates will be working for a company that's committed to innovation and facing challenges head on. Located in towns and cities all over the UK, Siemens offer a diverse range of graduate and internship opportunities where graduates will be given the freedom to make their mark and use fresh ideas to keep the business at the forefront of innovative technology.

Siemens does not offer a 'one size fits all' graduate programme – individuals join the company in all types of roles and business areas. The Engineering careers on offer are as diverse as the industry itself. There are roles in Renewable & Fossil Power Generation, right through to Rail Automation and Drives Technologies. There are some great training initiatives too, helping graduates reach Chartered Engineer status. Business graduates will help play a crucial role in helping the company run smoothly and the careers are on offer include Finance, IT, Project Management and Sales. So, for those who join as a Graduate Electrical Engineer working in Renewable Energy, or a Graduate Sales Trainee working in Rail Systems, Siemens will offer variety, challenging work and first class development.

GRADUATE VACANCIES IN 2016

ENGINEERING
FINANCE
GENERAL MANAGEMENT
IT
RESEARCH & DEVELOPMENT
SALES

NUMBER OF VACANCIES
80 graduate jobs

LOCATIONS OF VACANCIES

STARTING SALARY FOR 2016
£Competitive

UNIVERSITY VISITS IN 2015-16
CAMBRIDGE, IMPERIAL COLLEGE LONDON, LOUGHBOROUGH, MANCHESTER, NEWCASTLE, NOTTINGHAM, OXFORD, SHEFFIELD, STRATHCLYDE
Please check with your university careers service for full details of local events.

MINIMUM ENTRY REQUIREMENTS
2.2 Degree

APPLICATION DEADLINE
Year-round recruitment
Early application advised.

FURTHER INFORMATION
www.Top100GraduateEmployers.com
Register now for the latest news, events information and graduate recruitment details for Britain's leading employers.

SIEMENS

Advancing technology.
Advancing your career.

If you want a graduate career that makes a difference – join us.

Siemens is a leading global engineering company and has been finding innovative answers to some of the world's most challenging questions for 170 years.

From keeping cities at the cutting edge of technology, to providing greener energy solutions for the way we live, work and travel – we're providing the solutions for a sustainable future.

Whether you want to develop a graduate career in Engineering or Business, we offer early responsibility and continuous development; you'll be working for a company that's committed to innovation and facing challenges head on.

Head to our website to find out more.

siemens.co.uk/grads

sky

GRADUATE VACANCIES IN 2016

ACCOUNTANCY
CONSULTING
ENGINEERING
FINANCE
GENERAL MANAGEMENT
HUMAN RESOURCES
IT
MARKETING
MEDIA
PURCHASING

NUMBER OF VACANCIES
90+ graduate jobs

LOCATIONS OF VACANCIES

Sky is Europe's leading entertainment company and serves 21 million customers across five countries. They offer the best and broadest range of content, deliver market-leading customer service and use innovative technology to give customers a better TV experience.

As Sky grows they're looking for bright, talented graduates to make a difference to their ever-changing business. From launching new channels with record viewing figures to blazing a trail for technology, graduates will play their part keeping customers excited and inspired every day.

Those looking to develop their career at Sky will be part of a fast-paced business that's changing the game for the entire industry. Joining Sky at one of their state-of-the-art offices close to Central London, Leeds or Edinburgh, graduates will be right in the thick of it. Whatever their skills, wherever they join, from day one they'll be part of a network of friendly graduates that stretch right across the business. They'll work on real projects making decisions that really matter and help Sky do better than ever. And because successful graduates play such an important role for Sky, their mentors will make sure they have everything they need to develop. This includes working on a structured and tailored plan to progress their career through plenty of development opportunities. What's more, they'll have access to great rewards such as free Sky+HD and broadband, as well as enrolment in the Sky pension plan, health insurance and a wide range of retail discounts.

Sky offers a broad range of graduate programmes across their business and technology functions; from finance to software engineering, marketing to management and more. Whatever graduates are studying, there is a place for them to shine and create their own story at Sky.

STARTING SALARY FOR 2016
£25,000-£32,000

UNIVERSITY VISITS IN 2015-16
ASTON, BATH, BRISTOL, BRUNEL, CARDIFF, EAST ANGLIA, EDINBURGH, GLASGOW, HERIOT-WATT, KING'S COLLEGE LONDON, KENT, LEEDS, LEICESTER, LIVERPOOL, LOUGHBOROUGH, MANCHESTER, NOTTINGHAM, READING, SHEFFIELD, SOUTHAMPTON, ST ANDREWS, STRATHCLYDE, UNIVERSITY COLLEGE LONDON, WARWICK, YORK
Please check with your university careers service for full details of local events.

APPLICATION DEADLINE
Varies by function

FURTHER INFORMATION
www.Top100GraduateEmployers.com
Register now for the latest news, events information and graduate recruitment details for Britain's leading employers.

SLAUGHTER AND MAY

www.slaughterandmay.com

trainee.recruit@slaughterandmay.com

Slaughter and May is one of the most prestigious law firms in the world. They advise on high-profile and groundbreaking international transactions and have an excellent and varied client list that includes leading corporations, financial institutions and governments.

Slaughter and May has offices in London, Brussels, Hong Kong and Beijing and 'Best Friend' relationships with leading independent law firms around the world.

Slaughter and May has built a reputation for delivering innovative solutions to difficult problems. This reputation has been earned because each of their lawyers advises on broad legal areas, combining experience gained on one type of transaction to solve problems in another.

Core practice areas are Mergers and Acquisitions, Corporate and Commercial, and Financing. The firm also has leading practitioners in specialist areas including Tax, Competition, Dispute Resolution, Real Estate, Pensions and Employment, Financial Regulation, Information Technology and Intellectual Property.

Their lawyers are not set billing or time targets and therefore are free to concentrate to what matters most – expertise, sound judgement, a willingness to help one another and the highest quality of client service.

During the two-year training contract, trainees turn their hand to a broad range of work, taking an active role in four or five groups while sharing an office with a partner or experienced associate. Most trainees spend at least two six-month seats in the firm's market leading corporate, commercial and financing groups. Subject to gaining some contentious experience, they choose how to spend the remaining time.

Among their lawyers, 24 nationalities and over 70 different universities are represented.

GRADUATE VACANCIES IN 2016

LAW

NUMBER OF VACANCIES
80 graduate jobs
For training contracts starting in 2018.

LOCATIONS OF VACANCIES

STARTING SALARY FOR 2016
£41,000

UNIVERSITY VISITS IN 2015-16
ABERDEEN, BIRMINGHAM, BRISTOL, CAMBRIDGE, DURHAM, EDINBURGH, EXETER, GLASGOW, KING'S COLLEGE LONDON, LEEDS, LONDON SCHOOL OF ECONOMICS, MANCHESTER, NEWCASTLE, NOTTINGHAM, OXFORD, SHEFFIELD, ST ANDREWS, TRINITY COLLEGE DUBLIN, UNIVERSITY COLLEGE DUBLIN, UNIVERSITY COLLEGE LONDON, WARWICK, YORK
Please check with your university careers service for full details of local events.

MINIMUM ENTRY REQUIREMENTS
2.1 Degree

APPLICATION DEADLINE
Please see website for full details.

FURTHER INFORMATION
www.Top100GraduateEmployers.com
Register now for the latest news, events information and graduate recruitment details for Britain's leading employers.

Smriti, a lawyer in our Dispute Resolution group

How many lawyers do you see?

At Slaughter and May we train each of our lawyers to be a multi-specialist, equipped to advise on a broad range of legal matters that at other firms would be handled by a number of different lawyers.

We don't pigeonhole our people – we think that the broader the training and experience, the better the lawyer.

Our lawyers have a varied and interesting workload and ample opportunities to develop close relationships with clients and become their trusted advisers.

We have built a reputation for delivering innovative solutions to difficult problems. This has been earned because each of our lawyers advises on broad legal areas, combining experience gained on one type of transaction to solve problems in another.

We welcome applicants from all academic disciplines who achieve strong 2:1 results or the equivalent.

To find out more, you can apply for one of our Open Days, Work Experience Schemes or Workshops. For more information about a legal career with a difference, visit **slaughterandmay/joinus**

Great minds think differently

SLAUGHTER AND MAY

TeachFirst

faq@teachfirst.org.uk ✉
twitter.com/teachfirst 🐦 facebook.com/teachfirst f
youtube.com/TeachFirstUK ▶ linkedin.com/company/teach-first in

Teach First is an education charity working in partnership with others to end educational inequality. Young people in schools across England and Wales need leaders – exceptional people who can bring out the best in them and help them to become successful adults, whatever the circumstances of their lives.

The Teach First Leadership Development Programme (LDP) is a personalised programme encompassing high-quality training, supportive coaching, work experience and a PGCE qualification. The skills and experiences gained can be taken forward into any career. That's why schools and other organisations working in a whole range of sectors recognise the programme's ability to develop leaders. Put simply, they know that graduates who can engage, stimulate and inspire in the classroom can handle pretty much any situation.

The LDP is a two-year commitment, but the foundation of a life-long engagement with Teach First's work to ensure every young person has the education they deserve. As well as training inspirational leaders in the classroom, Teach First support their network of ambassadors – those who have completed the LDP – to drive forward change in education in influential leadership positions in education, business, social enterprise and beyond.

Some people join Teach First knowing they want to stay in education; some are sure that they don't; and others are uncertain about their plans. All of them find the experience of the Teach First Leadership Development Programme to be powerful, rewarding and enlightening. And all are changed by it.

Apply now and join thousands of others committed to ending educational inequality.

Teach First develops leaders for life.

GRADUATE VACANCIES IN 2016
ALL SECTORS

NUMBER OF VACANCIES
1,860 graduate jobs

LOCATIONS OF VACANCIES

STARTING SALARY FOR 2016
£Competitive

UNIVERSITY VISITS IN 2015-16
ABERYSTWYTH, ASTON, BANGOR, BATH, BELFAST, BIRMINGHAM, BRISTOL, BRUNEL, CAMBRIDGE, CARDIFF, CITY, DURHAM, EAST ANGLIA, EDINBURGH, ESSEX, EXETER, GLASGOW, HULL, IMPERIAL COLLEGE LONDON, KING'S COLLEGE LONDON, KENT, LANCASTER, LEEDS, LEICESTER, LIVERPOOL, LONDON SCHOOL OF ECONOMICS, LOUGHBOROUGH, MANCHESTER, NEWCASTLE, NORTHUMBRIA, NOTTINGHAM, NOTTINGHAM TRENT, OXFORD, OXFORD BROOKES, QUEEN MARY LONDON, READING, ROYAL HOLLOWAY, SCHOOL OF AFRICAN STUDIES, SHEFFIELD, SOUTHAMPTON, ST ANDREWS, STRATHCLYDE, SURREY, SUSSEX, SWANSEA, TRINITY COLLEGE DUBLIN, UNIVERSITY COLLEGE DUBLIN, UNIVERSITY COLLEGE LONDON, WARWICK, YORK
Please check with your university careers service for full details of local events.

MINIMUM ENTRY REQUIREMENTS
2.1 Degree
300 UCAS points

APPLICATION DEADLINE
Year-round recruitment
Early application advised.

FURTHER INFORMATION
www.Top100GraduateEmployers.com
Register now for the latest news, events information and graduate recruitment details for Britain's leading employers.

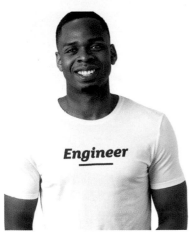
Engineer

Teacher

Social
Entrepreneur

Inventor

Principal

Cyber
Analyst

Accountant

Early Years
Teacher

Diplomat

LEADERS
FOR
LIFE

The young people in our schools need leaders – exceptional people who can bring out the best in them and help them to become successful adults, whatever the circumstances of their lives. Our world-class Leadership Development Programme will put you in exactly that position. You'll gain the skills and experiences to become an inspirational leader who drives lasting change, wherever your career takes you. Teach First develops leaders for life.

TeachFirst

Apply now for our Leadership Development Programme | teachfirst.org.uk/graduates

TESCO

Tesco's people are their biggest asset – over half a million of them worldwide! Tesco's success as the UK's largest retailer is shaped by the vision and ideas of the people who work there; and their ability to turn these ideas into a fantastic shopping experience for customers.

The customer is at the heart of everything Tesco does. They are continually striving to give customers a better shopping experience, whether that's through a seamless online experience or reducing the queuing time within stores.

Tesco is looking for talented individuals who share a passion for great service. People who have energy and enthusiasm for delivering, working collaboratively and managing large scale projects. People who can work under pressure, have excellent attention to detail, and enjoy solving problems. People who can communicate at different levels, thrive on working in teams, and have strong organisational skills. Of course, in return, Tesco provides plenty of learning and support along the way – with leadership development, mentors and buddies provided for graduates, as well as its renowned training academy.

Tesco is proud of its early career programmes, and the training provided. But they firmly believe that the most rewarding way to learn is to apply graduates' knowledge in real-life business situations. No two days at Tesco are ever the same. Their wide range of great graduate programmes can set graduates on a career path for life. They're all about taking responsibility, being entrepreneurial and making things happen.

Tesco has around 20 programmes and they're all designed to shape future leaders. They include: Stores, Distribution, Quality & Technical, Customer Analysis, Marketing, People, Property, Technology, Business Support, Supply Chain, Digital Retailing, Food, General Merchandise and F&F.

GRADUATE VACANCIES IN 2016

FINANCE
GENERAL MANAGEMENT
HUMAN RESOURCES
IT
LOGISTICS
MARKETING
PROPERTY
PURCHASING
RETAILING

NUMBER OF VACANCIES
200+ graduate jobs

LOCATIONS OF VACANCIES

STARTING SALARY FOR 2016
£22,000-£30,000

UNIVERSITY VISITS IN 2015-16
BATH, BIRMINGHAM, BRISTOL, DURHAM, KING'S COLLEGE LONDON, LANCASTER, LEEDS, LOUGHBOROUGH, MANCHESTER, NOTTINGHAM, READING, SOUTHAMPTON, SURREY, UNIVERSITY COLLEGE LONDON, WARWICK
Please check with your university careers service for full details of local events.

MINIMUM ENTRY REQUIREMENTS
2.1 Degree
300-320 UCAS points
Relevant degree required for some roles.

APPLICATION DEADLINE
31st January 2016
Applications will be dealt with on a first-come-first-served basis.

FURTHER INFORMATION
www.Top100GraduateEmployers.com
Register now for the latest news, events information and graduate recruitment details for Britain's leading employers.

TESCO
Careers

Govinda Kular –
Graduate
Food Programme

" **More ambition.**
More accountability. More opportunity to
make a difference for customers. "

Just a couple of months after joining us, Govinda spotted a brilliant way to put our brand new buying process into practice.

After talking to our expert product teams, he saw how our soft drink suppliers could source sugar for less.

A great achievement on its own.

But because Tesco graduates get real accountability, he soon found himself at the centre of negotiations with Europe's third biggest sugar supplier.

The result? Cost savings for our customers and great career development.

You could call it a win/win/win situation: for Govinda, the drink manufacturers, our business, and above all, our customers.

It's just one example of how we continue to place trust in our Tesco graduates – and how that's inspiring them to achieve great things. For everyone.

Learn more about our graduate opportunities at
www.tesco-graduates.com

Boris Johnson

**Transport for London (TfL) is an innovator in transport and its
services are now recognised from all around the world. From
its red buses and black cabs to Tube trains, TfL is responsible for
virtually every mode of transport in the city, and so without TfL
London would stand still.**

To keep the city moving forward, it will come as no surprise that it takes
over 27,000 staff to make it all happen so TfL invests as much in its people
as it does in London's infrastructure. There are not many other organisations
that give graduates the opportunity to see the impact their work has on the
capital city.

They could be engineers or quantity surveyors; go into general, project or
information management; have the analytical skills for transport planning or
traffic control; or support the business through procurement and marketing.
TfL will give successful applicants responsibility early on, no matter which of
the schemes that they choose.

TfL is in the midst of one of its greatest periods of investment and that means
there are many exciting projects that graduates could contribute to. Work
is now under way on Crossrail, a state-of-the-art underground line slashing
journey times from east to west London. TfL is making the iconic Routemaster
bus a 'green hybrid machine' and introducing low-carbon taxis. Not forgetting
the new Emirates airline and the upgrade programme, which is seeing the
development of major stations and underground lines.

Whether graduates want to dig, design, plan, manage or explore corporate
finance, they can expect all the personal and professional development
that they need at TfL. Join Transport for London to help 'Shape the Future
of London!'.

Shape the future of London – become a TfL graduate

Take a wider look at tfl.gov.uk/graduates

We want to be as diverse as the city we represent and welcome applications from everyone regardless of age, gender, ethnicity, sexual orientation, faith or disability.

MAYOR OF LONDON

Transport for London

UBS

www.ubs.com/graduates

sh-ubs-campusrecruiting@ubs.com

twitter.com/UBScareers facebook.com/ubscareers **f**

youtube.com/ubs plus.google.com/+ubscareers **g+**

UBS draws on over 150 years of heritage to serve private, institutional and corporate clients worldwide. They are present in all major financial centres, employing around 60,000 across more then 50 countries. UBS aims for excellence in all that they do, and this begins with their employees.

Who are they looking for? People with intelligence, integrity and drive. People with experience, or are eager to learn. People who are able to do good things for their clients, make a positive impact on their business, and help them as they continue to transform their firm.

Interested in Wealth Management, Investment Banking, Asset Management or Retail & Corporate Banking? Or how about IT, Legal, Compliance, Risk, Operations, HR or Marketing? At UBS, a world awaits. UBS offers talented individuals a wide range of programmes; from first year Insights or Horizons, through to Summer Internships, Industrial Placements and Graduate opportunities.

UBS programmes are designed to be a springboard for talented students and graduates. For those who are serious about their career and interested in international finance, UBS offers a stimulating, collaborative environment with opportunities to achieve success across many disciplines. So look around, get to know UBS. Wherever applicants are in their academic career, UBS invites them to make their future a part of the organisation's.

Don't have an economics or business degree, don't worry – there's a position for everyone at UBS to inspire and challenge for those who have drive and creativity.

UBS takes pride in attracting a wealth of diverse backgrounds into a world of career possibilities.

GRADUATE VACANCIES IN 2016

FINANCE
HUMAN RESOURCES
INVESTMENT BANKING
IT
MARKETING
SALES

NUMBER OF VACANCIES
300 graduate jobs

LOCATIONS OF VACANCIES

Vacancies also available in Europe.

STARTING SALARY FOR 2016
£Competitive

UNIVERSITY VISITS IN 2015-16
ASTON, BATH, BIRMINGHAM, BRISTOL, CAMBRIDGE, CITY, DURHAM, EDINBURGH, EXETER, IMPERIAL COLLEGE LONDON, KING'S COLLEGE LONDON, LEEDS, LONDON SCHOOL OF ECONOMICS, LOUGHBOROUGH, MANCHESTER, NEWCASTLE, NOTTINGHAM, OXFORD, READING, SURREY, TRINITY COLLEGE DUBLIN, UNIVERSITY COLLEGE LONDON, WARWICK
Please check with your university careers service for full details of local events.

MINIMUM ENTRY REQUIREMENTS
2.1 Degree
300 UCAS points

APPLICATION DEADLINE
Varies by function
Please see website for full details.

FURTHER INFORMATION
www.Top100GraduateEmployers.com
Register now for the latest news, events information and graduate recruitment details for Britain's leading employers.

Figuring out your future?

Let's shape it together.

We don't just look at what you're studying. (Really, we don't.) We care about your attitude. And it doesn't matter if you like things fast-moving or measured. You like reading people or plotting charts. Deliberating or deciding. Or some of all those things. It doesn't matter if you don't know yet. We can help you find out.

www.ubs.com/graduates

Unilever

GRADUATE VACANCIES IN 2016

ENGINEERING
FINANCE
GENERAL MANAGEMENT
HUMAN RESOURCES
IT
MARKETING
RESEARCH & DEVELOPMENT
SALES

NUMBER OF VACANCIES
50 graduate jobs

LOCATIONS OF VACANCIES

STARTING SALARY FOR 2016
£30,000

UNIVERSITY VISITS IN 2015-16
ASTON, BATH, BIRMINGHAM, BRISTOL,
CAMBRIDGE, DURHAM, EXETER, IMPERIAL
COLLEGE LONDON, KING'S COLLEGE
LONDON, LANCASTER, LEEDS, LIVERPOOL,
LOUGHBOROUGH, MANCHESTER,
NEWCASTLE, NOTTINGHAM, OXFORD,
TRINITY COLLEGE DUBLIN, UNIVERSITY
COLLEGE DUBLIN, UNIVERSITY COLLEGE
LONDON, WARWICK
*Please check with your university careers
service for full details of local events.*

MINIMUM ENTRY REQUIREMENTS
2.1 Degree
300 UCAS points

APPLICATION DEADLINE
Varies by function

FURTHER INFORMATION
www.Top100GraduateEmployers.com
*Register now for the latest news, events
information and graduate recruitment
details for Britain's leading employers.*

Unilever, a leading consumer goods company, makes some of the world's best-loved brands: Dove, Knorr, Magnum, Lynx, Sure, Tresemmé and Hellmann's to name a few. Two billion consumers use their products every day. Unilever products are sold in 190 countries and they employ 174,000 people globally.

Around the world, Unilever products help people look good, feel good and get more out of life. Unilever wants graduates with the will to lead others in driving these brands forward.

The Future Leaders Programme (UFLP) helps talent reach senior management – quickly. Graduates can apply to one of the following areas – Supply Chain Management, Customer Management (Sales), HR Management, Marketing, Business & Technology Management, Research & Development, Research & Development Packaging and Financial Management. Whichever area they join, graduates will make a big business impact.

The three year, world-class development programme is packed with variety and challenge, collaborating with both local and international teams. Graduates will have real responsibility from Day 1, with the opportunity of promotion to manager level after 2 years, and a support network to see them develop and attain their future professional goals. Unilever will support them in achieving Chartered status and qualifications such as CIMA, IMechE, IChemE, IEE, APICS, ICS, and CIPD.

Unilever's challenge? To double the size of its business, while reducing its environmental impact and increasing its social impact. Behind that ambition lie exciting challenges for the company and its brands, with the opportunity for graduates to make a real difference to Unilever's business and the wider world.

wellcome trust

www.wellcome.ac.uk

linkedin.com/company/wellcome-trust **in**   HR@wellcome.ac.uk ✉

The Wellcome Trust is a global charitable foundation dedicated to improving health. It provides over £700 million a year to support bright minds in science, the humanities and the social sciences, as well as education, public engagement and the application of research to medicine. Based in London, they have around 700 staff from all sorts of backgrounds, with all sorts of expertise.

Its £18 billion investment portfolio gives it the independence to support such transformative work as the sequencing and understanding of the human genome, research that established front-line drugs for malaria, and Wellcome Collection, the Trust's free venue for the incurably curious that explores medicine, life and art.

For recent graduates, the Trust runs a two-year development programme. It's a great career springboard, offering practical experience in a wide variety of areas with a world-renowned employer. The programme is flexible, giving graduates the chance to develop skills and knowledge that will enable them to move into the career they choose. The scheme offers rotations across a wide range of departments including funding, investments, policy, communications, IT, finance, HR, legal, and Wellcome Collection.

From the start, graduates are expected to use their knowledge and enthusiasm to drive projects forward that will make a difference to human health. Projects can include anything from assisting in the development of new funding schemes, to researching new investment opportunities or identifying innovative ways of engaging with the public.

People at the Trust are encourged to act boldy, making decisions and taking responsibility; to savour the mix of ideas, expertise and backgrounds across the organisation; to defy expectations, being ambitious and thinking creatively; and to enjoy the challenge of this vital work.

GRADUATE VACANCIES IN 2016

FINANCE
GENERAL MANAGEMENT
HUMAN RESOURCES
INVESTMENT BANKING
IT
LAW
MARKETING
MEDIA

NUMBER OF VACANCIES
10-12 graduate jobs

LOCATIONS OF VACANCIES

STARTING SALARY FOR 2016
£26,000

UNIVERSITY VISITS IN 2015-16
Please check with your university careers service for full details of local events.

MINIMUM ENTRY REQUIREMENTS
2.2 Degree

APPLICATION DEADLINE
Varies by function

FURTHER INFORMATION
www.Top100GraduateEmployers.com
Register now for the latest news, events information and graduate recruitment details for Britain's leading employers.

Experience our world. Develop your skills. Drive your future.

wellcometrust

Who we are

WPP is the world leader in communications services – including Advertising; Media Investment Management; Data Investment Management; PR & Public Affairs; Branding & Identity; Healthcare Communications; Direct, Digital, Promotion & Relationship Marketing; and Specialist Communications.

WPP has more than 155 companies setting industry standards and working with many of the world's leading brands, creating communications ideas that help to build business for their clients. Between them, WPP's companies work with 355 of the Fortune Global 500, all 30 of the Dow Jones 30 and 71 of the NASDAQ 100. WPP employs over 179,000 people (including associates) in over 3,000 offices in 111 countries.

WPP Fellowships develop high-calibre management talent with unique experience across a range of marketing disciplines. Over three years, Fellows work in three different WPP operating companies, each representing a different marketing communications discipline and geography. Fellows are likely to work in a client management or planning role, although some work on the creative side of an agency. Each rotation is chosen on the basis of the individual's interests and the Group's needs.

Fellowships will be awarded to applicants who are intellectually curious and motivated by the prospect of delivering high-quality communications services to their clients. WPP wants people who are committed to marketing communications, take a rigorous and creative approach to problem-solving and will function well in a flexible, loosely structured work environment. WPP is offering several three-year Fellowships, with competitive remuneration and excellent long term career prospects with WPP. Many former Fellows now occupy senior management positions in WPP companies.

GRADUATE VACANCIES IN 2016
MARKETING
MEDIA

NUMBER OF VACANCIES
1-10 graduate jobs

LOCATIONS OF VACANCIES

Vacancies available in Europe, Asia, the USA and elsewhere in the world.

STARTING SALARY FOR 2016
£Competitive

UNIVERSITY VISITS IN 2015-16
BRISTOL, CAMBRIDGE, DURHAM, IMPERIAL COLLEGE LONDON, KING'S COLLEGE LONDON, LONDON SCHOOL OF ECONOMICS, OXFORD, QUEEN MARY LONDON, UNIVERSITY COLLEGE LONDON
Please check with your university careers service for full details of local events.

MINIMUM ENTRY REQUIREMENTS
2.1 Degree

APPLICATION DEADLINE
5th November 2015

FURTHER INFORMATION
www.Top100GraduateEmployers.com
Register now for the latest news, events information and graduate recruitment details for Britain's leading employers.

WPP
The Fellowship 2016

Ambidextrous brains required

WPP is the world leader in marketing communications, with more than 155 companies setting industry standards in Advertising; Media Investment Management; Data Investment Management; Public Relations & Public Affairs; Branding & Identity; Healthcare Communications; Direct, Digital, Promotion & Relationship Marketing; and Specialist Communications.

We are manufacturers of communications ideas that help to build business for our clients, through creating and developing relationships with the people who buy and use their products and services. We do this through a demanding combination of hard work and flair; logic and intuition; left brain and right brain thinking.

The Fellowship was started, 20 years ago, to create future generations of leaders for our companies. Fellows tend to be intellectually curious people who are motivated by the challenges of marketing communications and by the prospect of working at the confluence of art and business. They spend three years on the program: in each year they work in a different WPP company, in a different marketing communications discipline and, usually, on a different continent.

Long-term prospects within a WPP company are excellent, with many former Fellows now occupying senior management positions.

Deadline for entry:
5 November 2015

Visit our website and apply online at
www.wpp.com

For further information contact:

Amelie Vignalou, WPP
T: +44 (0)20 7408 2204
E-mail: amelie.vignalou@wpp.com

Useful Information

EMPLOYER	GRADUATE RECRUITMENT WEBSITE	EMPLOYER	GRADUATE RECRUITMENT WEBSITE
ACCENTURE	accenture.com/top100	HOGAN LOVELLS	www.hoganlovells.com/graduates
AECOM	aecom.com/graduates	HSBC	www.hsbc.com/careers
AIRBUS	www.jobs.airbusgroup.com	IBM	www.ibm.com/jobs/uk
ALDI	www.aldirecruitment.co.uk/graduate	JAGUAR LAND ROVER	www.jaguarlandrovercareers.com
ALLEN & OVERY	aograduate.com	JOHN LEWIS PARTNERSHIP	www.jlpjobs.com/graduates
ARMY	army.mod.uk/officer	J.P. MORGAN	www.jpmorgan.com/careers
ARUP	www.arup.com/careers	KPMG	www.kpmgcareers.co.uk/times100
ASDA	www.asda.jobs/graduates	L'ORÉAL	careers.loreal.com/UKgrads
ASTRAZENECA	www.astrazenecacareers.com	LIDL	www.lidlgraduatecareers.co.uk
ATKINS	www.atkinsglobal.com/careers/graduates	LINKLATERS	www.linklaters.com/ukgrads
BAE SYSTEMS	www.baesystems.com/graduates	LLOYD'S	www.lloyds.com/graduates
BAIN & COMPANY	www.joinbain.com	LLOYDS BANKING GROUP	www.lloydsbankinggrouptalent.com
BAKER & MCKENZIE	www.bakermckenzie.com/londongraduates	M&S	www.marksandspencergrads.com
BANK OF AMERICA MERRILL LYNCH	www.baml.com/campusEMEA	MARS	mars.co.uk/graduates
BANK OF ENGLAND	bankofenglandearlycareers.co.uk	MCDONALD'S	www.mcdonalds.co.uk/people
BARCLAYS	joinus.barclays.com	MCKINSEY & COMPANY	www.mckinsey.com/careers
BBC	www.bbc.co.uk/careers/trainee-schemes	METROPOLITAN POLICE	www.metpolicecareers.co.uk
BDO	www.bdo.co.uk/careers	MI5 – THE SECURITY SERVICE	www.mi5.gov.uk/careers
BLACKROCK	www.blackrockoncampus.com	MICROSOFT	www.beyourfuture.net
BLOOMBERG	bloomberg.com/careers	MONDELĒZ INTERNATIONAL	careers.mondelezinternational.com/Europe
BOOTS	www.boots.jobs/early-careers	MORGAN STANLEY	morganstanley.com/campus
BOSTON CONSULTING GROUP	careers.bcg.com	MOTT MACDONALD	mottmac.com/careers/graduate
BP	www.bp.com/grads/uk	NESTLÉ	www.nestlecareers.co.uk/academy
BRITISH AIRWAYS	www.britishairwaysgraduates.co.uk	NETWORK RAIL	www.networkrail.co.uk/graduates
BT	www.btgraduates.com	NEWTON EUROPE	www.newtoneurope.com/careers
CANCER RESEARCH UK	graduates.cancerresearchuk.org	NGDP FOR LOCAL GOVERNMENT	www.ngdp.org.uk
CENTRICA	www.centrica.com/graduates	NHS	www.nhsgraduates.co.uk
CITI	www.oncampus.citi.com	NORTON ROSE FULBRIGHT	www.nortonrosefulbrightgraduates.com
CIVIL SERVICE FAST STREAM	www.gov.uk/faststream	OXFAM	www.oxfam.org.uk/getinvolved
CREDIT SUISSE	www.credit-suisse.com/careers	P&G	uki.experiencepg.com
DANONE	www.danone.co.uk/graduates	PENGUIN RANDOM HOUSE	www.penguinrandomhousecareers.co.uk
DELOITTE	www.deloitte.co.uk/graduates	PWC	pwc.com/uk/careers
DIAGEO	www.diageo-careers.com	RBS	www.yourpassionyourpotential.rbs.com
DLA PIPER	www.dlapipergraduates.co.uk	ROLLS-ROYCE	rolls-royce.com/graduates
DYSON	www.dysongraduates.com	ROYAL NAVY	www.royalnavy.mod.uk/careers
EUROPEAN COMMISSION (EU CAREERS)	eu-careers.eu	SHELL	www.shell.co.uk/graduates
EXXONMOBIL	ExxonMobil.com/UKRecruitment	SIEMENS	www.siemens.co.uk/grads
EY	ey.com/uk/students	SKY	skystartingout.com
FIRST DERIVATIVES	www.firstderivatives.com/careers	SLAUGHTER AND MAY	www.slaughterandmay.com
FRESHFIELDS BRUCKHAUS DERINGER	www.freshfields.com/ukgraduates	TEACH FIRST	teachfirst.org.uk/graduates
FRONTLINE	www.thefrontline.org.uk	TESCO	tesco-graduates.com
GLAXOSMITHKLINE	www.futureleaders.gsk.com	TRANSPORT FOR LONDON	www.tfl.gov.uk/graduates
GOLDMAN SACHS	www.goldmansachs.com/careers	UBS	www.ubs.com/graduates
GOOGLE	www.google.com/students/emea	UNILEVER	www.unilever.co.uk/careers-jobs/graduates
GRANT THORNTON	www.grant-thornton.co.uk/trainees	WELLCOME TRUST	www.wellcome.ac.uk
HERBERT SMITH FREEHILLS	www.herbertsmithfreehills.com	WPP	www.wpp.com